Quee

Queer Screams

*A History of LGBTQ+ Survival
Through the Lens
of American Horror Cinema*

ABIGAIL WALDRON

McFarland & Company, Inc., Publishers
Jefferson, North Carolina

This book has undergone peer review.

ISBN (print) 978-1-4766-8742-1
ISBN (ebook) 978-1-4766-4765-4

Library of Congress and British Library
cataloguing data are available

Library of Congress Control Number 2022031917

Front cover images © 2022 Shutterstock

Printed in the United States of America

*McFarland & Company, Inc., Publishers
Box 611, Jefferson, North Carolina 28640
www.mcfarlandpub.com*

Table of Contents

Acknowledgments

To my parents, Brad and Tanya: thank you for allowing me to watch rated-R movies at a young age, without which I would not have had early access to some of the best parts of the horror genre, and for loving me unconditionally. To my sister, Emma, to whom I first came out as queer: thank you for always supporting me, my obsessions, and watching horror movies with me. To Sarah Montplaisir for your invaluable feedback, and to Kaja for your artistic talents.

To my graduate school editors, peers, and friends: Dr. Karen Li Miller, my advisor, and huge support system, working hard with me to edit my ramblings and to keep me from overusing the word "myriad," and to Dr. Gabriella Soto, Dr. Dan Mrozowski, and Stephen McDonald for reading my work and encouraging my thought process. Additionally, to my McFarland editor Dré Person, for helping me along with the publication process.

To my friends for their unwavering support, and for bearing with me as I discussed horror movies non-stop for the past few years ... and will continue to do so for the rest of my life: Zainab, Chris, Emily, Cara, Heather, Emma, Noémie, and the countless other friends who willingly open the extensive historical queer horror can of worms.

For the late John Palencsar and Jen Giasone.

Preface

Cult filmmaker John Waters once expressed that "without obsession, life is nothing." I began the writing of this book back in graduate school in 2019 as I was planning the topic of my American Studies master's thesis. Through reflection, I found that who I am is a combination of obsessions, two of the most passionate being American history and horror films. Since I was a child, I have been instinctively drawn to horror films. Combing through the horror selection at Blockbuster Video was both terrifying and thrilling, with images of Chucky from *Child's Play* and Freddy Krueger of *A Nightmare on Elm Street* imprinting themselves on my subconscious. I started realizing I was queer as a young teen. That too was terrifying and thrilling. Back then, I was unaware that who I was and the horror genre itself would become intertwined, as I found in my research that queerness is rooted in horror, and vice versa. My obsessions and my queerness are at the center of this book; I would not be able to write this had I not been queer and a horror lover.

Queer Screams is about queer representation in American horror films, and how queer folks can and should reclaim the horror genre as their own. Through the reclamation process, queer folks will find catharsis. The main objective of *Queer Screams* is to show *how* queer people find catharsis in the horror genre, mainly by using "gay sensibility," as coined by queer film historian and activist Vito Russo, to identify queer characters and storylines in horror cinema. Based on a history of marginalization and trauma due to homophobia and transphobia, the fantasy of the horror genre, along with it being deeply rooted in queer sensibility, allows queer folks to see themselves within the frame of the bloody silver screen. Although not all representations are obvious or positive, the genre is rich in queer history as it reflects societal fears. For decades, the fear of the queer has permeated the horror genre, and many queer folks are now taking claim of horror—an act of reclamation, just as the term "queer" and the pink triangle designated to gay men during the Holocaust has been reclaimed.

I follow the queer experience chronologically through history. Based on the specific decade, horror films reflect the fears of that decade. This includes the fear of the Lavender Menace of the Cold War 1950s, the fear of HIV/AIDS as depicted in homoerotic vampire films of the 1980s, and the revenge through representation of the anti-queer Trump era. I examine films through their historical lens and correlate them to the American queer experience. This book begins by outlining the various ways in which I analyzed horror films for queer representation. As film is used by scholars to study history, horror films are a key component in this research. Horror films are created to scare, haunt, shock, and horrify. As such, turbulent times in American history are often subjects of horror films or at least inspirations. Throughout the twentieth century, America has used social Others such as queer folks to instill fear in the majority, particularly straight white Americans. Queers have been demonized, pitied, ridiculed, and studied for mental illness for decades, resulting in real life and on-screen violence. This violence was perpetuated through film, specifically horror films, to cause fear and panic in the minds of heterosexual Americans, and often leaving the queer for dead. As I will explain in the subsequent chapters, queers took the form of monsters, aliens, deviants, and perverts— they were villains. However, due to film censorship and the Hays Code (a set of regulations that will be discussed in Chapter 1), often these monsters were not outright queer but rather subtextual queers. The subtextual queer would be used for decades to villainize Otherness, i.e., queerness.

Despite this history of on-screen horror violence and its effects on the minds of Americans both queer and straight, there is a silver lining that has grown in the past few decades: catharsis through reclamation. Horror figures like Frankenstein's monster (his queerness will be elaborated in Chapter 1) and the ever-frequent horror cliché of the Final Girl (the often-lone survivor and killer of a horror film's antagonist) have been reclaimed by queer horror fans as queer characters. They have become positive symbols of determination, survival, outsiderness, and destroyers of oppressive forces.

Of the books I have studied in preparation for writing *Queer Screams*, I have not discovered a book devoted to queer representation in horror from the past two decades. The books I have found do not mention current LGBTQ+ issues, such as transgender rights, marriage equality, or non-binary representation. My book bridges the gap between the ground-breaking works on queer film that have come before, such as Harry M. Benshoff's invaluable *Monsters in the Closet: Homosexuality and the Horror Film* (1997) and Vito Russo's pivotal *The Celluloid Closet:*

Homosexuality in the Movies (1982), and offers a unique focus on queer film, theory, horror, and the American queer experience.

As a queer horror film fan, I have always been fascinated by the draw to horror, especially for queer folks. While an avid fan of the genre, I found countless other queer folks who themselves are drawn to the fantastical and the macabre. I began to research to pinpoint why there is such a pull to the genre for us queer folks and began finding specific films of queer focus. Throughout my research, I found that homophobic slurs in horror films were frequent, leading me to believe that the majority of horror film history was one of transphobia and homophobia. However, I began to turn my focus toward subtextual elements of queerness and found amazingly diverse representations of queer folks throughout the horror canon. I scoured hundreds of films from the 1930s to 2021, keeping note of *seen* and *unseen* queerness on the silver screen. Through my personal Instagram account, where I connect and interact with fellow horror-obsessed queers, I reached out to the horror community for input on why they, as queer folks, love horror. As I am a bisexual cisgender white woman, my insight is only one view in the diverse spectrum of queerness. With my questionnaire, I have included the responses from non-binary, gay, queer, and lesbian folks who adore horror for all sorts of reasons, some differing from my own, in the concluding chapter of this book. Ultimately, their input supports my argument for the invaluable cathartic nature of horror.

Unlike queer horror publications of the past, my research aims to evaluate several representations of the LGBTQ+ community, particularly transgender, gay, lesbian, bisexual/pansexual, intersex, and non-binary representation. I devote an entire chapter and additional moments in other chapters to the representation of transgender, intersex, and non-binary folks in horror and the use of the trans body *as* horror by writers and directors. For this research, I dove into a study conducted in 2018 that evaluated the use of transgender bodies as titillating fodder in film and its effect on the general American population on the perception of real transgender people, especially transgender women of color.

Regarding queer BIPOC in this book, there will appear to be a glaring dearth of representation. Though I have scoured hundreds of films, queer BIPOC characters were scarce and only steadily included in horror scripts in the 2000s. A good resource to dive deeper into BIPOC representation, specifically black representation, in horror films is Robin R. Means Coleman's *Horror Noire: Blacks in American Horror Films from the 1890s to Present*, which touches upon queer black representation in horror films as well as popular culture.

My goal in writing this book is to spark renewed interest in queer film studies, specifically the impact and benefits of the horror genre for queer folks. Additionally, the aim of *Queer Screams* is to find those who have been apprehensive about the horror genre and supply them with the knowledge to better analyze, understand, appreciate, and enjoy the genre. With this knowledge, I hope that queer viewers find themselves on the bloody silver screen, and with that discovery, achieve pride and catharsis.

The bibliography for my work includes dozens of ground-breaking scholarly publications. This includes, as stated earlier, *The Celluloid Closet* and *Monsters in the Closet: Homosexuality and the Horror Film*, two of the more prominent publications on queer film history and horror film history. My bibliography also includes *A Queer History of the United States* by Michael Bronski, *How to Survive a Plague: The Story of How Activists and Scientists Tamed AIDS* by David France, *Horror Noire: Blacks in American Horror Films from the 1890s to Present* by Robin R. Means Coleman, *Behind the Screen: How Gays and Lesbians Shaped Hollywood, 1910–1969* by William Mann, publications by gender and sexuality theorists Judith Butler and Jack Halberstam, and several articles from horror magazines *Fangoria* and *Rue Morgue*. The bulk of my primary sources are films, of which I watched and evaluated over 200, with a special focus on over ninety individual films. I identified signs of queer subtext, homophobic language, and LGBTQ+ representation both negative and positive.

The organizational style of my book is chronological, interweaving film, cultural history, and theory through the 1930s to 2021. I provide a timeline at the beginning of each chapter to help organize the historical periods, each breaking down years of importance to American queer history and horror films. My educational background is American Studies; thus, I have tried to refrain from going beyond the United States, despite there being a wide breadth of horror films with queer representation produced and distributed in several countries including Canada, the United Kingdom, France, Mexico, and Italy.

The reasoning behind my drive to write this book over the course of three years is the desire to both historically link horror to queerness and to today's American society. The shared American past is unfortunately saturated with racism, misogyny, and queerphobia. With the rise of #MeToo, the Black Lives Matter movement, and the growing open discourse of queer life over the past decade, Americans find value in critiquing the past to create a more equitable present and future. Celebrities are being scrutinized for past problematic speech and behaviors, just as the American powers that be are being scolded for the upholding of white supremacist historical figures through the hero-washing of historical monuments and texts. One of my goals in writing *Queer Screams* is for the text to be an exposition of problematic storylines and figures (as well as progressive horror film moments) to help facilitate a better future for the horror genre. Readers can dive into the issues with past horror scripts, learn from them, and demand both mainstream and independent film productions be better through the means of more diverse hiring practices and storytelling. History is meant to be used as an educational tool—let's use the queer history of horror as a tool to bring about positive change.

I conclude this preface with a brief note regarding how I feel about the magnificently gruesome, fantastic, ground-breaking, and enlightening films featured in this publication. As a historian, I have looked at the following films objectively when discussing their intentional or accidental queerphobia and past comments and interviews of actors, writers, and directors reflecting on their films. My critique of these films is often harsh, and this is not meant to indicate that I do not have a great appreciation for the actors, filmmakers, and writers of the thousands of films in this incredible genre. I grew up watching, celebrating, cringing at, and cowering from these films, and I hope my historical analysis of these cultural primary sources act not only as criticism but as hope for better treatment of queer folks by the horror genre. By the end of this book, you will see that the genre itself is already honoring my hopes.

Introduction

"Growing up gay [...] you are often made to feel like you are an abomination. Therefore, when I watch horror films, I can identify with both the monster and the final girl fighting for her life, because I am, by my very nature, both."—Jeffrey, 27[1]

Stereotypes in Film as Historical Reflection

Films transform and reflect audience reality. They can evoke myriad emotional responses such as empathy, love, anxiety, and fear. Overall, as there is a deep history of misogyny and racism in film, homophobic tones have also been present for decades. Gay men have been typecast as eccentric, flamboyant, unintelligent, and sissy, and lesbians have been typecast as manly, unattractive, predatory, and brutish. Additionally, non-binary and transgender folks have been either monstrous or entirely invisible. These stereotypes often accompany a central character theme, such as the comedic role or that of a villain, and they persist in all genres of films released in the twentieth century. Horror films often use and have used these stereotypes for a darker purpose and evoke the more negative emotions emitted through film.

Horror films examine fear, anxiety, relief, rage, and hope, though they lean toward human discomfort responses overall. Often, these fears are projections of mass societal anxieties that touch upon politics, psychology, sociology, and relationships between vastly different life experiences of a community or country. The horror genre always reflects social anxieties and fears. Examples include the 1950s' invasion anxiety as seen in *Invasion of the Body Snatchers* (1956), the 1980s' contagious queers conveyed in *The Hunger* (1983) and *Fright Night* (1985), the racism of the 1960s illuminated in the final moments of *Night of the Living Dead* (1968), and the post–9/11 anxiety of societal apocalypse like the alien invasion of New York City in *Cloverfield* (2008). As historical dramas reflect on major historical events and movements like World War II, the antebellum South, and 1960s social unrest, horror uses the fantastic to develop the internal fears of these same and countless other historical periods, resulting in an extrapolation of shared realities.

Unfortunately, American horror films have a history of divisiveness. Theories have developed equating horror films to historical and contemporary violent events and tendencies, thus conjuring fear and anxiety in viewers. Some people simply cannot stand the idea of fear as entertainment due to its violent nature, causing discomfort, and would rather turn to a comedy or historical drama. Often, the trauma inflicted upon characters on-screen deeply affects viewers long after the final credits. For populations with a deep history of traumatic experiences such as the LGBTQ+ community which includes lesbian, gay, bisexual, transgender, pansexual, and countless other queer identities that fall on the queer spectrum, a film can either trigger or help resolve the issues related to that traumatic history. This book will discuss the power of film in reflecting and igniting societal fears, how horror films in particular showcase these fears, and how heterosexual and queer audiences alike are affected by them. The fears in question are the ones aimed toward some of the most prominent Others, those that are disenfranchised, oppressed, and outcast in a dominant heterosexual, cisgender, patriarchal, white American society: lesbian, gay, bisexual, transgender, non-binary, and queer folks.

Films have been a means to perpetuate stereotypes and social attitudes since the inception of modern film in the early twentieth century. Films have often typecast certain minority groups to assert power over such groups to create and reflect hierarchy within American society. For example, stereotypes formed through minstrel shows and the creation of blackface were used to showcase the supposed inferiority of Black Americans, as did unintelligent and hyper-feminine attributes became commonplace with the portrayals of women. For queer folks, the sissy and butch were formed to oppress gay men and lesbians through painting all gays and lesbians with one broad brush. This is a recurring theme in both mainstream and horror films. As asserted by authors Elizabeth and Stuart Ewen in *Typecasting: On the Arts and Sciences of Human Inequality, a History of Dominant Ideas*, "Typecasting, is not simply about representation; it is the language of power."[2] Power over minority groups keeps these groups from asserting personhood and is key to suppressing their influence over the minds of the majority. Queer folks were not being shown as the people they were, but rather, some*thing* to be feared, especially in horror films: perverts, serial killers, science experiments gone wrong, an affront to God, a "screaming queen or interior decorators."[3] To quote film studies scholar Richard Dyer,

> Where gayness occurs in films it does so as *part of* dominant ideology. It is not there to express itself, but rather to express something about sexuality in general *as understood by heterosexuals* ... how homosexuality is thought and felt by heterosexuals is part and parcel of the way the culture teaches them (and us) to think and feel about their heterosexuality. Anti-gayness is not a discrete ideological system, but part of the overall sexual ideology of our culture.[4]

The pervasive anti-gayness that ran throughout American institutions and mediums from the early to mid–1900s resulted in ideas of heterosexual supremacy, homosexual demonization, often through monsterization, and created a sexual Other that would be blamed for many of society's ills. Queer and straight folks were, and are, both personally and socially affected by homophobic psychology, laws, and stereotypes.

The common stereotypes of queer folks that dominated a majority of twentieth-century America included mental illness, pedophilic tendencies, and over-sexualization. As a result, thousands of queer and transgender folks were institutionalized, at the mercy of dominant religious thought that told them they were sinners and monsters. Dominant psychology would label them confused, deviant, predatory, and mentally ill. They were "queer monsters." Both religion and science dictated how society should see queer people: monsters to be feared and pitied, and in many cases, they should be destroyed physically, emotionally, or mentally through bullying, conversion therapy, lobotomy, and murder. Monsters like the queer monster were on the silver screen to terrify audiences. They were outcasts, those that lurk in the shadows, and otherworldly creatures that did not fit in with "normal" society. Queer folks have been the key figures of horror films both in physical and subtextual terms, a continuous trend through the twenty-first century.

Roots of Apathy: The Misrepresentation of the Queer and the Invention of Otherness

Though American horror films focus on both human and non-human monsters, there is a contradictory nature within classic monster tropes: you sympathize while also fearing the villains and anti-heroes. Monsters such as the Wolfman or Frankenstein's Monster are loved and feared by audiences, yet their lives are meant to be pitied for their misfortunate appearances, their fate of violent deaths, and ultimate curses. Those whom we pity are not seen as "one of us," but rather as an Other. This results in dehumanization. The death of the monster is not meant to be the main concern at the end of the film. Rather, their death signifies relief: the "normal" couple or lone hero, the antithesis of Otherness, is finally safe from the monster's oddness and violence.

The Other is needed for comparison to the dominant idea of normality in society, where "without gays, straights are not straight."[5] The Other, normalcy's opposite, becomes a subject of interest for all audiences of a horror film. Questions arise of its true nature, intent, or level of threat. While being reviled as villainous or scary, the Other is simultaneously titillating, as evident in classic monster movies. Audiences are fascinated by the who, what, where, when, and how of horror monsters: they are terrifying as well as exciting to watch due to their intriguing Otherness. Unfortunately, the Otherness placed upon the monster has adverse effects on how viewers see the diversity among humanity. Otherness in horror films is not just intriguing, but terrifying. Linking the two emotions results in the placement of fear and anxiety upon both fictional characters and human beings that are seen as abnormal.

Queer people have perpetually been seen as an Other. As a result, society has deemed them less-than or something to be feared, sowing the seeds of apathy toward queer lives and experiences. As films are influencers and reflectors of social thought, those that use queer characters as an accompanying Other to the "normal" protagonist drive the audience to react apathetically to a queer person on screen. Much of this Othering was and is orchestrated by cisgender (denoting or relating to a person whose sense of personal identity and gender expression corresponds with the sex assigned to them at birth), heterosexual, and usually white males, resulting in queer characters that are highly inauthentic and presented with harmful stereotypes. "[Queer] films," explains Boze Hadleigh, author of *The Lavender Screen: The Gay and Lesbian Films—Their Stars, Directors, and Critics*, "depict not so much a homosexual world or lifestyle as straight society's assumptions."[6] The assumption of the queer community by heterosexuals is that of lust. Queer stereotypes in media persist with gay men jumping from relationship to relationship, bent on sexual exploits rather than long-lasting romantic relationships. Queer women are painted as moving too fast, their U-Hauls in tow after the first date, only for the relationship to fizzle out after the loss of the initial butterflies. Straight folks, on the other hand, have thousands of romantic comedies dedicated to their relationships. If we're lucky, they will have a fun queer sidekick. The film and media stereotype of lustful queer folks that do not exhibit or deserve the same love as their heterosexual counterparts perpetuates apathy toward queer life. If it is perceived that queer folks are only about sex and not love, a universal human emotion, they are viewed as less than human, effectively Othering them. Apathy accompanies this idea, making queer folks' very existence easy to dismiss. Among the most violent of dismissals are the brutality, abuse, and murder of queer folks. Hadleigh asserts that "it's often been theorized that there is a direct relationship between treatment of gays in the media and growing anti-gay violence."[7] Though horror films rarely spare anyone, it is the Othering of queer folks in film that fosters anti-gay attitudes, leading to real-life violence.

Homophobia in Film and Real-Life Violence

The violence that is associated with anti-gay sentiments in media is not only external, such as murder, bullying, and institutionalization, but also internal. Not all, but many queer folks suffer from depression, addiction, anxiety, self-harm, and suicidal thoughts.[8] As such, sexuality expression and gender anxiety have been used *as* horror in American horror films, reaping external and internal traumatic violent results.

How a person deals with trauma vary based on the individual. Queer folks' traumatic history in America has lent itself to therapy, the formation of non-biological queer families, and other means of finding solace in one's body, mind, and place in the world. Not every queer person has experienced violence, but the vast majority are familiar with the emotional, mental, social, and physical violence inflicted upon people across the queer spectrum. Being queer is nothing to fear, but queer folks have been systemically taught to fear the Other, the queer, the strange and unusual—ultimately, themselves. In this effect, queer folks often find themselves on the bloody silver screen in various monstrous bodies, either being chased through the mountainside or wielding fangs, inflicting harm on perceived innocents. As they have been taught by religious institutions and dominant social creeds throughout the twentieth century, to be queer is to be monstrous.

American horror films attract a diverse audience that seeks to be transported into a world of fear, just as a viewer of a romance wants to be transported into a love story. The horror film is not attractive to everyone. However, it has become evident that a large portion of queer cinephiles adore horror. Based on historical fears, and the nature of horror films being about the monstrous, queer folks find solace in a genre that aims to frighten. *Queer Screams* examines the reasons why queer folks are drawn to the genre. The paramount reason is the subtextual elements that allow queer folks to see themselves in horror characters and themes.

Subtextual Queerness in the Fantastic

In the early days of horror during the 1930s and 1940s, film studios expected that horror audiences would identify with the victims and survivors, all of whom were white and apparently heterosexual, the more "normal" characters of a horror film. However, time and time again, movie monsters and other perceived villains were often far more relatable than their "normal" counterparts, especially to societal outcasts such as queer people. The monsters of this era, and the numerous monsters to follow, are complex: they are feared yet sympathized with, loved and hated, heroes and villains. Where normalcy represents the average heterosexual couple or classic nuclear family, the Other signifies a threat, deviation from the norm, or a strange phenomenon. This is the nature of the Other. We all have differences in our lives that make us "abnormal" in some shape or form. The heterosexual couple at the end of a creature feature is too normal for a horror audience. The Other is far more fascinating, therefore relatable, especially to societal outcasts. The Other represents what society suppresses within itself, whether it is a physical deformity, a fascination with the macabre, or a romantic impulse that is not perceived as normal by the heterosexual patriarchy. Those feelings that get suppressed are often attributed to those we oppress in American society. In Mark Jancovich's *Horror, the Film Reader*, film theorist Robin Wood argues that "'the true subject of the horror genre is the struggle for recognition of all that our civilization represses and oppresses.'" As indicated by Jancovich, Wood posits that

> the appeal of horror is primarily due to our identification with the Other, that which our society represses and defines as monstrous. As Wood puts it, "Central to the effect and fascination of horror films is their fulfillment of our nightmare wish to smash the norms that oppress us."[9]

Horror allows the oppressed to see normality destroyed on screen, enabling them to be more at ease with their perceived abnormalities. This is especially the case with queer folks who have been oppressed in American society for nearly all the twentieth century and told to suppress their sexual and romantic feelings for those of the same sex. With a genre rooted in the fantastic, horror is a place in which queer folks can see themselves either explicitly or in the film's subtext.

The fantastic nature of the horror genre allows for independent interpretation, revelation, and imagination through and beyond the silver screen. Particularly for queer audiences of horror, a queer lens can provide them with the vision to see parallels between their experiences and the experiences of a plethora of horror canon characters, whether it is victim, Final Girl, killer, or monster. The realm of the fantastic defies normalcy, allowing for various facets of Otherness such as "androgynes, transsexuals, gender-switching people, and alien sexuality that is clearly not heterosexual."[10] As a genre, horror is the perfect avenue to confront societal fear of diversity, exhibited by the Other. Not only does horror *show* Otherness, but truly examines it. Many horror films are used as social commentary to extrapolate what is normal, what isn't, and why not.

Wood offers a formula for which we can understand the horror film through social norms and Otherness. To begin, Wood's formula acknowledges that normality is threatened by the Monster.[11] There are three variables in Wood's horror film formula: normality, the Monster, and the relationship between the two. Normality is represented by the heterosexual couple, suburban family, and social institutions such as the Catholic or Christian church. Normality is boring—the cliché heterosexual couple and monotonous actions of police and clergy are nothing fantastic. The fantastic lies in the Monster. The Monster is also, as Wood states, "much more protean, changing from period to period as society's basic fears clothe themselves in fashionable or immediately accessible garments—rather as dreams use material from recent memory to express conflicts or desires that may go back to early childhood."[12] Wood's theory asserts that horror film villains or thematic elements represent the fears of current society. Horror films, thus, reflect "normal" society's anxieties of the Other that would put normalcy in jeopardy. Viewing these monsters from a contemporary standpoint, it is easy for minority populations to identify with Otherness as the Monster reflects how society feels about them, the minority, in certain periods of history. However, it is not always clear what the monster's Otherness may represent.

For the majority of the twentieth century in America, queer folks have been disenfranchised, abused, bullied, murdered, and alienated by a world that caters to the heterosexual body and sensibility. It is like being trapped in a horror film: a villain, visible or invisible, is wreaking havoc on you and your friends, or the villain is just like you, but their attributes are designed to place fear in the hearts of society, resulting in self-alienation and loathing. Identification in horror films for queer folks is based on historical prejudices, "an articulation of these histories," explains historian Alexander Doty.[13] Horror theorist Andrew Tudor continues,

> If we really are to understand horror's appeal, and hence its social and cultural significance, we need to set aside the traditionally loaded ways in which "why horror?" has been asked. For the question should not be "why

horror?" at all. It should be, rather, why do *these* people like *this* horror in *this* place at *this* particular time? And what exactly are the consequences of their constructing their everyday sense of fearfulness and anxiety, their "landscapes of fear," out of such distinctive cultural materials?[14]

Subtext accompanies the fantastic. Without subtext, a fantastic genre such as science fiction or horror would be rendered too simple, not fantastic enough. Through subtext, all audiences can extrapolate plot devices and character tropes to find a representation of themselves. Queer audiences use subtext to their advantage. Too many films are whitewashed into being only available and applicable to straight, white audiences, whether due to studio executives' say in the project, writers that only show one point of view and alienate other populations, or a lack of understanding for multiple life experiences based on sexuality, race, economics, or gender identity. Minority populations are thus less likely to relate to what they are seeing in mainstream films. Understanding and using subtext can be the remedy—subtext allows anyone to become involved in a film and find themselves among the characters.

Queer readings of horror films are vital to representation where representation has traditionally been whitewashed. Unfortunately, queer readings of films have been accused of analyzing "too far into things" for the sake of making a film queerer. This is not the case. Queer folks are simply using their queer sensibility to find queer characters or plot points due to a decades-long lack of outright representation. Doty stresses that queer readings of films "aren't 'alternative' readings, wishful or willful misreadings, or 'reading too much into things' readings. They result from the recognition and articulation of the complex range of queerness that has been in popular culture texts and their audiences all along."[15] Queer folks recognize queerness and thus identify subtext that may not be obvious to heterosexual viewers. Additionally, as noted by film scholar Richard Dyer, "Audiences cannot make media images mean anything they want to, but they can select from the complexity of the image the meanings and feelings, the variations, inflections and contradictions, that work for them."[16] For queer folks, this is a powerful idea, in that, they can create their own survivors and monsters, making the process and those chosen quite personal.

bell hooks' *The Oppositional Gaze* describes the dilemma that marginalized spectators face when they look at harmful film representations. Whether offensive, derogatory, or deeply stereotyped, repulsion to damaging images of ourselves in film characters is common. The act of not looking can be a form of resistance against the power structures that conjured up this negative depiction.[17] However, hooks points to Annette Kuhn's *The Power of the Image* where Kuhn acknowledges the power of saying "no" to the oppressive images but also identifies the power of deconstructing those images. Kuhn advocates that

> the acts of analysis, of deconstruction, and of reading "against the grain" offers an additional pleasure—the pleasure of resistance, of saying "no"; not to "unsophisticated" enjoyment, by ourselves and others, of culturally dominant images, but to the structures of power which ask us to consume them uncritically and in highly circumscribed ways.[18]

When queer folks are critical of the images of themselves that were handed to them by the white, cisgender, and hetero-dominated film establishment, they are their own activists for better representation. If they ignore the shameful queer representations of the past, the status quo will remain, and their perceptions of cinema would continue to be negative. Whereas if queer people are critical to their representations, they hold the power to use these images to create new ones. The damsel in distress can become the ass-kicking heroine, the hideous monster can be gentle and misunderstood, and a troubled stereotypically coded queer boy with a killer inside him can be redeemed as a hero to thousands of young queers who relate to him and his demons. Through the critical reading process advocated by Dyer, Doty, hooks, and Kuhn, catharsis can be achieved for queer folks in their viewings of American horror films.

Finding Catharsis in Horror Through Final Girls and Reclamation

A horror film taps into the psyche of audience members and forces them to sit in a dark room watching their fears unfold before their eyes. As once stated by horror author Stephen King, "It may well be that the mass-media dream of horror can sometimes become a nationwide analyst's couch."[19] Horror can be therapeutic for a nation and its people that have dealt with suffering. Especially susceptible to horror stories are those Americans who have dealt with severe trauma not just on several occasions, but throughout their entire personal and public lives: minority populations. Whether due to racism, sexism, homophobia, or transphobia, minority populations have a unique American history of suffering based on something out of their control. American queer folks have a history of trauma. An extrapolation of traumatic pasts will follow throughout this book. Historically, queer lives have been dominated by the fear held by others toward queer people, and queer folks have had to fight to keep themselves safe. Safety is not often awarded to the protagonists of horror films; thus, the audience members are thrust into an uncomfortable space that allows them to confront their fears or trauma. Queer folks and horror films have a complicated relationship—both comfort and discomfort are found on the bloody silver screen, and it is with this relationship that catharsis can be found.

No life is explicitly violent or free from it. However, internal and external violence affects queer and transgender folks at a higher rate than many other communities in America, such as the heterosexual, cisgender, and white majority. Horror films deal with violence openly and showcase murderers, demonic creatures, and otherworldly animals wreaking bloody havoc on society. Psychological horror reflects the internal violence people go through, as well as how it is inflicted upon others. Through the avenue of the horror film, folks that have dealt with or are afraid of such violence can see their fears on screen from a safe distance, perhaps making it easier to cope with or understand. The monsters on screen, for the most part, are not real, as they are fictional characters. Although not real, the realm of fiction allows viewers to place themselves in the shoes of a monster, victim, or both. Queer folks, then, can take their experiences and correlate them to the on-screen horror and violence, either negatively or positively. As queer people in America have a long history of violence, misunderstanding, and abuse, as well as triumphs, queer folks can find catharsis through the horror film. Based on queer history, queer folks additionally have the right to *claim* perceived or outright queer characters in horror, for reclamation is an important part of the healing process. To heal from history, sometimes the oppressed must claim it for themselves, as to control the narrative. Queer folks have been labeled as monsters for centuries, and thus they have the authority to claim these same problematic monsters and their metaphors as their own. Complicated vampires or film slashers, once claimed by the queer community, can shed new light on their own experiences and can be a means to deal with the specific problems faced by the queer community.

Not only do queer folks identify with the clear Otherness of film monsters, but also with their victims. The Final Girl, who is frequently the sole survivor of the monster or slasher's rampage, is often quite androgynous and has equally feminine and masculine characteristics. The ability for the Final Girl to have these non-binary features makes her accessible to all, and her ability to rise above an oppressor is identifiable for queer folks and their experiences as being oppressed. Thus, Final Girls are quite queer, and queer folks have as much of a right to claim them as they do the monsters. As stated by author Allison Graham in her examination of horror through the lens of Freudian theory that she believes offers the most accessible way to understand the roots, and for the purposes of this book, the undeniable queer roots of the genre,

> madness (from *The Cabinet of Dr. Caligari* to *Psycho* to *The Shining*), monsters—whether "natural" (*Nosferatu, Jaws, Gremlins*) or "synthetic" (*Frankenstein, The Car*)—and satanic possession (*Rosemary's Baby, The Exorcist*) can be interpreted as dramatizations of our fear of our own "double" nature, the projecting upon another (a dead mother, shark, a car, the devil) the terrors and desires we cannot enact outside the realm of art or dream.[20]

Along with a perfect explanation of American society's general draw to the horror genre, whether Graham knows this or not, she is perfectly describing the queer viewing experience, especially those of history's past that could not safely be open about their identities. The "double" nature of a queer person is the dueling desires and fears within: to be out is to be both liberated and targeted. Through horror, queer folks can project themselves into the monsters and Final Girls on-screen, themselves also free, triumphant, defeated, and caged, encompassing dozens of emotions that are shared between character and viewer. Additionally, many queer folks cannot express themselves openly. Therefore, they can project their fears and even courage onto those in film, as Graham explains, the feelings they cannot enact outside of their own art or dreams.

For the sake of finding peace with oneself or fulfilling a desire to see queer folks on screen, reading and understanding horror as an extremely queer genre can allow for queer catharsis. Trace Thurman, a featured writer for *Gayly Dreadful*, an online publication dedicated to queer horror, and co-host of the podcast *Horror Queers*, identifies the anger that queer folks have which has accumulated after decades of oppression. This anger can be channeled into creating and viewing art, specifically the horror genre.

> Horror films provide a necessary catharsis for viewers who are able to handle (or stomach) their content, and this is something that, quite honestly, queer viewers need. It would never be argued that growing up queer is easy, and watching horror films is just one of the cathartic ways (among many others) to deal with the stresses of simply being queer.[21]

Seeing a coded queer character get revenge on a room full of bullies, a hideous monster escaping the clutches of the angry mob, or a terrified young woman rise from the ashes to defeat the man that has been chasing her for an hour and thirty minutes gives queer folks, especially young ones, hope that they too can survive whatever life may throw at them. *This is catharsis.*

Horror Representation

When I discuss the topic of this book with any audience, there is always one person who begs the question "Are there even any gay people in horror movies?" The rise of this question excites me, for then I have the opportunity of enlightening someone to the wide range of queer characters and themes in horror. But I soon began to ask why this question is posited in the first place. Where does the idea of no queer folks in horror come from? It could be for the simple fact that queer people hardly appear in movies at all, let alone horror. However, two ideas come to mind as to why this question is frequently asked: (1) the audience member lacks what film historian and gay activist Vito Russo calls a "gay sensibility," and (2) unremembering due to trauma.[22]

"Gay sensibility" is the ability to spot subtextual clues that corroborate the existence of a queer character or theme. This point mostly refers to cisgender, heterosexual audience members who may not fully understand the queer experience, thus may not be able to readily identify it. Queer folks have developed the skill of identification since childhood, looking for one another in a crowd, amongst family and friends, to find others like them with simply a look, a glance. Brian Pronger describes this identification tactic best in his book *The Arena of Masculinity: Sports, Homosexuality, and the Meaning of Sex* (1990):

> In Stanley Kubrick's film *The Shining* [(1980)], there is a similar recognition between an older man, a chef, and a little boy [...] it is of a special gift of insight.... The gay look and deportment are the products of the knowledge of paradox and estrangement, and of adjusting oneself to a world which doesn't fit. Having had this experience, gay men can recognize it in each other. "It takes one to know one."[23]

Queer folks have socially evolved to use such identification methods to find one another, find community. Therefore, this ability to recognize one another in real life is then transferred to on-screen representations and/or invisibility. Cisgender, heterosexual folks have not grown up with the need to have a skillset to identify one another as they have been the default for centuries. Their ability to sense queer people on screen is consequently lacking in strength. This point also reflects on the fact that early films, and subsequent films due to decades of subtextual practices, were not permitted to be open about queer characters due to the censorship by the Hays Code which will be discussed in Chapter 1.

The point of unremembering due to trauma can be most associated with queer audience members who grew so accustomed to oppression, societal indifference to crises such as the HIV/AIDS epidemic, and violence against queers in film that they cannot identify or remember any positive portrayals. The painful past of seeing characters die by suicide because of being queer and seeing them shunned by family and society hits too close to home, which results in unremembering as a defense mechanism. Christopher Castiglia and Christopher Reed, authors of "Queer Theory Is Burning: Sexual Revolution and Traumatic Unremembering," acknowledge that "the positive aspects of a traumatized past (what can be half-remembered around the edges of lack) are recast as future aspirations (what one wants when one 'works through' trauma). This might lead to either a romanticizing of futurity or its vilification as the time of unachievable reparation."[24] The result is the idea that queer characters never existed at all in film. Queer folks seem to have forgotten the shame these queer characters felt, their struggles, and their demise because they wished to no longer see themselves being taken advantage of or killed on the big screen.

This amnesia of the queer person's experience in film is a result of these two points of thought. By shedding light on all the ways and instances in which queer folks have been present on the silver screen, queer folks can reclaim the moments of queer character destruction and turn them into something new for the future. Castiglia and Reed urge "a return of/to memory as a means to resolve queer theory's persistent melancholy, to reanimate its connections with the social and rhetorical innovations of previous generations of gay and lesbian thinkers (or with current generations that still identify with that past)."[25] It is through memory that queer folks can reclaim their past. The horror genre is an avenue in which to do so. Harmful representations of queer characters in horror have existed throughout the history of film. Though many are openly stereotypical including being sissy, flamboyant, pathetic, underdeveloped, or hollow, such characters can be reclaimed by those they were meant to hurt. Additionally, this book discusses the myriad queer characters in horror that are quite positive, both from past and present films. These positive characters, most of whom will be discussed in the later chapters, are themselves a form of reclamation and a response to the decades of negative portrayals.

Why queer folks enjoy horror is a vague and often contradictory question. Why does a population with a diverse range of sexual orientations and gender identities tend to come together and enjoy a genre that is explicitly violent and often traumatic? To pinpoint this pull toward the horror genre for queer folks, it must be examined why a group of people identify with horror in a particular period, as advocated by theorist Andrew Tudor. Each decade of the twentieth century experiences different struggles, with some that last only for the decade or continue. Queer struggles and movements have lingered far beyond their starting points, and these struggles tend to revolve around societal fear of the Other and an effort to change minds through activist movements. Horror films help navigate each decade for they reflect what is feared during the time of their inception: plague, aliens, monsters, serial killers, or demons. Horror films should not be analyzed at face value, however. As once expressed by theorist Gilles Deleuze, it is not what a piece of art is, but rather what it does.[26] The art examined in this book are horror films, but the research that is exhibited is not just the characters, actors, writers, or directors in the film itself. *Queer Screams* also analyses how these film components have made and continue to make queer audiences feel, and how they affect and reflect history. The nature of a horror film is to get a reaction from the audience, usually one of shock and fear. Queer audiences are affected differently: they can find validation and catharsis in horror stories and films because of the genre's ability to reflect the fears, violence, and triumphs of LGBTQ+ realities within their historical experiences.

Queer Screams covers a time span of horror films from *Frankenstein* (1931) to the films of 2021 chronologically with extrapolation of corresponding historical experiences. A timeline will be provided at the beginning of each chapter to visually conceptualize the connections between a film and the decade or era it was released. Each film's corresponding decade or era will be examined for moments of minor, though meaningful, or significant queer experiences, whether politically, medically, socially, and/or personally. Ultimately, the decade in which a film is made speaks through the film itself and provides a lens through which to view and study American queer history. Insight by horror actors, writers, directors, historians, and fans will be included as examples of how horror affects multiple facets of life beyond the bloody silver screen. Prominent throughout is Mark Patton, queer activist and star of *A Nightmare on Elm Street 2: Freddy's Revenge* (1985). His life is contemporaneous with Hollywood homophobia, the HIV/AIDS epidemic, and the reclamation of a once painful past. Patton's story along with the various stories throughout this book, all of which are linked to the horror genre, reflect the diverse experiences faced by a queer person: pain and pleasure, hell and heaven.

CHAPTER 1

The Queens of Hollywood

Queer Roots, Censorship,
and the Lavender Menace
(the 1930s–1940s)

Queer Monsters and the Beginning
of the Production Code

1922 ▸ Dr. Wilhelm Stekel publishes *The Homosexual Neurosis*

1929 ▸ U.S. enters Great Depression following stock market crash

1930 ▸ Hays Code established

1931 ▸ *Dracula*   *Frankenstein*

1932 ▸ *The Old Dark House*   *Freaks*

1933 ▸ Dr. Hirschfield's Institute of Sexual Research is destroyed by Nazis in Berlin   *The Invisible Man*

1934 ▸ Production Code Administration is implemented

1935 ▸ *Bride of Frankenstein*

1936 ▸ *Dracula's Daughter*

1937 ▸ J. Edgar Hoover writes "War of the Sex Criminal," *The New York Herald Tribune*

Figure 1

Vaudeville, a theatrical show that incorporated singing, dancing, acting, and comedic performances, was a means to entertain the
masses before the development of the moving image, and the interim
between silent films and the innovation of sound in feature films by the
mid–1920s. Theater troupes put on performances often incorporat-
ing queer subtext into their shows with the likes of gender-bending and

cross-dressing musical and comedic acts. Queer folks were among the ranks of these troupes, many of whom would go on to star in motion pictures and torrent into the film industry. Vaudeville provided an avenue for people who were not professionally trained enough for the main stage but who wanted to make their presence known among the underground, while still entertaining the public. Many conservative Americans viewed the theater world as seedy and a defiance of traditional American gender roles. Entertainment through the avenues of theater, burlesque, vaudeville, and film was, as stated by queer historian Michael Bronski,

> understood by many public moralists to be an environment of sexual promiscuity, criminal activity, and gambling [...] For public moralists, the problem was not just that theaters bred immorality and crime, but that they let the imagination flourish ... promoted instability and immorality by allowing deviations from sexual and gender norms to materialize onstage.[1]

This sort of atmosphere spawned the careers of numerous queer people who would go on to star on the silver screen, such as Ernest Thesiger in *Bride of Frankenstein* (1935) and James Whale, the director of *Frankenstein* (1931), *The Invisible Man* (1933), and *Bride of Frankenstein*. Tod Browning, director of *Dracula* (1931) and *Freaks* (1932), though heterosexual, was also an alumnus of vaudeville, who, along with folks like Whale, help to solidify horror's vaudeville roots.

To combat the overt queerness of film actors and creators like Thesiger and Whale, motion picture executives devised a code that would regulate behavior, something not done in vaudeville especially. The Code would oversee and regulate film writers to ensure no deviance, such as men dressed as women or storylines involving queer love, would be on display for ordinary Americans—an attempt to guarantee that there would be as little left to the imagination as possible. Of course, this was not always effective. However, the newly developed Hays Code, also known as the Production Code, was established in March of 1930 by Will H. Hays. The regulations set by the Hays Code demanded that all films "shall not imply that low forms of sex relationship are the accepted or common thing," implying that adultery and pre-marital sex should not be shown in a positive light.[2] Additionally, all references to "sexual perversion" were forbidden. There is no doubt that sexual perversion included homosexuality. The basis for this idea of homosexuality as sexual perversion can be linked in part to the work of Dr. Wilhelm Stekel and his publication *The Homosexual Neurosis* (1922). In his book, Dr. Stekel, an Austrian psychoanalyst and pupil of Dr. Sigmund Freud, refuted many claims in psychoanalysis that described homosexuality as an immature stage of adult sexuality and an inborn condition that can be cured with psychoanalytic treatment. He associated homosexuality with epilepsy, a condition he understood as a "particular form of hysteria [...] as well as with sadism, masochism, incestuous desires, jealousy, paranoia, criminality, and regression to baser animalistic instincts."[3] Along with the flawed scientific rationale for the Code, the Catholic church provided moral guidance for Code regulations. William Mann explains in his book *Behind the Screen: How Gays and Lesbians Shaped Hollywood, 1910–1969,* "'What emerged [in the Code] was a fascinating combination of Catholic theology, conservative politics, and pop psychology—an amalgam that would control the content of Hollywood films for three decades.'"[4]

The Roaring Twenties, in which Dr. Stekel published his work, was regarded as one of the most opulent, wild, and sexually free decades of the twentieth century. Writers and artists of the decade flocked to beacons of artistic expression such as New York City, Paris, and Berlin to participate in new ways of personal expression, where homosexuality, bisexuality, and genderfluidity were prevalent. Theater and vaudeville flourished, and the personal and sexual expressions of the decade were on full display. Berlin during the 1920s, for example, was the hub for queer study and sexology thanks to the research conducted by Dr. Magnus Hirschfeld, an openly gay Jewish physician. By 1918, Berlin was one of the most hospitable German cities toward homosexuality. Dr. Hirschfeld established the Institut für Sexualwissenschaft (The Institute of Sexual Research) in 1919 and would go on to publish nearly two hundred pieces on human homosexuality. Unfortunately, the party ended with the crash of the American stock market and the onset of Nazism throughout Europe in the 1930s, where Dr. Hirschfield's institute, which housed an invaluable collection of documents about sex and sexuality, was ransacked by fascist students, and later set ablaze on May 6, 1933. With the American Great Depression, conservative gender roles were encouraged, and the Roaring Twenties were seen as a point that could be blamed for the country's ills. Men were out of work and no longer in firm control of the family unit, causing their masculinity to be put into question. Women who had previously been housewives were thrust into the workplace to support the crumbling finances of said family unit. Traditional gender roles had quickly become a thing of the past, and blame was thrown at the hedonists of the 1920s: sophisticates and queers. Observed by historian George Chauncey, "The revulsion against gay life in the early 1930s was part of a larger reaction to the perceived 'excesses' of the Prohibition years and blurring of the boundaries between acceptable and unacceptable public sociability."[5] "In the 1930s," adds William Mann, "homosexuals took on greater menace because by their nature, they called into question such fundamental

societal cornerstones as male supremacy, gender and social arrange-
ments, and the sanctity of church and family."[6]

Harry M. Benshoff, author of *Monsters in the Closet: Homosexuality and the Horror Film*, notes that the myriad alleged homosexual
attributes described by Dr. Stekel in *The Homosexual Neurosis* comprise
the themes and obsessions within classic Hollywood horror films.[7] The
1930s monster films of major studios, as stated by historian Vito Russo
in his groundbreaking work *The Celluloid Closet: Homosexuality in the
Movies*, portray queers as "predatory twilight creatures."[8] Ironically, at
the helm of several of these early monster films was openly gay director James Whale, born from England's vaudeville scene, who inserted
his sexuality and societal fear thereof into his dark masterpieces. His
films serve as firm roots for the horror genre and will be discussed later
in detail.

To understand the allure of horror, one must understand subtext,
particularly gay subtext or sensibility, as an art form. The horror genre is
born from the fantastic and is firmly rooted in the imagination. Due to
its fantastic roots, the horror genre can be used as a means to allude to
psychological and personal experiences without openly acknowledging
them to the audience. When codes were put in place to ensure homosexuality would not be seen in a favorable light, if at all, queer filmmakers used the power of their gay sensibility to infuse their films with a
queerness not clearly perceptible to the straight eye. As described by
Vito Russo,

> a gay sensibility can be many things; it can be present even when there is
> no sign of homosexuality, open or covert, before or behind the camera. Gay
> sensibility is largely a product of oppression, of the necessity to hide so well
> for so long. It is a ghetto sensibility, born of the need to develop and use sec-
> ond sight that will translate silently what the world sees and what the actu-
> ality may be. It was gay sensibility that, for example, often enabled some
> lesbians and gay men to see at very early ages, even before they knew the
> words for what they were, something on the screen that they knew related to
> their lives in some way.[9]

Gay sensibility allowed queer folks to see themselves in a medium such
as film that tried desperately to keep them out. Often, they found themselves in a genre that told stories of outcasts, misfits, and supposed
monsters, all of which were representative of either queer feelings,
experiences, or societal queer fear that was well understood by queer
folks. One such story and landmark in horror cinema and film history is
James Whale's *Frankenstein* (1931).

Universal Pictures' *Frankenstein* is a film adaptation of Mary Shelley's 1818 *Frankenstein; or Modern Prometheus*. Shelley herself has

been speculated to be queer, as seen in her letter to close friend Edward Trelawny in 1835 after her husband's death, "I was so ready to give myself away—and being afraid of men, I was ready to get tousy-mousy for women." "Tousy-mousy" sometimes simultaneously written as "tuzzy-muzzy" is a slang term for vagina, states historical lexicographer Jonathan Green. Since his inception, Frankenstein's Monster has continuously been created and recreated by queer folks.[10] Brought on as director for the feature was James Whale, a British actor and director, whose vision of protagonist Dr. Frankenstein's Monster would ultimately become an iconic image of horror, monsters, and Halloween motifs. Whale was openly homosexual, a fact known by most in film and theater communities, earning the epithet the Queen of Hollywood "deserved not for effeminacy or stereotypical mannerisms, but for Whale's challenge to the system and his eccentric yet nonetheless dignified persona."[11] Whale's queerness would seep into nearly all productions of which he was part. For *Frankenstein*, following Universal's *Dracula* (1931), Whale was enthusiastic about the possibilities of the picture. His vision of a melancholy, misunderstood monster, "the key to the film's heart," came from his lover, producer David Lewis "who, after reading the novel, told [Whale]: 'I was sorry for the goddamn monster.' And so, *Frankenstein* became not a tale of a demon, as *Dracula* had been, but rather the story of a frightened, misunderstood, ostracized, *different* child."[12] The queer Other of Hollywood horror was born.

From the onset, both Whale and Lewis, who openly attended Hollywood premieres together as a couple, could see the parallels between their experiences as gay men and what is signified by the Monster's very existence. Understood as sinful and violent, queer folks in the 1930s were themselves viewed as monsters who needed to be destroyed, abandoned, and feared. Subsequently, the "birth" of the Monster and its relation to its creator can be similarly viewed as a parent-child relationship, but to a queer audience, it can signify the parent-queer child relationship in which the creator (parent) abandons his creation (child) due to its monstrosity. Queer children for centuries have been abandoned by parents for numerous reasons: shame, disgust, and fear of judgment from others. These parents who abandoned or abused their queer children, whether verbally, physically, or emotionally, would turn to either religion or science to support their homophobia. Both religion and science come to a head in *Frankenstein* as Dr. Frankenstein simultaneously defies God *and* science through the creation of his creature. Harry Benshoff explains:

> In the horror film ... debates rage over questions of normality and nature, self and Other, minoritization and universalization. On the one hand,

Boris Karloff as Frankenstein's Monster (left) enjoying a cigarette as James Whale touches up his make-up on the set of *Bride of Frankenstein* (Universal Pictures, 1935).

medical science is often responsible for constructing monsters [...] On the other, science is repeatedly invoked in these films in order to show that there are things within the natural world which should be reckoned with and ultimately accepted [...] In the classical Hollywood horror film, science is sometimes used to suggest that "normality" needs to update its thinking on queer matters, but these discovered "truths" are usually shown to lead to tragedy.[13]

Though Dr. Frankenstein proved that he could create life outside of procreation, an idea that has followed through the history of science fiction as well as in the Christian Bible with the birth of Jesus without the copulation of Mary and Joseph, Shelley's accompanied characters would regard the doctor as having defied God. With regards to those who strictly follow the teachings of the Christian Bible, where debates have raged for centuries over the Bible's stance on homosexuality, many heterosexual Christians and Catholics consider gay men as being a sin against nature and God. A verse often discussed is Romans 1:26–27 of the Christian Bible, which states, "Because of this, God gave them over to shameful lusts [...]. Men committed indecent acts with other men, and received in themselves the due penalty for their perversion." Matthew Vines, author of *God and the Gay Christian: The Biblical Case in Support of Same-Sex Relationships*, explains that in this verse "while Paul labels same-sex behavior 'unnatural,' he uses the same word to criticize long hair in men in 1 Corinthians 11:14, which most Christians read as a synonym for 'unconventional.'"[14] Nevertheless, many followers of the Catholic and Christian religions assert that verses such as these make concretely the faith's condemnation of homosexuality. Frankenstein's Monster is a metaphor for the Christian predisposition of sins against nature and leads to the idea that the creature must be destroyed to bring safety and normality back. The monster is scary, violent at times, and feared by all ... to God-fearing folks. To queer folks, they see themselves in the monster who is feared and said to be an afront to God. That bond is made throughout the film, particularly in ones involving Dr. Frankenstein's reaction to his sinful creation.

After creating his monster, Dr. Frankenstein is ecstatic with his scientific triumph. He had created life and was as proud as a new parent, a father gazing at his infant son. However, Dr. Frankenstein ultimately rejects his creation due to fear and shame of what the creation was: an abomination. His cruelty for the Monster culminates in the creature's desire for the love and sympathy of his creator. Lester D. Friedman and Allison B. Kavey explain in "It's Still Alive: The Universal and Hammer Movie Cycles":

> In the touching moment that follows Frankenstein locking out the sunlight—a fitting visual metaphor for his depriving the Creature of emotional warmth and intellectual light—this mute being tenderly holds out his hand like a supplicant, silently begging for more light, more knowledge, more love. But Frankenstein refuses.[15]

Creating life and rejecting it is reminiscent of the experiences faced by queer children if they are rejected by a parent upon proclaiming their queerness. Additionally, the creature's struggle for light is an analogy for the closet. "For the Creature, light is both death and enlightenment," as is coming out to one's family about one's queerness.[16] A queer child could be begging for the closet door to be open, to fulfill the desire for freedom and happiness. Yet if the closet door opens to people who refuse to accept and love, the light beyond the closet could be deadly both emotionally and physically. The creature's desire for the light parallels the real-life desire to be free from the closet, and the fact that Dr.

Frankenstein refuses light for his creature, refuses love, strikes a chord within the queer experience, especially those closeted or who have faced parental abandonment.

Frankenstein ends with the Monster being chased through the countryside by a violent lynch mob. The Monster would plummet to his death, while his creator returned to the arms of his fiancée. Heteronormativity is restored. Hollywood would do its own purging of queerness in the years following the film. After the successes of his groundbreaking films, including the queer-coded *The Old Dark House* and *The Invisible Man*, Whale was eventually abandoned by Hollywood due to his open homosexuality after his last main success, *Bride of Frankenstein*. He would go on to produce seventeen more films but never surpassed the accomplishments of his first few horror pictures. He was found dead in his pool in 1957 of an apparent suicide. Director Robert Aldrich recollects that "Jimmy Whale was the first guy to be blackballed because he refused to stay in the closet [...]. Whale said, 'fuck it, I'm a great director and I don't have to put up with this bullshit'—and he was a great director."[17]

Following *Frankenstein*, before the Production Code was fully enforced, *Freaks* (1932) made its way to the big screen to shock audiences across the world. Following his seminal *Dracula*, Tod Browning's *Freaks* revolves around a band of literal freaks in a traveling circus. The "freaks" ranged from a strong man and bearded lady to people with missing limbs and animalistic characteristics. Many of these characters themselves were vaudeville and circus performers, giving the audience "authentic" freaks and circus acts. Here, Browning used his queer vaudeville roots to his advantage, giving his film queer subtext. The essence of *Freaks* lies in the freak code: offend one of us, offend all of us. The freaks find solidarity in one another, a surrogate family with whom they can bond over shared trauma and experience.

Apparently, the world was not ready for a band of self-assured freaks who would kill to protect themselves and their family. Ultimately, the film was reviled and banned across the world for alleged moral indecency. Extreme abnormality was not well received during the Depression, a time when America especially yearned for a return to normalcy during one of the biggest pitfalls of its financial system. Audiences wanted the comfort of retreating into another world while at the movies. *Freaks* gave them the opposite—ultimate discomfort. Author Joseph Maddrey elaborates:

> Browning drops us into a closed community of freaks who cannot relate—physically or emotionally—with polite society. The nightmare begins when this community is breached by outsiders. Because the stars of the film were

genuine carnival sideshow performers, audiences could not help feeling guilty for invading the closed community. The most guilt-inducing moment comes when Hans [a little person who falls in love with a woman of average height, Cleo] turns on Cleopatra [who belittled and lied to Hans], and us [as she snarls], "Dirty ... slimy ... freak."[18]

The final scene of the film is the ultimate horror for film audiences. Cleo had offended Hans—she offended them all, "she is stalked by the 'monsters'—a transvestite, a pair of Siamese twins, an emasculated clown, and a limbless 'human worm' who writhes in the mud after her with a knife in his teeth."[19] They cut off her legs, carved out her voice box, and covered her in hundreds of feathers. "*Freaks* was perceived as an outright assault on moral decency, and it was denounced by audiences across the globe."[20] Due to the outcry of discomfort and disgust by *Freaks*, the officials of the Hays Code took notice and would work on ways in which their code of ethics would be enforced in future films. *Freaks* was the last hurrah of the no-holds-barred film industry of the 1930s.

Implementation of the Code and Bride of Frankenstein

In 1934, the Production Code Administration (PCA) was implemented to enforce the Hays Code established four years earlier. The PCA played a stauncher role in censorship activities for Hollywood motion pictures. No sexually perverse characters or storylines were permitted unless they met their demise by film's end or were explicitly villainous. Sexually perverse, of course, included homosexuality and any variation of queerness. As explained by Olga J. Martin, secretary of the PCA, in 1937, "'No hint of sex perversion may be introduced into a screen story. The characterization of a man as effeminate or a woman as grossly masculine would be forbidden for screen portrayal.'"[21] If the "love that dare not speak its name" could not be explicitly seen, openly-queer characters were rendered both invisible and voiceless under the PCA. Boze Hadleigh, author of *The Lavender Screen*, explains:

> Homogeneity and conformity were the desired ends of the Code, and for decades to come gay people were invisible on the silver screen. In the words of gay writer Christopher Isherwood, "The heterosexual dictatorship played out a sexual genocide against homosexual people on the screen. By making us invisible, they could pretend we didn't exist. By making us unmentionable, they made us appear more contemptible."[22]

Before the PCA, films were more able to skirt the Hays Code's set of censorship guidelines, whereas the PCA set out to restrain directors and writers who formerly could sneak past the Code. However, these same directors now had to become creative by hinting at queer characters and other "perverse" plot points. This led to the flourishing of subtext, "'unspeakable' (or unseen) horrors and the 'love that dare not speak its name' moved into closer proximity through silences imposed by the Production Code Administration."[23] The unspeakable and invisible nature of the PCA queer created literal monsters of queer folks. If the only way to have queer characters was to have them be monstrous, then so be it.

Queer writers, directors, and actors faced additional challenges with the implementation of the PCA. To have lucrative careers, or to even simply survive in Hollywood, queer film professionals had to hide themselves just as their characters were forced into hiding per the PCA's moral clauses. Will Hays compiled a "doom book" which was home to one hundred and seventeen names of those deemed "unsafe" due to their homosexuality.[24] Never one to be forced back into the closet, out-queer director James Whale continued to proudly proclaim his queerness within his films and in his public and private life. The result of this rebellion would be one of his most iconic creations: *Bride of Frankenstein.*

Picking up where *Frankenstein* left off four years earlier, *Bride of Frankenstein* begins in the countryside where its residents are relieved to see Frankenstein's Monster dead. The Monster emerges bumped and bruised from his suspected grave, left to wander the countryside and woods while his disheveled creator returns to his castle and fiancée. Ailing Dr. Frankenstein is met by Dr. Septimus Pretorius, an eccentric experimenter who has found the secret to reanimation, much like the doctor. He wants Frankenstein's help with implementing his own plan upon a new body, a female body, based on Frankenstein's own creation. Meanwhile, the Monster finds a hermit in the woods who takes him in. He does not fear the Monster for he cannot see him due to blindness. In his secluded cabin, the man teaches the Monster words like "friend" and "good." Their outsider-ness forms a bond, an honest friendship. Their friendship is cut short after two lost hunters encounter the pair, resulting in the Monster fleeing into a crypt where Pretorius is stealing the corpse of a woman. Pretorius approaches the Monster, telling him he plans to create a mate for him: a friend. Ultimately, Pretorius and Frankenstein succeed in creating a female mate for the Monster, and the Bride of Frankenstein is born. She is animalistic, knows no words, and is fearful of her male counterpart when he tries to approach her. Ashamed, the Monster proclaims that he and his bride "belong dead," and tells Frankenstein to flee.[25] The Monster pulls a lever, destroying the laboratory, himself, and his bride.

After the success of *Frankenstein* and the implementation of the Code, Whale was able to adapt post–Code to continue creating his art. Author William J. Mann explains, "[h]aving had the good fortune to enter the industry at a time when their services were in greatest need—the transition to sound—[queer filmmakers] quickly mastered not only the techniques of moviemaking but of studio politics as well."[26] Luckily, Whale was effectively his own producer for *Bride of Frankenstein*, as the head of Universal was away in Europe. This gave Whale free reign on his sequel to implement subtextual hints at queerness, as well as any other plot device he wished. While some historians claim that Whale's queer sensibility was not imparted upon his films, Mann feels that Whale imprinted his queerness on his art, and the result are films that poke fun at heterosexual sensibilities while uplifting queer life motifs, such as Otherness, with much success.

> But it is not a gay agenda—with that word's implication of politics and modern identity—that is so apparent in Whale's films. Rather, it is a consciousness inspired by Whale's idiosyncrasy, which continues to resonate with gay audiences.... Monika Morgan called the *Bride of Frankenstein* "a homosexual joke on the heterosexual communities Whale—a gay man—served."[27]

Whale's queerness was implemented both directly and indirectly. Whether conscious or not, *Bride of Frankenstein* has myriad queer signifiers, one of which was decided directly by Whale: the actors. Due to his roots in vaudeville, which itself is queerly rooted, he found the actors he wished to prominently use in his film, particularly Ernest Thesiger. Whale met Thesiger through the theater world of London and the two became friends. Thesiger, though married to a woman, was not secretive with regards to his homosexuality. "'He was camp and feminine and proud of it,' observed historian Anthony Slide, 'long before such attributes became fashionable in certain quarters of the gay community.'"[28] Susan Sontag defined Camp in a 1964 essay in *Partisan Review*: "Camp sees everything in quotation marks. It's not a lamp, but a 'lamp'; not a woman, but a 'woman.' To perceive Camp in objects and persons is to understand Being-as-Playing-a-Role. It is the farthest extension, in sensibility, of the metaphor of life as theater."[29] Thesiger was a vessel for camp in his performances, especially *Bride of Frankenstein*, thus a vessel for queerness. Whale's use of actors who, like him, were open about their queerness, was a means to make queers visible. Mann elaborates:

> Straight directors used sissies, too, but usually as the butts of jokes or slapstick comedy relief. The sissies of [...] Whale, on the other hand, are shrewd, coy, and arrogant: comic, yes, but in positions to command some power. Thesiger's Dr. Pretorius actually holds the key to life itself: he has the power

to lure Henry Frankenstein away from his bride and command him to do his bidding.[30]

Pretorius, brought to life by Thesiger, is a queer artist and madman who was primarily viewed as the latter by heterosexual audiences. Joseph Breen of the PCA, however, did notice some queer messages in Whale's film, though he focused on the blasphemy exhibited in the script. As stated by Mann, Breen, who was responsible for clearing all scripts prior to filming, had "no initial objection to the character of Dr. Pretorius as a pansy."[31]

> [A]lthough Breen seems to have suspected something queer in Pretorius' line "We are all three infidels, scoffers at all marriage ties." Whale agreed to change the word "infidels" to "skeptics," and "marriage" to "normal." Breen was placated, and filming was allowed to begin.[32]

Thesiger brought Pretorius to (queer) life. His character is the most explicit evidence of queerness, but it is the subtextual elements that make the film truly queer. Mann continues, "Yet *Bride*'s final cut is about as queer as can be, with Pretorius' arch effeminacy (and yes, quite obvious perversion) coming through without use of lipstick or specific dialogue. It was all done through Ernest Thesiger's eyes and the lilt of his voice, and Whale's subversive direction."[33]

Bride of Frankenstein is a tale of Otherness, rejection, and friendship through Other status, mainly through the storyline of the blind hermit and the Monster. The hermit who invited the Monster to join him in drink and smoke was so enthralled to finally have a friend that he thanked God for answering his prayers. Queer reality is often one of mistrust yet need for friendship. A queer person cannot know whether a person would accept them or not, but the friendship between Others of society can create honest companionship between two yearning souls. As outcasts, they can bond together, protect one another from the harshness of the world, regardless of queerness, blindness, or undead status.

The Monster's suicide at film's end can also be viewed as a queer signifier: the Monster, the queer, has been told by society that they are wrong, bad, perverted in some way as to cause self-loathing. The tragic end to the Monster and his bride portrays the pain from rejection and anti-queer societal propaganda that many queer folks face, from 1935 through the twentieth century. "The monster in *Frankenstein*," explains Vito Russo, "bears the brunt of society's reaction to his existence, and in the sequel, *Bride of Frankenstein*, the monster himself is painfully aware of his own unnaturalness."[34] Following the rejection of someone, an Other whom he thinks should accept him for what he is as had the

Director James Whale (left) and Ernest Thesiger as Dr. Septimus Pretorius sipping tea on the set of *Bride of Frankenstein* **(Universal Pictures, 1935).**

blind hermit, the pain is too hard to bear, resulting in the Monster's suicide and martyrdom. Whale would share a similar fate with the monster who dominated his career and art for decades. Twenty-two years after *Bride of Frankenstein*, Whale committed suicide by jumping headfirst into his swimming pool.

Whale was a master in his art and lived openly as a gay man in a time when such a lifestyle was deemed perverted and unnatural. Through his art, queer folks can find themselves hidden in the shadows as well as in the bright spotlight. His legacy lives on in the work of other queer film artists, most prominently in *Bride of Chucky* (1998) helmed by queer writer and director Don Mancini, sixty-one years after Whale's *Bride of Frankenstein* gracefully and grotesquely hit the silver screen. *Bride of Frankenstein* marked an end to untethered queer art in cinema for decades to come. The PCA would run rampant for the next few decades, ready to demonize and destroy sexual perverts to save America.

Popular Psychology and the Countess

As indicated by the Production Code Association, homosexual characters were sex perverts and deviants. If they were to be shown, it was only to have them be destroyed or be grotesquely villainous. During the 1930s and 1940s, Universal horror reflected not just the Code, but the American social thought of queer people being threatening creatures of the night. The societal vision of a homosexual was also one of mental illness. Queer folks were sent off to institutions, sanitariums, and to the psychiatrist's couch to be purged of their sexual deviancy. Most psychologists at the time believed a person with homosexual tendencies could be cured through psychoanalysis while some began to believe in aversion therapy. Aversion therapy uses, among other stress methods, intense electrical shocks simultaneously with arousing stimulus to create a mental connotation with pain and homosexual pleasure. The first documented use of electric aversion therapy was conducted by Dr. Louis W. Max in 1935. At a meeting of the American Psychological Association, Dr. Max said of his young male patient after the experiment, "That terrible neurosis [after intense electroshock rather than low levels of electricity] has lost its battle, not completely but 95% of the way."[35] Electroshock would gain momentum in the 1940s. Though by this time many psychologists had more sympathy for queer folks than in the past, there was still use of words such as "deviancy" and "perversion" that gave way to pity rather than anger. Some "deviants" went willingly into therapy, bending to social pressures, while others were forced against their will. In many cases, homosexual men bore the brunt of societal disgust, but queer women were seen from a more psychological angle. Lesbian and bisexual women were pained as threatening seductresses in need of psychiatric help. The intersection of psychiatry and lesbianism/bisexualism during this era is perfectly packaged in the story of Countess Marya Zaleska, the daughter of Dracula.

Dracula's Daughter (1936), written by Garrett Fort and directed by Lambert Hillyer, stars the glamorous Gloria Holden as a mysterious Hungarian countess and artist. Originally, Whale was brought on as director but was ultimately scrapped from the production due in part to his lack of interest in making two horror films in a row, seeing that this film would have been on the heels of *Bride of Frankenstein*.[36] The film begins with the death of Count Dracula (based on his demise from *Dracula*) in London. Upon confirming his death through Scotland Yard, Countess Zaleska, having been turned into a vampire, thought that with the death of the head-vampire Dracula, she could become human again. She only had to burn his body. She had hoped of breaking the vampiric spell, to be "free to live as a woman, free to take my place in the bright world of the living, instead of among the shadows of the dead [...]. I can live a normal life now, think normal things."[37] Alas, the wish of freedom would not be granted as the spell proved to be unbreakable, despite Zaleska destroying Dracula's body. She would have to reluctantly continue living as a vampire, seducing men *and* women with her piercing eyes and hypnotic gleaming ring that lures her victims into a state of trance.

As an intriguing foreign artist, Zaleska mingles with other prominent society figures and meets psychiatrist Dr. Jeffrey Garth, who, while on a holiday hunting trip in Scotland, he reminisced about his work back in London, glad to be away from his treatment of "neurotic women."[38] The audience is introduced to his main realms of thought, specifically those regarding his friend Von Helsing and his obsession with vampires. Dr. Garth believes that Helsing's obsession with vampirism is a disease of the mind that can be cured through the mind's will, as with any obsession. Upon hearing this, Zaleska is entranced by the possibility of a "release" from obsession and asks Dr. Garth to discuss his thoughts further in private. She confides to Dr. Garth that "someone … something [Dracula, her queerness] … reaches out from beyond the grave and fills me with horrible impulses," to which Dr. Garth tells her that her mind has the power to stop these forces.[39] As what is done to alcoholics to make them face their addiction, explains Dr. Garth, so too must Zaleska face hers: "Next time you feel this influence, don't avoid it. Meet it. Fight it."[40] Garth demands Zaleska use her willpower to cure herself of her cursed illness, a concept that is very much of the times in 1930s–1940s psychology. As stated by Dr. La Forest Potter in 1933 regarding a lesbian patient who was not dedicated to being cured of her lesbianism, "no homosexual *can be cured*, or even relieved of his or her abnormality, *who will not whole-heartedly cooperate towards this end.*"[41]

Though she hopes to be cured of her "illness" and obsessive compulsion to drink human blood, Zaleska still must consume human blood to survive until she has the "will" to be "cured." Zaleska's manservant Sandor entices a woman named Lili to pose for a painting by Zaleska for money. As Lili prepares herself, Zaleska asks her to remove her blouse, as she looks on longingly. It must be noted here that to bite someone's neck, as with a vampire, there is no need to remove the entire blouse. "Why are you looking at me that way?" asks Lili.[42] Zaleska tries to enchant Lili with her hypnotic ring, and Lili asks to leave. Zaleska approaches, to which Lili screams in terror as the scene fades to black. Zaleska's queer undertones are evident in this scene, and the Breen Office, part of the PCA, took notice. When the final script was approved

Nan Grey as Lili (left) is hypnotized by Countess Marya Zaleska, played by Gloria Holden, in *Dracula's Daughter* (Universal Pictures, 1936).

by the PCA, the Breen Office advised that the seduction scene between Zaleska and Lili would

> need very careful handling to avoid any questionable flavor.... The whole sequence will be treated in such a way as to avoid any suggestion of perverse sexual desire on the part of [Zaleska] or of an attempted sexual attack by her upon Lily.[43]

"Yet, for the attuned spectator," Benshoff asserts, "the lesbian implication is [...] unavoidable."[44] It was clear to the censor board that this scene was especially queer and feared that it would be conveyed so onscreen. After the attack on Lili, Zaleska appears at Dr. Garth's home the next evening for an examination. "I had to come," Zaleska states, trembling. "You're the one person who stands between me and utter destruction [...]. There is nothing ahead for me but horror."[45] She explains her violent encounter with Lili the night before: "When you left me last night, I determined to put myself to a test as you suggested. I failed. It came over me again, that overpowering command. Wordless. Insistent. And I had to obey."[46] Dr. Garth suggests putting her under hypnosis, a psychiatric analysis to drum up deeply hidden memories or repressed feelings. "It is too late for experiments!" Zaleska pleads.

"I need you Dr. Garth.... I need you to save my soul!"[47] Dr. Garth tells her that she is hiding something from him and won't dare tell him the truth about herself. This hidden aspect of herself, though meant to signify vampirism, emits utter queerness. "Primarily lesbian," states historian Boze Hadleigh,

> Countess Zaleska's private life is utterly private, and in public she must disguise her true nature. Her alienation from "decent" society causes her to prey upon it. She is a virtual parasite, who cannot breed, but adds to her ranks by seductive conscription. Her unions are "unholy"; she hates her life and would gladly trade it for a commonplace existence.[48]

This entire confrontation between Zaleska and Garth is a coaxing by the doctor to get her to tell him that she is a vampire, for he suspects it to be so. This scene can be read as someone pushing a queer person to out themselves, to expose the horror and monstrosity within, to exit the closet.

Zaleska wants Garth to leave London with her, for him to "save" her as she escapes the repercussions from attacking Lili. Discovered by authorities, Lili lies in a coma after the attack. Through hypnosis, Lili reveals clues to Dr. Garth indicating Zaleska was her attacker. Garth finds Zaleska in his apartment where she is adamant that he leaves London with her. He refuses and demands she come with him to Scotland Yard to be turned in to the authorities. Desperate for help but firm in her demands that he leaves with her, Zaleska admits to Garth that she is Dracula's daughter. However, Zaleska no longer pleads for her freedom but has become predatory. Zaleska kidnaps Garth's beautiful secretary Janet, and now that Garth knows the truth about Zaleska, he summons Von Helsing to ambush her in Transylvania. There, Zaleska waits with an unharmed Janet for Garth's arrival. "What do you want with Garth?" asks Sandor. "Release? Still release?" "No," Zaleska answers. "I know that's impossible now. I want him [...]. For life. Eternal life with me!"[49] This turn of events *straightens* Zaleska's story and attempts to bring her story into the realm of heterosexuality by film's end. Just as Garth agrees to give Zaleska his life for Janet's, Zaleska is impaled by a wooden arrow. It was Sandor, her manservant, upset that Zaleska would no longer grant him the eternal life promised to him, setting him free, who killed her.

By the film's end, Zaleska no longer wished for a cure of her vampirism, her queerness, and was content with bringing Garth into her world instead. A world of darkness, evil, and of course, queerness. She accepted herself for what she was, and for that, she was vanquished, letting Garth and Janet remain in the world of the normal heterosexual. The predatory queer is dead, allowing the heterosexuals to survive.

The taglines for this film connotated queerness. Among them were "She gives you that weird feeling!" and "Save the *women* of London from Dracula's Daughter!"[50] There is little doubt that the studio or writers knew of Countess Zaleska's coded queerness. She is a queer murderous villain, a blood-sucking vampire preying on the innocent (straight) women of London. Her queerness signifies the anxieties surrounding female sexuality of the 1930s, specifically male anxieties of female sexual desire. As advocated by Andrea Weiss, author of *Vampires and Violets: Lesbians in Film* (1993), the queer female vampire "provokes and articulates anxieties in the heterosexual male spectator, only for the film to quell these anxieties and reaffirm his maleness through the vampire's ultimate destruction."[51] This is the case with *Dracula's Daughter*'s central male characters, Garth and Sandor. Sandor, Zaleska's manservant, destroys his master, reaffirming his manhood, while Garth and Janet are reunited in safety from the malevolent vampire.

Despite the all-too-familiar demise of the evil queer in the film's final moments, queer women can and should reclaim the Countess, if not for reclamation of once terrible connotations between queer women and mental illness but for the power she wields. Weiss posits the merits of the female vampire as a vessel for queer power: "The lesbian vampire is the most powerful representation of lesbianism to be found on the commercial movie screen, and rather than abandon her for what she signifies, it may be possible to extricate her from her original function, and reappropriate her power."[52] I assert that the character of Countess Marya Zaleska can and should be reappropriated for her power as a queer woman much like Carrie White of Brian De Palma's *Carrie* (1976), which I discuss further in Chapter 7. What was once a harmful vessel for horror and mental illness, the female vampire, inherently queer, can be used as a source of strength for women who love women, despite her "dangerous" powers given to her through vampirism. Unlike many women at the time of the film's release, Zaleska has the ability and power to charm and have authority over others. It is a shame that she wished to be cured of such faculties, but of course, that was the male-dominant fantasy of the era: control over perceived uncontrollable women. Zaleska was doomed from the opening credits.

Unfortunately, the empowering vision for the Countess is a relatively modern idea, one that was not on the radar of Hollywood executives and government officials of the 1930s. The year following *Dracula's Daughter*, F.B.I. director (and oft-regarded closeted queer) J. Edgar Hoover echoed the sentiments of the film's underlying fear of the queer in an article titled "War of the Sex Criminal" in *The New York Herald Tribune*: "The present apathy of the public toward perverts, generally regarded as 'harmless,' should be changed to one of suspicious scrutiny. The harmless pervert of today can be and often is the loathsome mutilator and murderer of tomorrow."[53] Horror films of this period reflect an American society on the brink of a domestic and international war against what was seen as both villainous and abnormal behavior.

Gender Crisis and World War II–Era Queer Activism

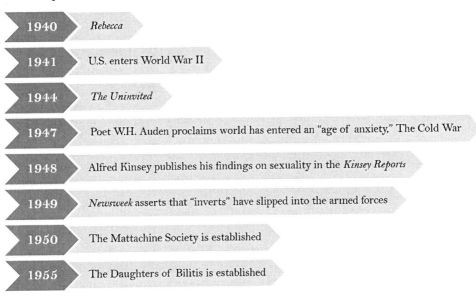

1940   *Rebecca*

1941   U.S. enters World War II

1944   *The Uninvited*

1947   Poet W.H. Auden proclaims world has entered an "age of anxiety," The Cold War

1948   Alfred Kinsey publishes his findings on sexuality in the *Kinsey Reports*

1949   *Newsweek* asserts that "inverts" have slipped into the armed forces

1950   The Mattachine Society is established

1955   The Daughters of Bilitis is established

Figure 2

On the cusp of American involvement in World War II, the country was facing an economic and apparent gender crisis. The Great Depression disrupted the gender norms of the period, where men were out of work, which had been their birthright for centuries and evidence of their masculinity. Men's masculinity was put into question. Up until this point, it was effeminacy that was an indicator of male homosexuality.

When America officially entered the war on December 8, 1941, scores of men became impassioned to join the war effort and entered the armed forces. Ironically, this further disrupted gender norms under the guise of being a part of the *manliest* endeavor for an adult male. These men would become fellow soldiers, bunkmates, and sometimes lovers where "the same-sex environment of the Armed Services might lead 'normal' men and women into such vices."[54] In 1949, *Newsweek*

had reported that "although army regulations forbade drafting homosexuals, scores of inverts managed to slip through during the war."[55]
The use of the phrase "slip through" is key, for it signifies the supposed
deceptive nature of the homosexual and a queer person's ability to cloak
themselves within a largely heterosexual, *manly* atmosphere. The magazine article continues with tips for identifying a male homosexual, as
encouraged by psychiatrists: "(1) By their effeminate manner and dress
[and] (2) By repeating words from the homosexual vocabulary and
quickly looking for signs of recognition."[56] Similarly, the Women's Army
Corps (WAC) had guidelines in place to detect and eject women from
the corps who were too masculine presenting. This became a challenge
for women in WAC: the army, meant to be a masculine endeavor for
men due to its brutish history, was now smoothing out its rough edges
for the sake of upholding strict feminine gender roles. Masculine presenting women were watched closely for other perceived lesbian attributes as they were believed to be dangerous to the legitimacy of the
corps. WAC enlistment and discharge criteria went so far as to assume
that women who expressed a strong desire to join the army were themselves queer because "'real women,'" states historian Leisa D. Meyer,
"would not want to be 'soldiers' at all."[57]

Not only were military men and women being surrounded solely
by the same sex during the war, but additionally, some women who had
been left at home by husbands and boyfriends had realized same-sex
feelings as a result of being surrounded primarily by women. While
men were at war together, women were finding one another and finding
themselves, thanks to both the leaving of men for combat and the subversion of their gender stereotypes.

Film played a part in women finding their same-sex attraction. The
act of going to a dark theater and sharing an experience with strangers who wish to enter a realm of fantasy facilitates comradery, especially for a horror audience. You scream together, cower together, and
are delighted together when experiencing the things that go bump in
the night. During World War II, those experiencing films together were
largely people too young to go to war, and those explicitly left out of the
armed forces. The theater became a meeting ground for friends to flee
the fear of war and escape into fantasy. Women in particular became
central patrons of movie theaters during wartime. "The formation
of lesbian communities during the war," explains historian Rhonda J.
Berenstein, "could have been accompanied by social practices that bore
directly on film spectatorship—lesbians may have told each other about
films in which a lesbian theme might be discerned."[58] Film showings
for *The Uninvited* (1944) capture this phenomenon. *The Uninvited* is a

ghost story that focuses on mother-daughter relationships in life and death. However, there was a queer sensibility that permeated the feature that made the mother-daughter plot seem like a cover-up narrative device for lesbianism.

Berenstein examines the ghostly lesbianism in *The Uninvited* in her *Cinema Journal* piece "Adaptation, Censorship, and Audiences of Questionable Type: Lesbian Sightings in *Rebecca* (1940) and *The Uninvited* (1944)." During these films' era, the Production Code Administration cracked down on scripts that showed evidence of sexual perversion in characters. While *Rebecca* was a thriller directed by Alfred Hitchcock, the director referred to his film as horror. "The term," Hitchcock explains in an interview, "meaning originally 'extreme aversion,' has loosely applied to films which, supply the desired emotional jolt, exploit sadism, perversion, bestiality, and deformity."[59] This perversion was scrutinized by Joseph Breen of the PCA who wrote a four-page letter that described the instances in *Rebecca* that invoke "inescapable inferences of sex perversion."[60] The film, however, is subtextually queer, meaning queerness is assumed and suspected but largely unseen. The same goes for *The Uninvited,* which was directly related to Hitchcock's *Rebecca* in advertisements and film taglines.[61] Queer women flocked to this ghost story feature. The Legion of Decency was more frightened of this group phenomenon than the women were while seeing *The Uninvited.* The Legion wrote a letter to Paramount Pictures complaining that the film was influencing "questionable" behavior of "large audiences of questionable type" who attended the film at unusual hours.[62] Queer women and women discovering their queerness were able to find one another through film showings of horror movies like *The Uninvited* that had queer motifs.

The ghostly lesbians of *The Uninvited* echoed the societal ideas of the spinster, a specter on the fringe of society who did not conform to American traditional gender norms of marriage and the desire for such. "All lesbians are outsiders, the films said," notes Vito Russo in *The Celluloid Closet,* "and in each film the myth of the predatory but lonely lesbian was reinforced."[63] The queer women going to movie theaters to see *The Uninvited,* those living in a country that enforced marriage and strict female gender roles, could perhaps see themselves among the lonely ghostly lesbians onscreen. They identified with the ghosts, for they too felt unseen and relegated to the shadows of society.

Lesbian ghosts, though retouched in production to be only subtly queer and be villainized to showcase the dangers of such a lifestyle, were able to slide past the PCA based on the already misunderstood nature of the queer American woman. Gender and sexuality theorist

Judith Butler elaborates on the idea of the unseen lesbian in her queer discourse. She states in "Imitation and Gender Insubordination" from *Inside/Out: Lesbian Theories, Gay Theories*, "Lesbianism is not explicitly prohibited in part because it has not even made its way into the thinkable, the imaginable, that grid of cultural intelligibility that regulates the real and the nameable."[64] How fitting then that the queer female horror characters of the World War II era had been largely invisible ghosts and specters. Queer women spectators of these films could see themselves in the un-seeable, in understanding their social status of invisibility, and the loneliness that accompanies it.

This loneliness felt by queer folks during the early twentieth century would be changed socially with the publications by Alfred Kinsey on human sexuality. In 1948, Kinsey, an American biologist and sexologist, and his associates published *Sexual Behavior in the Human Male*. *Sexual Behavior in the Human Female* would be published five years later. The two volumes would be known as the Kinsey Reports. *Sexual Behavior in the Human Male* broke ground as one of the first publications to go into minute detail about human male sexuality and experiences, to the shock and fascination of the general American public. For the first time, sexuality, particularly homosexuality, was being discussed openly thanks to the intrigue generated by the 1948 book, and to much surprise, homosexuality and bisexuality were more common than previously thought. Unfortunately, however, of the 17,000 men surveyed, all of whom resided in the American northeast, Kinsey completely ignored black folks in his analysis of sexuality, and focused on mathematical statistics rather than placing queer folks in a cultural and social context.[65] Ultimately, *Sexual Behavior of the Human Male* noted that as of 1948,

> 37 percent of all males had some form of homosexual contact between their teen years and old age; 50 percent of males who remained single until the age of thirty-five had overt homosexual experiences to orgasm; 10 percent of males were more or less exclusively homosexual for at least three years between the ages of sixteen and fifty-five; 4 percent of males were exclusively homosexual throughout their lives.[66]

The arrival of the Kinsey Report to social consciousness caused two central reactions: (1) queer folks discovered that they were not the only ones who felt same-sex attraction, and (2) the reports frightened the heterosexual world with the idea that queer people existed everywhere and anywhere. The latter caused, among other things, purges of suspected queer U.S. government employees as advocated by Senator Joseph McCarthy, himself an alleged queer man.[67] To McCarthy and other government officials, homosexuals were a risk to national security. In 1948, McCarthy explained his reasoning for outing an alleged homosexual government employee who had become part of the Central Intelligence Agency: the "perverts" who infiltrate agencies of the CIA are security risks because they were "subject to blackmail."[68] This is a reference to the idea that queer folks often lied about themselves and their sexuality, thus, if someone found out about their sexuality, especially an enemy of the U.S., queer folks could be blackmailed into spilling government secrets in exchange for the enemies keeping quiet about the government employee's perversion. This frame of mind would playout for the rest of the twentieth century but particularly in the 1950s through the 1970s.

Borne out of the first Kinsey Report was the Mattachine Society, established in November of 1950. Harry Hay, a gay labor organizer with Communist leanings, was searching for a group of like-minded individuals to discuss the newly published Kinsey Report. He wished to form a community dedicated to political action in addition to finding sexual partners and camaraderie, seeing such as "not only logical but vital [...]. Using Marxist cultural theory, Hay understood homosexuals to be a distinct and oppressed class of people able to combat ignorance with education and organize against the prejudice of the dominant culture."[69] The Daughters of Bilitis, formed in 1955 in San Francisco, was another group that was borne from the need to find community among like-minded queers and form political and personal bonds.

Queers, realizing that more people like them existed, felt a desire to create explicitly queer art, especially in the realm of underground film. Swift backlash came to the emergence of queer identity in the form of strict mass conformity and brutality toward Others and queers. Mainstream film representations of psychotic, dangerous, and pitiful queers destined for alienation and death would flash on the bloody silver screen throughout the Cold War.

CHAPTER 2

Psychos, Aliens, and Ghosts

Mass Conformity, Gay Liberation,
and the Underground Response
(the 1950s–1970s)

The Cold War and the Psychological Response to Queerness

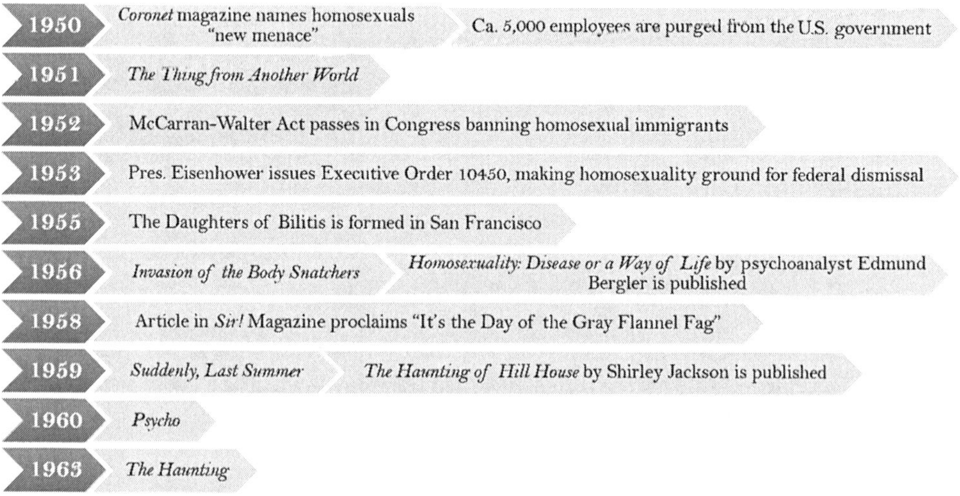

1950 — *Coronet* magazine names homosexuals "new menace" — Ca. 5,000 employees are purged from the U.S. government

1951 — *The Thing from Another World*

1952 — McCarran-Walter Act passes in Congress banning homosexual immigrants

1953 — Pres. Eisenhower issues Executive Order 10450, making homosexuality ground for federal dismissal

1955 — The Daughters of Bilitis is formed in San Francisco

1956 — *Invasion of the Body Snatchers* — *Homosexuality: Disease or a Way of Life* by psychoanalyst Edmund Bergler is published

1958 — Article in *Sir!* Magazine proclaims "It's the Day of the Gray Flannel Fag"

1959 — *Suddenly, Last Summer* — *The Haunting of Hill House* by Shirley Jackson is published

1960 — *Psycho*

1963 — *The Haunting*

Figure 3

"I don't have any bad memories of the fifties," reminisced world-renowned horror author Stephen King in a 1984 interview with science fiction writer Randy Lofficier. "Everything was asleep. There was stuff going on, there was uneasiness about the bomb, but on the whole, I'd have to say that people in the fifties were pretty loose."[1] King's easy-going, sleepy fifties memories are like those experienced by other cisgender straight white men of nearly any era in American history. For minority populations, including queer folks, the fifties were far from easy. The Cold War was in full swing by the late–1940s, and queer poet W.H. Auden described it as an "age of anxiety" in 1947:

> The Cold War fired the starting gun on two parallel contests: the arms race and the space race, fostering a culture of suspicion, surveillance, and spying, all of which impacted strongly on the art, design, film, and literature of the period [...]. At the cinema, too, fears were turned into pleasures, with popular themes including alien invasion, communist infiltration, spies, and the space age.[2]

Just as they had been monsters, vampires, and ghosts, the genuine lives of queer folks continued to be physically invisible on and off-screen into the 1950s and 1960s. The American Dream post–World War II would not allow an intruding queer to destroy the fabric of the burgeoning nuclear family. Vito Russo describes this atmosphere of toxic heterosexuality, where queers were

> subtextual phantoms representing the very fear of homosexuality. Serving as alien creatures who were nonetheless firmly established as part of the culture in every walk of life, they became the darker side of the American dream. In a society so obsessed with the maintenance of sex roles and the glorification of all things male, sissies and tomboys served as yardsticks for what was considered normal behavior.[3]

Both alien invasion and communist infiltration were reflected in the fear of the homosexual, "that new menace," as stated in a 1950 issue of *Coronet* magazine.[4] This new menace was a threat to an era that encouraged mass conformity through patriarchal heteronormativity. Gays did not fit the ideal familial/societal mold, but if white, could pass in suburban settings and the mainstream. This presented a problem for anxious heterosexuals: how could a queer person be detected? Are they living among us? Articles in *Coronet, Newsweek,* and *Time* advised "normal" Americans how to identify homosexuals, including recognizing "gay" language and "extreme narcissism" as indicators of homosexuality.[5] In the March 1958 issue of the men's magazine *Sir!,* one could read an article titled "It's the Day of the Gray Flannel Fag." The piece warns that "Not All Homos Are Easy to Spot. Many Have Muscles, Are He-Man in Everything—Except Sex."[6] For the conservative 1950s, abnormality lay in men who did not act like their expected normal hypermasculine selves, in addition to women who were perceived as more masculine than their expected biological traits. Fashion choices, mannerisms, and even occupations could have been homosexual indicators in the eyes of vigilant heterosexual Americans. In the age of anxiety, vigilant heterosexuals were wary of hidden homosexuals among them.

Films about alien invaders such as *The Thing from Another World* (1951) and *Invasion of the Body Snatchers* (1956) are clear allegories of the suspicions straight Americans felt towards a *strange* neighbor, *funny* coworker, or *flamboyant* teacher. A queer person could be anywhere just as these human-like aliens were in horror/sci-fi films; thus, there was a retreat to psychological texts to aid in identifying these alleged predators bent on destroying the family unit and causing harm to vulnerable children. The result would be the removal of perceived queer government employees, known as the Lavender Scare. Along with the Red Scare that targeted those accused of being communist sympathizers, thousands of queer government employees were fired from their jobs. In 1950, *The New York Times* had published an article, written by Republican National Committee chairman Guy George Gabrielson, in which he asserted that "sexual perverts who have infiltrated our government in recent years are perhaps as dangerous as actual Communists."[7] Nearly 5,000 perceived communist or queer government employees were purged from the U.S. government by the December of 1950, and in 1953, President Dwight D. Eisenhower issued Executive Order 10450 that made homosexuality grounds for federal termination. Not only were these people fired from their jobs, but thousands of those that were perceived as queer were forced into hospitalization where they were at the hands of "sympathetic" psychiatrists trying to cure them of their homosexuality. Benshoff describes the psychiatric atmosphere of the Cold War:

> [P]sychiatry's most damaging and cruel legacy is to be found in the "sympathetic treatments" it has prescribed throughout the twentieth century for its diagnosed homosexuals: shock treatment, castration, vasectomy, testicular irradiation, ovariectomy, nerve section, gender realignment therapy, electrical or emetic aversion therapy, hormone injections, and even lobotomy.[8]

The fear of the homosexual had grave consequences for queer Americans. They were effectively othered and targeted by homophobic psychiatric practices and prevalent social homophobia. These fears were projected in the films of the 1950s that spoke of alien invasions and aliens that blended among American society: "these human-seeming monsters are like the emotionless pod people of *Invasion of the Body Snatchers* (1956), outwardly human but actually a totally different form of life."[9] This overwhelming fear of the Other additionally culminated legislatively for the *alien*-Other in the Immigration and Nationality Act, also known as the McCarran-Walter Act, passed by Congress in

1952, effectively banning homosexual people from immigrating to the United States.

In the horror films of the 1950s, while many monsters were explicit in their attempts to destroy the nuclear family and often took the form of regular human beings, the homosexual menace was used as a metaphor for perversion and a subtextual method of threatening the nuclear family. While subtext was used to get homosexual themes through the PCA, if outright queer characters were to exist, they would have to be destroyed by film's end. The hidden (quite literally) homosexual menace who must be destroyed due to his sexuality was on display in *Suddenly, Last Summer* (1959), which was based on a play by Tennessee Williams, a gay playwright. The play is explicit in character Sebastian Venable's homosexuality. However, the Catholic Church through the Legion of Decency, influencer of the PCA, took action to censor Gore Vidal's film script just enough to still convey Venable's deviant lifestyle and "voracious sexual appetite" as his undoing by film's end.[10] "My script was perfectly explicit," said Vidal, who like Williams was also a gay man, "and then the Catholic Church struck. Since the film illustrates the horrors of such a [queer] lifestyle, it can be considered moral in theme even though it deals with sexual perversion."[11] What is left of the film is the story of a family grappling with the mental instability of their brother and son: Sebastian. He is sexually promiscuous and enlists his family members, mainly his beautiful sister played by Elizabeth Taylor, to attract young men into his midst. For the entirety of the film, Sebastian is faceless, invisible, though he is played by then-closeted gay actor Montgomery Clift. He has no physical presence on screen, resulting in an ominous, creeping villain that clouds the whole picture. Vito Russo described the screen character of Sebastian as a representation of homosexuality and "evil incarnate, the symbol of a sterile decadence that is punishable by death."[12] Sebastian's homosexuality is indeed punished by death from an angry mob, much like Frankenstein's Monster: "As for Sebastian's particular fate, it is unlikely that many homosexuals have died at the hands of cannibalistic Spanish-speaking street children. More have died at the hands of 'fag bashers' in American cities."[13] Sebastian was painted as a sick man, an aberration "against God and nature," whose destruction at the end of the film signifies the need for society to purge itself from predatory Others.[14] Sebastian's sickness, his homosexuality, would soon be used in multiple films in the 1960s as representative of the deviant and dangerous Other: the mentally-ill homosexual. Mental illness and homosexuality would be equated with one another.

Cold War psychological analysis of queer folks often portrayed them as being psychotic. Psychoanalyst Edmund Bergler wrote in his

1956 book *Homosexuality: Disease or a Way of Life* that "homosexuality is a neurotic condition [...]. Specific neurotic defenses and personality traits that are partly or entirely psychopathic are specifically and exclusively characteristic of homosexuals."[15] The psychotic homosexual crept its way into Hollywood films. Though not explicitly labeled as homosexual, Norman Bates in Alfred Hitchcock's *Psycho* (1960) is evidence of this method of thinking, of a homosexual as mentally disturbed and, quite clearly, *psycho*.

Psycho (1960) follows Marion, a woman on the run who stops at an eerie motel for the night, only to be dramatically murdered in the shower by an unknown knife-wielding woman. The owner of the motel, Norman Bates, played by closeted queer actor Anthony Perkins, lives with his domineering yet unseen mother. Bates is later investigated by police after Marion is alleged to have gone missing, having been disposed of by Bates after he acknowledges that his mother murdered her. It is revealed by the film's end that Bates believes himself to *be* his mother. Her body was being preserved by him in the basement. Bates dressed as his mother while he murdered Marion. He is a mentally and emotionally disturbed single man, obsessed with his mother, and cross-dresses as he commits murder—a trifecta of perceived sexual perversion for early 1960s' audiences.

Single adult men of the 1950s, already seen as strange for being single in an age of compulsive heterosexual coupling, were also viewed as perverted, homosexual, and/or predatory by psychologists of the decade. Therefore, Norman Bates, a single adult male living with his mother, would be rather strange to heterosexual audiences raised in the 1940s and 1950s:

> The hyper heterosexuality of 1950s American culture contained a deep distrust of the single man. This perspective was reinforced by the professional psychologists. Hendrik Ruitenbeek, a respected psychoanalyst, noted in 1966 that "contemporary America seems to have no room for the mature bachelor [...]. A single man over thirty is now regarded as a pervert, a person with severe emotional problems, or a poor creature fettered to a mother."[16]

During this time, such rumors began to spread of hunky actor and bachelor Rock Hudson. In 1955, *Life* magazine's cover story of Hudson urged the bachelor to get married "or explain why-not" to his legions of fans curious about the wealthy, attractive, and shockingly single thirty-year-old.[17] A swift marriage was subsequently arranged by Hudson's also-queer agent Henry Willson for fear that the tabloids, particularly the lurid *Confidential*, would expose Hudson's homosexuality and effectively ruin his career. Willson set up Hudson with his secretary, Phyllis Gates, and the two were married in 1955 and divorced in 1958.

Anthony Perkins as knife-wielding Norman Bates, dressed in his mother's clothes and a woman's wig, about to murder Marion Crane (Janet Leigh) as she showers in the Bates Motel in *Psycho* (Paramount Pictures, 1960).

When Bates was revealed to be a cross-dressing maniac, the bachelor theory held firm in the eyes of 1950s audiences: he is a mentally unstable homosexual man.

The Mama's Boy of the silver screen is coded as queer, especially in the 1950s and 1960s. This is due in part to dominant social thought of boys and young men being emasculated by their mothers: "A boy's best friend is his mother," advocates Bates.[18] As promoted by Dr. Benjamin Spock in 1946, a mother's role in her son growing up to be effeminate and therefore assumed queer lies in her overbearing parenting and making her son her close confidant, resulting in his emasculation.[19] This popular theory of the time aligns with Norman Bates' relationship with his mother and would not be lost on a 1960s audience.

As achieved with Sebastian Venable of *Suddenly, Last Summer* (1959), invisible or rather chameleon queers presented a new horror on screen. By the early 1960s, the specter of queerness flooded stories of mentally unhinged men and women. An amendment was made to the Code where homosexuality was permitted if handled "'with care, discretion, and with restraint.'"[20] In reality, queer folks were being severely affected by the hyper-sexualization of gender identity. Men had to be men, and women had to be women, or else they were viewed as confused and sick. "Gays dropped like flies in the Sixties," asserts Russo in *The Celluloid Closet*, "and for as many reasons as there were tragedies. Sometimes the sexuality of lesbians and crazed gay men victimized others, threatening the status quo; sometimes it caused self-hatred enough to make them suicidal."[21] As queer bars continued to be raided and children were encouraged to "smear the queer" on school playgrounds, many queer folks were alienated, abused, and some even harbored their own internal homophobia. Their queerness followed them everywhere, haunted them like ghosts in the night. Such ghosts were even situated on the silver screen with films such as *The Haunting* (1963). As with *The Uninvited*, the lesbian specter was the focus of *The Haunting*. Though *The Haunting* is a British horror film set in Massachusetts and shot by the UK MGM sister company MGM British Studios, the film would be a great influence in American horror cinema and spawn American adaptations such as the remake *The Haunting* (1999) and *The Haunting of Hill House* (2018), a Netflix original television series. Each of these adaptations highlight the subtextual queerness of the original, especially with the character of Theo who, in both adaptations, is openly bisexual.

Based on the Shirley Jackson novel *The Haunting of Hill House* (1959), *The Haunting* follows three volunteer subjects Eleanor (Nell), Theodora (Theo), and Luke as they are being observed in a study of the supernatural activity in a secluded New England mansion by Dr. Markway. On the surface, the film appears to be a simple ghost story. However, the film is rife with lesbian undertones for both female leads, Nell and Theo. Claire Bloom plays Theo, a sophisticated, beautiful woman who not-so-subtly hints at her own queerness toward her "friendship" with Nell. "The affectionate term for Theodora is Theo," states Theo. "We are going to be great friends, Theo," responds Nell.[22] Nell's new friendship wavers on sexual desire throughout the beginning of the film. At the first dinner of their stay, Nell proposes a toast to "companions," to which the camera pans to the two women, "'To my new companion,' replies Theo with inimitable, elegant lasciviousness."[23] We begin to see that Nell is both enchanted and fearful of Theo. Nell, a reserved and anxious woman, enjoys the company of Theo but grows uncomfortable by her presence at times. This is illustrated by the first night at Hill House, which shows the first supernatural experience of the film. Theo walks Nell to her room and invites herself in to do Nell's hair. Nell is at first wary, but on account of supernatural phenomena, the two women huddle in Nell's bed together as a sinister knocking on the door and walls frighten them. After the episode, Luke and the doctor appear in the doorway to check on them. They find Nell and Theo giggling at their own fear. Theo leaves for her room, and Nell is alone: "Eleanor, realizing a mixture of relief and anxiety that she is alone locks her door ('Against what?,' she muses)."[24] The camera work of this scene, as well as the dialogue between the two women, lends itself to a queer reading. Not to mention, when Patricia White, author of "Female Spectator, Lesbian Specter: *The Haunting*," watched the film on television, she noticed that this scene was cut out completely.[25] The paranoia meant to stem from supernatural haunting is placed upon Nell's growing paranoia of Theo's intentions. Nell begins to view the doctor in a romantic light, perhaps as a means for her to forget about a possible desire for Theo. Theo takes notice.

> When asked what *she* [Theo] is afraid of, Theo responds, "of knowing what I really want." Her words make Eleanor uncomfortable on several levels. Eleanor misreads her own desire, as I suspect some feminist film critics would, as a desire for a man ... she [Nell] begins to see Theo as a persecutor.[26]

Several scenes later, Nell radically calls Theo the true "monster of Hill House."[27] Nell's fear of Theo reflects Nell's anxiety toward her own sexuality, her queer desires.

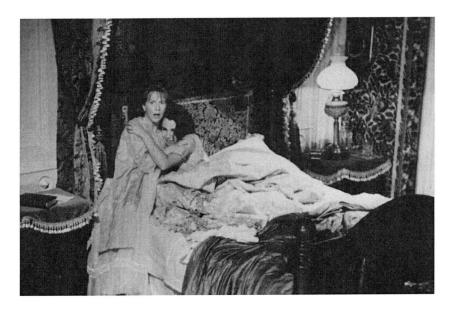

Julie Harris as Nell (left) cowering in bed with Claire Bloom as Theo in *The Haunting* (Metro-Goldwyn-Mayer, 1963).

Multiple lesbian indicators or hints at mental illness being equated to homosexuality are abundant in the ways the doctor refers to Hill House itself. He calls the house "diseased, sick ... crazy, if you like. A deranged house ... your aunt thinks that maybe Hill House was born bad."[28] Queer sexuality has been linked to sickness and mental illness in film since *Dracula's Daughter* in 1936. Queer folks, like straight folks, exist with mental illness, but it is queer folks who are seen as inherently mentally ill, much like Hill House that "was born" as such. All the ghosts in Hill House are women, and those most affected by the house's madness are women. This is to say that the women of Hill House have an effect over one another and pull living women into a trap of homosexual anxiety. It is when a living woman dies in the house that the significance of this idea is magnified. The ending of *The Haunting* shows Nell having died by the house, that is, die by the homosexual nature of the house. Her fears of Theo throughout the film, the fear of being attracted to or loving other women, resulted in her death. The house, representative of homosexuality, claimed her sanity and took hold of her fear. Nell had finally succumbed to her homosexual desires, and thus, had to die by their influence. She had to die rather than live as a queer woman, echoing the influence of the Hays Code mandate of having queer folks die by the end of their film to show the dangers of such a lifestyle. However, *The Haunting* was sneaky in its storytelling, leaving much interpretation up to the viewer. Nell narrates the end of the film as the camera floats around Hill House, "Whatever walked here, walked alone. We who walk here, walk alone."[29] "We" signifies the lonely queers who walk the earth, walk Hill House, damned to a life of sadness.

Queer women, like ghosts, are invisible to those who are unfamiliar with queerness. "Lesbianism," explains Vito Russo, "is rendered invisible because it is purely psychological. And since most lesbians were invisible even to themselves, their sexuality, ill-defined in general, emerged onscreen as a wasted product of a closeted lifestyle."[30] Perhaps Russo's analysis of *The Haunting* provides a theory as to why Theo, the most explicitly queer character, survives Hill House. She knew what she was; hence, the ghosts did not affect her. The ghosts pestered those, like Nell, who fled from their sexuality and haunted them for it. Though Theo never uttered an outright confirmation of her queerness, her actions toward the men and women in the film are indicative of her queerness and bisexuality. It would not be until the 1999 remake of *The Haunting* that horror fans get confirmation of Theo's sexuality where she is given a more acceptable and flirtatious image as an out bisexual woman. Though sexually promiscuous, which is stereotypically placed upon bisexual women, she is still valid as representation.

Social Unrest, Queer Rebellion, and the Break-Down of the American Nuclear Family in the Late 1960s and 1970s

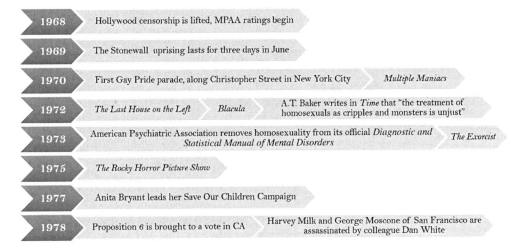

1968 Hollywood censorship is lifted, MPAA ratings begin

1969 The Stonewall uprising lasts for three days in June

1970 First Gay Pride parade, along Christopher Street in New York City   *Multiple Maniacs*

1972 *The Last House on the Left*   *Blacula*   A.T. Baker writes in *Time* that "the treatment of homosexuals as cripples and monsters is unjust"

1973 American Psychiatric Association removes homosexuality from its official *Diagnostic and Statistical Manual of Mental Disorders*   *The Exorcist*

1975 *The Rocky Horror Picture Show*

1977 Anita Bryant leads her Save Our Children Campaign

1978 Proposition 6 is brought to a vote in CA   Harvey Milk and George Moscone of San Francisco are assassinated by colleague Dan White

Figure 4

In 1968, the Hollywood censorship code was lifted, beginning the Motion Picture Association of America rating system, the MPAA. This did not affect how queers were being presented on film. Villainization continued with the onset of the queer revolution. The 1970s started promisingly for queer folks. The sexual liberation of the 1960s allowed repressed individuals to find communities with members like themselves. Gay youth were finding one another and experienced what they have rarely publicly had in the past: free love. "The era of Gay Liberation began a process of discovery," proclaims historian David France. "To act flauntingly on one's sexual appetence was essentially an act of rebellion, but also of self-affirmation, identity exploration, and community forging. What from the outside might have looked like pure carnal zeal was the rudimentary first pass for this emerging youth culture."[31] The first gay pride parade was held along Christopher Street in New York City in 1970, one year after the revolutionary Stonewall Uprising, where transgender women of color and butch lesbians, among other queer subgroups, confronted police brutality head on amidst bricks and Billy clubs. They were responding to the Mafia control of New York's gay clubs, in which police raids were frequent and often unprovoked, as well as the regular abuse of queer folks and sex workers. The 1970 gay pride parade was a symbol of triumph and hope that was emulated after the three days of riots at the Stonewall Inn, and for the first time, queer folks were able to celebrate openly along city streets. The parade was also meant to be an event of activism, in which queer attendees displayed political signs, often pointing out the hypocrisy of American attitudes toward the gay community. One such sign from the 1971 Gay Pride Parade reads, "We are your worst fear. We are your best fantasy."[32] The sign reflects the simultaneous fetishization and demonization of queer folks by heterosexual people.

Many films of the 1970s that showcased queer characters often used this idea to point out the irony of heterosexuals being fearful yet fascinated by the homosexual lifestyle or what they perceived such a lifestyle to be. Queer artists understood that straight folks saw their new queer revolution as a sick, over-sexual circus when to them it was a bold, enlightening new reality. To the straight onlookers, this would be a horror film, with crazy homosexuals inflicting psychological pain on their straight existence. A 1968 *Time* magazine film column discussed how "unashamedly queer characters are everywhere ... [but] most of the homosexuals shown so far are sadists, psychopaths, or buffoons. If the actors are mincing more than the dialogue these days, that may only be because Hollywood has run out of conventional bad guys."[33] What better way for an independent film to spoof Hollywood tropes, proclaim the evident truth that "traditional normality no longer exists," and the extreme fears of heterosexual Americans than through outright and outlandish sadistic queer characters.[34] In comes the young queer filmmaker John Waters, the Pope of Trash and King of Filth, and his fellow filthy queers to showcase *Multiple Maniacs* (1970).

John Waters' early body of work, especially *Multiple Maniacs*, is representative of the rise of social and pop-culture commentary. Waters uses "camp" to critique mass conformity and shed light upon queer culture. The breakup of the nuclear family during the 1960s, in part due to the increasing sexual and queer revolutions, led to one of the biggest generation gaps in American history, where children significantly differed intellectually, politically, and socially from their parents. Children would find their own families of similar lifestyles and interests. As was the case with the majorly female audience of *The Uninvited* (1944), many of the wandering children of the sixties found their families in the cinema and through film. Despite mass conformity culture throughout the 1950s and 1960s, underground groups of beatniks, punks, and queers were developing and reclaiming modes of entertainment purposed for their subcultures and orientations. Filmmakers, such as the openly queer Andy Warhol and a young John Waters, were making low-budget art films, cultivating pure camp. Camp was a cheeky revival of formerly mass-produced and popular fixtures of conformist America, whether gaudy lamps, cheap jewelry, bright exaggerated eye makeup, or iconic no-longer-hip ensembles. Classic films and early rock n roll usually accompanied camp, along with exaggerated forms of gender expression. Pop culture of decades past was reclaimed by the Others of society, those that seldom fit into the molds the objects or dress meant to evoke. There was humor in the reclamation, causing viewers to think as to why this particular style was being revamped by queers. Susan Sontag, a lesbian cultural critic, stated that "the essence of Camp is its love of the unnatural: of artifice and exaggeration. And 'Camp' is esoteric—something of a private code, a badge of identity."[35] In most cases, this "badge of identity" through camp signified queer art to queer audiences. Camp art, such as midnight movies named because they were typically low-budget features shown only during the late hours of the night, became sources of which queer folks could find one another, bond, and even go out for a night of fun and safety due to camp films attracting similar company. Camp would become a staple of 1970s queer culture, and camp would encroach on the realm of horror films by the beginning of the decade.

Multiple Maniacs was manifested by Waters' twisted mind in 1970. Up until *Multiple Maniacs*, Waters was known for his low-budget productions and inclusion of his group of fringe queer friends, including Harris Glenn Milstead, known as Divine, a drag queen. Divine, who starred in nearly all of Waters' films until his death in 1988, was described by Waters as not "playing a man who was dressed as a woman. He was playing a woman. Divine was Jayne Mansfield and Godzilla coming together to scare hippies."[36] Waters, Divine, and the Dreamland gang sported bizarre clothes, spoke profanely, and mocked the "peace-and-love" generation of whom they seemed to be the antithesis. Sex and violence intermingled with sacrilege and bad taste. *Multiple Maniacs* follows Lady Divine and her Cavalcade of Perversion: straight folks are brought into a circus tent to gaze upon "sluts, fags, dykes, and pimps" and the perverse queer lifestyle that includes two men passionately kissing.[37] Upon being lured into a wooded area to view this circus of freaks, the patrons are tied up and murdered by Lady Divine.

The film makes multiple references to the Manson Family Murders that happened less than a year before the film's release, with Lady Divine and fellow criminal David admitting to participating in the murders.[38] Charles Manson, cult leader and convicted felon, ordered four of his followers to break into a Los Angeles residence and murder all occupants to ignite a race war in 1969. Of the victims was a pregnant

Sharon Tate, actress and wife of famed director Roman Polanski. Manson and his followers were regarded as hippies, and thus it was these murders that led to the acknowledgment of the end of the Free Love and hippie movements in America. This cynicism is echoed throughout Waters' *Maniacs*. Lady Divine, a buxom drag queen who "turns" lesbian after a sexual encounter with a woman in a church, which involved a rosary being inserted into her anus, represents the terrifying image of what society will become (or, perhaps, what society *should* become if it were up to Waters). This was frightening to some, but revolutionary and exciting for others, mainly, queer folks. Waters' outlandish and trashy *Multiple Maniacs* is one of the first films of the midnight film phenomenon that included nearly exclusively queer characters, albeit serial killers and predators. This trend of queer characters in midnight films would continue through the 1970s, making the evening film experience very much a queer affair.

Although *Multiple Maniacs* does not follow most of the guidelines for it to be considered a horror film, Waters uses Divine as a monster in and of herself: the ending shows her on a murder spree where she kills and eats her boyfriend, becomes maniacal, foams at the mouth, is subsequently raped by a giant lobster, then wreaks havoc on the city of Baltimore. Divine chases a herd of people down the street while wearing a dark fur coat and making animal grunts. This is a clear nod by Waters to legendary horror monsters King Kong and Godzilla. Eventually, Divine is executed by the National Guard to the tune of "America, the Beautiful." Divine is a queer menace. This, of course, is a compliment from Waters, purely intentional. When Waters sent a copy of his deranged film to the Ontario Film Review Board, they quite literally destroyed the copy. Waters was thrilled: "That was the best review I ever got."[39]

Unlike the disgustingly delightful films of John Waters, many films of this era did not use queer people as allegories for the fear straight folks have toward them. Waters, a queer man himself, knew how to create films with tongue firmly in cheek. Straight directors of the 1970s used tired tropes for horror that enlisted a queer menace for the sake of villainy. Like *Multiple Maniacs*, Wes Craven's *The Last House on the Left* (1972) is a reaction to the peace and love generation's downfall. The film follows two young women, Mari and Phyllis, who are on their way to a concert by the fictional band Bloodlust. While trying to score drugs, the girls become the captors of a maniacal group of escaped mental patients, one of whom is a bisexual woman named Sadie. Sadie and the gang torture their captives. Sadie is the quintessential predatory bisexual: she attempts to kiss the girls, gropes Phyllis' breasts, and orally rapes Mari. As Phyllis tried to flee her captors, she screams, "Stupid dyke!" to

Sadie.[40] Later, Sadie is murdered by Phyllis. To suggest that Craven gave Sadie a more uplifting narrative would be outrageous, as she is a sadistic torturer. But it is the fact that Craven makes this gruesome character queer in the first place that is problematic and continues stereotypes of the predatory queer.

Another persistent stereotype that has existed throughout the history of film has been the sissy. A sissy is an effeminate gay man typically used for comedy. However, the horror of the 1970s used the sissy as a victim for whom no empathy was meant to be felt.

A manic Divine, played by Harris Glenn Milstead (Divine), having just been raped by a giant lobster in *Multiple Maniacs* (New Line Cinema, 1970).

"In a kill 'em or cure 'em climate," Vito Russo explains, "violence by and toward homosexuals onscreen escalated at the end of the 1960s and became the keynote of the 1970s. Sissies were now cured, killed, or rendered impotent in suitable nasty ways."[41] During this time, as America was in a Post-Stonewall era, contradictions in public discourse began to surface with onlookers of the growing gay rights movement struggling with internal homophobia that had been accruing for decades. Tolerant Americans became more vocal about their support for gay rights, yet the systemic homophobia of American society caused internal struggles for many, including journalists and scholars such as A.T. Baker who wrote in a 1972 issue of *Time* that "'the treatment of homosexuals as cripples and monsters is unjust [...]' noting the cultural construction of the monster queer, even as he goes on to demonize homosexuals as 'biologically inaccurate and socially unsound.'"[42] The post–Stonewall years were riddled with this kind of contradictory homosexual opinion. On the one hand, people were noticing the film industry's attempts at painting queer folks as monsters and vice versa, and seeing that as a problem, but many people simultaneously demonized queer folks personally. This contradiction would continue into a new kind of queer person in horror films who was visibly not a monster, yet became a victim of the monster's violent attack, echoing old horror's homophobia but through victimization.

Two stereotyped gay men, an interracial couple, were the first victims of Prince Mamuwalde in *Blacula* (1972). Bobby and Billy are interior decorators importing Prince Mamuwalde's coffin, assuming it is empty, after purchasing a lot from Dracula's castle. When they bring the coffin with them to Los Angeles, Blacula rises from his coffin, killing the men. Bobby and Billy are in a loving relationship. However, their love is not meant to be admired. Dr. Robin Means Coleman in her book *Horror Noire: Blacks in American Horror Films from the 1890s to the Present* elaborates on this idea:

> Romantic love in *Blacula* is narrowly defined as heterosexual. In the film, the brave, savvy Dr. Gordon Thomas, with the help of his medical assistant/girlfriend Michelle, uncovers Mamuwalde's secret. Together they are a good team, and also in a loving relationship. Yet, Bobby and Billy, who are similarly doting on one another, and even equal partners in a thriving business, are reduced to "two faggot interior decorators" in the movie. Later, when Bobby's body disappears from a funeral home because he has turned into a vampire, police raise the question, "Who the hell would want a dead faggot." And, in yet another scene, a racist stereotype, "they all look alike," is shifted to gay men, furthering the film's dismissive, heteronormative rhetorical violence.[43]

Means Coleman also discusses the "sissified" gay man.[44] Sissification, which includes dressing a gay male character in an effeminate fashion and demeanor (and in the case of Billy and Bobby, even their professions as antique dealers is a nod to the sissy, as such a profession is a stereotype of gay men), renders a character unserious; thus, audiences can distance themselves when that character becomes a victim. In a film that broke so many barriers not just in horror films but cinema at large, *Blacula* added to anti-gay discourse in film and American society, and this addition will continue to plague American horror films.

In 1973, the American Psychiatric Association removed homosexuality from its official Diagnostic and Statistical Manual of Mental Disorders. This was thanks in part to the activism of militant gay groups such as The Lavender Panthers, formed by the Rev. Ray Broshears in San

Lovers Bobby, played by Ted Harris (left), and Billy, played by Rick Metzler, are attacked by William Marshall as Prince Mamuwalde (center) in *Blacula* (American International Pictures, 1972).

Francisco "to strike terror in the hearts of 'all those young punks who have been beating up my faggots' by arming the group with chains, whistles, Billy clubs, and red spray paint."[45] The rise of militant queer folks was inspired by their militant civil rights comrades. Queer folks would use this same energy to confront Hollywood homophobia for years to come. Homosexuality had been a mental disease for a majority of the American twentieth century. Still, queer folks in film were being used to push anti-gay agendas and used as "perfect" victims—perfect in the sense that queer characters, coded or outright, were usually seen as villainous or pathetic, therefore an audience would either cheer or be indifferent to their death. Underground films, however, presented a different image from the mainstream queer characters created. The militancy of queer groups in the 1970s rubs off on the punk queer filmmakers of the underground who channeled the militancy through the unabashed inclusion of queer protagonists, anarchist queer essence, and a subversion of traditional ideas of sexuality, often to surprising (though latent) mainstream success.

A pop version of John Waters' twisted *Multiple Maniacs* arrived with Richard O'Brien's *The Rocky Horror Picture Show* (1975). Adorned in camp, sex, and a sweet transsexual from Transylvania, *The Rocky Horror Picture Show* follows the boring heterosexual couple, Brad and Janet, as they enter a castle to seek help for their broken-down car in the middle of the night. They happen upon a freaky cast of characters complete with singing, dancing, and unabashed queerness. Dr. Frank-N-Furter, played by Tim Curry, is the androgynous alien queer anti-hero who forces Brad and Janet, not so subtly, out of their hetero comfort to give themselves "over to absolute pleasure" in the means of sex and intrigue of multiple genders.[46] Though the film initially flopped commercially, *The Rocky Horror Picture Show* went on to become a cult midnight movie classic, especially among those in the queer community. Audiences flocked to midnight showings thanks to the fan-created tradition of audience participation. Unfortunately, the large gathering of queer folks at showings would result in homophobic gangs targeting the early screenings resulting in anti-gay violence at some theaters. Eventually, the gangs subsided, and the film would go on to earn approximately nine million dollars annually by 2001.[47]

Like *Multiple Maniacs*, the film caters to the queer sensibility through camp and satire of straight society due to the overt queerness of writer O'Brien: "As both catalogue and spoof of old monster movies and science fiction films," explains Russo, "*Rocky Horror* becomes almost dizzying in its references, but its most expert satire is of the age-old fear with which straight society encounters deviant sexuality."[48] Included in reference is Dr. Frank-N-Furter wearing a pink triangle on his lab coat, which signifies the persecution of queer folks by Nazi Germany, and lighter references from movies such as *King Kong* (1933) and *The Wizard of Oz* (1939).[49]

Though the film concludes with the demise of the most sexually-adventurous queer character Frank-N-Furter, as well as his lover/creation, the film succeeds in channeling an inner queer within the film's straight couple. "At its sybaritic climax," explain Lester D. Friedman and Allison B. Kavey in "Mary Shelley's Stepchildren: Transitions, Translations, and Transformations," "the formerly prim Brad and Janet meld into a balletic, hedonistic underwater orgy where male, female, and newly created bodies blissfully touch, kiss, and intermingle without shame, guilt, or gender distinctions."[50] *The Rocky Horror Picture Show* advocates for sexual freedom, as well as being your authentic self. "Don't dream it," demands Frank-N-Furter. "Be it."[51]

The rarity of *The Rocky Horror Picture Show*, other than its embrace of queerness, lies in its ability to have catapulted into mainstream culture despite its underground status (though the film only grossed just

Patricia Quinn as maid Magenta (left) and Tim Curry as the "sweet transvestite" Dr. Frank-N-Furter shivering with anticipation for the arrival of the hunky creation in *The Rocky Horror Picture Show* (20th Century–Fox, 1975).

over a million dollars in domestic box office revenue during its 1975 theatrical release). While the horror genre rose to prominence throughout the 1970s with blockbuster hits like *The Amityville Horror* (1979), *Alien* (1979), and *The Omen* (1976), two horror films soared beyond the rest, generating hundreds of millions of dollars: *Jaws* (1975) and *The Exorcist* (1973). *Jaws*, the story of three men hunting a killer great white shark, is a straightforward action/horror film where there is little to no analysis necessary. *The Exorcist*, on the other hand, touches upon a fractured family unit, the demonic possession of a pubescent twelve-year-old girl, and a troubled priest whose faith is wavering and seems to have much on his mind beyond his duties as a clergyman in the Catholic church.

Based on the 1971 novel by William Peter Blatty, *The Exorcist* tells the story of young Regan MacNeil, whose happy preteen years have been corrupted by a malicious demon inhabiting her body. Once-cheery Regan becomes a snarling, vicious, and crude monster through no fault of her own. The growing violence of the demon whilst using Regan as a vessel causes Regan's mother Chris to seek help beyond the confounded doctors who cannot seem to find an answer to Regan's strange and frightening behavior, not to mention her outrageous body contortions, simultaneously masturbating and mutilating herself with a crucifix, and her colorful vehement vocabulary. She is suggested by her doctors to consult with an exorcist. They believe, however, that it is not the exorcism that will cure Regan but rather her belief in being possessed, which would allow an exorcism to be successful, will be her remedy. This is similar to the early forms of psychiatry used to treat homosexuality in patients during the 1930s and 1940s: as long as the patient believes the therapy will work, they shall be cured of their ailment through their own will.

The Exorcist is not merely a story of a young girl possessed by a malevolent demon, but rather the story of the troubled Father Karras. Throughout the film, Karras is weighed down by the guilt of leaving his ailing mother in a mental institution. After her passing, alone, Karras is distraught. Another priest, Father Dyer, comes to comfort him in his room on the Georgetown University Campus where Karras was hired as both religious and psychiatric counsel. In the brief scene, these men exhibit affinity for each other. Karras grabs Dyer's arm before he leaves, wordless but poignant in touch. In Blatty's novel, it is revealed that Dyer, a friend to Chris MacNeil, feels she is the key to leaving the priesthood, along with Karras. "She ... can help us with my plan for when we both quit the priesthood." "Who's quitting the priesthood?" Karras asks. "Faggots. In droves."[52] This dialogue is not included in the film but explains Karras and Dyer's seemingly tender friendship. After the film's climactic exorcism, Karras, sacrificing himself to the demon Pazuzu to save Regan, throws himself out her bedroom window, effectively vanquishing the evil entity. Dyer finds Karras at the bottom of the steps which he tumbled down outside the window. Dyer goes to Karras' side and asks him if he wants to make his confession. Dyer continues as Karras opens his hand as a signal of "yes." "Are you sorry for having offended God and for all the sins of your past life?" Once again, Karras opens his hand for "yes."[53] Dyer cries as he gives Karras his last rites before dying. In the film's final moments, as Chris and Regan MacNeil, now free of the demon, move out of their Georgetown home, Chris spots Dyer lingering near the house. Just as she and Regan are about to leave their old, cursed home, Chris gives Dyer the necklace Regan pulled from Karras' neck during the exorcism. "I thought you'd like to keep this," she says as she hands the religious necklace to Dyer.[54] The film ends with Dyer visiting the staircase at which Karras fell to his death.

It is also fascinating to note how Father Karras in Friedkin's film is initially hesitant to conduct the exorcism at the insistence of Chris MacNeil. During his first visit with Regan, already in the throngs of demonic possession, Regan mentions Karras' mother's death, a fact that Regan herself would not know of, proving that something sinister and all-knowing is living inside the girl's body. After the encounter, Karras refuses to perform the exorcism. His reluctance could signify his fear of being exposed as gay or queer at the hands of the all-knowing demon or perhaps the devil himself. When he finally agrees to conduct the exorcism with the aid of Father Merrin, a priest with exorcism experience, Merrin warns Karras that the demon will "psychologically attack" them and will mix "lies with truth" to provoke the priests.[55] During the exorcism, Regan only hurls homophobic insults such as "cocksucker" and "faggot" toward Father Merrin, though the demon does shout, "Fuck him, Karras!"[56] One piece of important dialogue cut from the film, though it exists in the book, is an exchange between the demon and Karras of which is Karras' last straw before he begins to taunt the demon into taking him, not Regan, as a sacrifice. The demon begins, "'Even *worms* will not eat your corruption, you...' Karras heard the words of the demon and began to tremble with a murderous fury. [...] '...homosexual.'"[57] When tying together both book and film versions of Karras, *The Exorcist* becomes a tale of not just a demonic child but of a troubled religious leader who holds guilt not only for his mother but also for himself. Although Karras, a seemingly queer man, becomes a hero for saving young Regan from the grips of the demon, he *becomes* a demon himself, and dies with the evil still in him. Perhaps it is best that the film trod lightly on Karras' sexuality, lest the queer once again become the scapegoat for evil.

The Rocky Horror Picture Show advocated for queer self-expression and bloomed in an era that proclaimed the queer as deviant and heterosexuality as Godly, while a film such as *The Exorcist* encouraged a need for a return to traditional societal values of good over/versus evil, of saving society from demonic forces, many of which were believed to be caused by homosexuality according to the growing Moral Majority. When discussing the film in his 2000 piece for *History Today*, author Nick Cull explains that Blatty wrote the book and produced the film to "scare a new generation of Americans back into church."[58] His attempt, in a sense, worked. But, instead of a new generation of God-fearing folk, the film, along with the intensifying feminist, queer, and sexual revolutions across the United States, emboldened older generations who had grown fearful of a perceived devolution in societal morals. The budding queer rights movement was high on the Moral Majority's radar due to the deeply rooted belief that homosexuality was sin and intrinsically linked to child abuse and pedophilia. This belief is encapsulated in part by the Save Our Children campaign in 1977, headed by ultra-religious

Anita Bryant and followers of the growing Moral Majority. Joined by homophobic pastors and personalities such as Jerry Falwell, Bryant preached bigotry toward queer folks and pronounced that queer people, particularly gay male teachers, were recruiting children to become homosexual. "[R]ecruitment of children," asserts Bryant in the *Miami Herald* in 1977, "is absolutely necessary for the survival and growth of homosexuality—for since homosexuals cannot reproduce, they must recruit, must freshen their ranks."[59] Famously averse to the homophobic taunts of folks like Bryant was Harvey Milk, the first elected gay city official of San Francisco. Milk and his fellow queer activists fought against homophobic legislation such as California's Proposition 6 (1978) which would "prohibit lesbians and gay men, as well as any teacher who was found 'advocating, imposing, encouraging or promoting' homosexuality, from teaching in public schools."[60] Activists helped defeat the proposition by a 58.4 to 41.6 percent margin. Tragically, twenty days after this victory, Milk and then-mayor of San Francisco George Moscone were assassinated by their conservative former colleague Dan White. The 1970s ended with a huge blow to the queer community and an uplifting of the Moral Majority. The assassination of Harvey Milk would be the tip of the iceberg for the struggles and setbacks queer folks would face in the 1980s. The worst was yet to come.

CHAPTER 3

Villainization

AIDS and Casual Homophobia (the 1980s)

> Americans learn basically through stories. To human-ize [AIDS] is crucial. Without humanization, education is thwarted [...]. Gay people have been characterized for years as being only gay, only for glitter, only for party. The AIDS crisis has shown that gay people have a strong, hard, solid underside that can deal with the ultimate issue in life, which is death—strongly, powerfully, heroically.— Boze Hadleigh, *The Lavender Screen: The Gay and Les-bian Films—Their Stars, Directors, and Critics*, 2001[1]

Predatory Leather Daddies and Pedophilic Clowns: Villainous Stereotypes in Mass Media

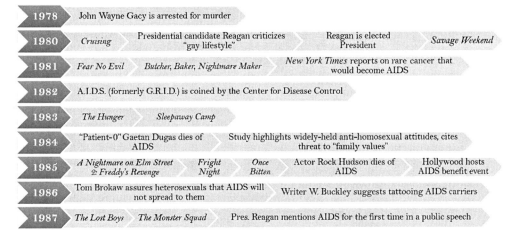

Figure 5

Without uplifting narratives in the era of AIDS, viewers would continue to see queer characters as punchlines and villains. Portrayals of gay men in the 1980s continued the stereotypes generated throughout the 1960s and 1970s. The stock-footage of queer men consisted of sissies, sexual deviants, and leather-clad queer men, and these characters were usually played and written by straight folks. Such is the case with the gay caricature of Nicky, played by straight actor Christopher Allport, in *Savage Weekend* (1980). Nicky is a sissy Bronx native whose snarky quips and flamboyant gestures conjure up the decades-old gay male stereotype used by all genres of film. The dialogue written for him drips with homophobic effeminacy, with lines such as "I don't know about you girls, but Mother Nicky is gonna get herself watered," referring to a nearby bar.[2] The homophobic dialogue continues moments later, taking a jab at the "risky" sexual behavior said to be prominent of gay men at the time: "Jesus, you think my life is easy? I can't even escape my lovers in the men's room."[3] Film reviewer Joe Baltake for the *Philadelphia Daily News* was a fierce opponent of the film's portrayal of the sole gay character upon its release, going so far as to assert that Nicky is "the foulest movie character of recent memory, enough to set Gay Rights activism back several decades. In contrast to him, the goings-on and characters in [*Cruising* (1980)] are charming."[4] One of the only redeeming factors of *Savage Weekend*'s gay character is his ability to win a bar fight against two homophobic rednecks.

As mentioned in Baltake's review, movies such as *Cruising*, a slasher-thriller about a serial killer preying on gay men in New York City, painted a gay underground filled with leather, BDSM sex acts, and risky public sex (as alluded to by Nicky in *Savage Weekend*). Such a depiction was strikingly similar to a *Life* magazine article from 1964 of queer leather subculture and included

> a double-page photo spread of men at the Tool Box, a gay biker bar [...] captioned, "These brawny young men in their leather caps, shirts, jackets and pants are practicing homosexuals, men who turn to other men for affection and sexual satisfaction. They are part of what they call the 'gay world,' which is actually a sad and often sordid world."[5]

This article used the queer leather subculture to make a blanket statement about *all* queer men: their world is deviant, seedy, and depressing. *Cruising*, in fact, did depict a world in which lay a seedy individual, most specifically, a murderer of gay men. The film tells the story of a macho-straight cop Det. Steve Burns, played by Al Pacino, who must go undercover in the world of New York City gay leather bars to catch a serial killer who targets gay men amid bold sex acts meant to shock viewers. Director William Friedkin was inspired to pursue work on the film adaptation of Gerald Walker's book *Cruising* (1970) after reading a series of news articles about unsolved murders in New York's lower east side gay leather bars (these mysterious deaths were later attributed to the AIDS virus).[6] Det. Burns is plagued with the thoughts of what he has seen in the gay world, and he becomes so alarmed by fear of himself being gay that the film includes sex scenes with his girlfriend whenever he comes back from his gay undercover work to prove to himself, and surly some audience members, that he is heterosexual.

Like *Cruising*, many narratives of queer folks are written, acted, and directed by straight people. It seemed that the heterosexual world, amid queer revolution and increasing visibility, became obsessed with the homosexual world, its alleged antithesis. "To heterosexuals," explains Darrell Yates Rist in his 1986 piece "Fear and Loving and AIDS," "male homosexuality is a catalogue of mythic understanding. Elegance and beauty sallying with decadence and torment, insouciance with fear. Good and evil. Gays are mystery incarnate [...] the spritely androgyne in drag queens ... and annihilism, black and cold, in sadomasochistic leather men."[7] Films like *Cruising* are representative of this intrigue and misunderstanding of a diverse community. *Cruising* is a film for straight people to look inside a gay world, as told by fellow straight people.

The stereotypes of *Cruising*, shaped and enforced by heterosexual people, were debated among those of the queer community. On different ends of the spectrum were those who found the blanket statements of gay male city life offensive and those, many being part of the leather/BDSM scene, who found them to be quite accurate. Literature scholar Jack Halberstam examines the nature of film stereotypes and stresses the importance of acknowledging which stereotypes are used to exploit a minority group of which are used to identify a minority group to a broad audience using easily recognizable characteristics. "However," he explains, "stereotyping does not always and only work on behalf of a conservative representational agenda: the stereotype does often represent a 'true' type [...] that does exist within the subculture."[8] William Friedkin (*The Exorcist*), director of *Cruising*, conducted his film research at actual New York City gay leather bars, and nearly all of the men in those bars throughout the film were real patrons. "I met the managers, the bartenders, and a great many people who frequented the bars," says Friedkin for an interview with *Venice Magazine* in 2007. "I went back a number of times. They knew I was doing research for the film, and they're the ones you see in those scenes. There are no screen extras guild members. These guys were paid as extras, but they were just there, doing their thing."[9] Thus, *Cruising* is quite an authentic film, but

Several extras in *Cruising* (United Artists, 1980). Many of these extras were real patrons. Filming took place in *The Hellfire Club*, a BDSM nightclub in the Meatpacking District of Manhattan, New York City. This location was designed to resemble the Mineshaft, another NYC leather bar, that would not allow filming.

only for those that know of the true research collected by Friedkin and the film's usage of actual leather bar patrons. For those unaware of the accuracy of the on-screen depictions, viewers may see *Cruising*, a film directed by a heterosexual man, as a mockery of queer subcultures or a caricature of the lifestyle.

Ultimately, the film was picketed while in production by local activists in the vicinity of the filming. These queer activists felt the film negatively portrayed homosexual men as deviant sex criminals. As a result, film production was stalled frequently, with edits and reshoots needed to phase out background protests and whistles, which ultimately added to the film's overall production costs. Additionally, Friedkin, in an effort to keep his movie from further activist onslaught, included a disclaimer at the beginning of the film that read "[t]his film is not intended as an indictment of the homosexual world. It is set in one small segment of that world which is not meant to be representative of the whole." Unfortunately, this attempt at soothing tension with queer activists made matters worse, where many, including Vito Russo, saw this as an admission of guilt: "What director would make such a statement if he truly believed his film would not be taken as representative of the whole?"[10] Such polarizing on-screen depictions of queer men continued the decades-long narrative of the predatory homosexual. Legal discourse was not dissimilar from pop-cultural ideals toward gay men. The criminal homosexual stereotype was used as fodder in the trial of real-life serial killer John Wayne Gacy from 1978 to 1980.

Anti-homosexual attitudes, including the lack of empathy for gay victims of crime and the stereotype of the violent and deviant homosexual, were exhibited in the trial of notorious serial killer John Wayne Gacy, the Chicago sociopathic/psychopathic pedophile "killer clown." Gacy also happened to be queer. Gacy would eventually admit to his wife that he was bisexual, though it was clear his sexual preference was for males. His wife found numerous gay magazines hidden by Gacy, and Gacy himself only targeted males for his rapes and murders. Gacy raped, tortured, and murdered at least thirty-three young men and boys from 1972 to 1978.

In 1978, Gacy slipped up in his years-long murder spree by setting one of his victims free: Jeffrey Rignall. Rignall was picked up by Gacy on his way to a gay bar in March of 1978. He was then taken by Gacy to his home, where he was drugged, beaten, tortured, humiliated, and raped. After Rignall came to consciousness in a park late at night after the brutal attacks inflicted upon him by a man he did not know, he went directly to a police station. According to Rignall, "the police were so uncooperative that he had to spend weeks tracing the identity of his attacker."[11] Once he was able to identify Gacy as his attacker, Rignall again went to the police, but felt that he was not taken seriously and that the police were discriminating against him: "Rignall believed police treated his case as routine after he told officers that he was homosexual [...]. Rignall claimed that when he complained about the sexual assault, the police treated him as if he were on drugs, even though the police knew that Gacy previously had served a prison sentence for sodomy."[12] Although there was clear evidence of sexual assault by Gacy from his past conviction, police would not fully believe Rignall's testimony. In addition, as alleged by a police officer involved in the investigation, the parents of the missing boys under investigation as potential victims of Gacy "did not send in dental and medical charts on their missing sons because they did not want to find out that their children had been involved in a case with homosexual overtones."[13] Not only were Rignall and other victims of Gacy treated with bias based on their sexualities from both loved ones and detectives, the press and investigators also used anti-gay rhetoric and stereotypes toward Gacy, a man who should have been tried without bias for the sadistic rapist and murderer he was. While the young boys kidnapped may or may not have been homosexual, they were taken against their wills regardless of their sexual preference and were stereotyped for their victim association with homosexuality.

From the start of the investigation, police and investigators stressed Gacy's homosexuality. During Gacy's trial, prosecutors denying Gacy's defense claims of insanity noted in a rebuttal that he "consciously chose to be a homosexual, consciously chose his victims, consciously decided to kill."[14] This idea of homosexuality as a choice would follow throughout the trial to disprove Gacy's plea of insanity. Gay media outlets caught on to what the prosecutors were trying to do with the case, specifically queer Chicago residents who were furious with the constant references to Gacy as a gay man. In a letter to the editor of the *Chicago Sun-Times*, one member of the queer community shot back at the continual mention of Gacy's homosexuality and encouraged media outlets to look at the slayings not as "'homosexual murders,' but simply 'murders.'"[15]

Despite the outcry from Chicago's queer community, the portrait of the homosexual pedophile serial killer persisted. Gacy was a sadistic pedophile killer. However, media coverage of Gacy and court testimony on his case linked his homosexuality to his violent pedophilic and murderous impulses. This image of Gacy, a volunteer clown who entertained at children's events, promoted the fear of the sick homosexual-next-door who was a threat to your children. This is true of him, but his homosexuality had nothing to do with his desire to inflict pain, especially on children. Activist Larry Kramer mentions the media's equating of homosexuality with Gacy's crimes in his seminal 1983 article on the growing AIDS crisis for the *New York Native* titled "1,112 and Counting." This article is a message to queer men that their world is being torn apart from the inside, and only they can help one another because the American population has seen and still sees queer people, especially gay men, as perverts deserving of infectious downfall.

> Frightened populations are going to drown out [the truths about the AIDS epidemic] by playing on the worst bigoted fears of the straight world, and send the status of gay rights back to the Dark Ages. Not all Jews are blamed for Meyer Lansky, Rabbis Bergman and Kahane, or for money-lending. All Chinese aren't blamed for the recent Seattle slaughters. But all gays are blamed for John Gacy, the North American Man/Boy Love Association, and AIDS.[16]

The effects of the media portrayal and vocabulary in the trial of John Wayne Gacy had devastating effects on how America treated those who contracted HIV/AIDS during the 1980s and 1990s. Unfortunately, since the horror genre is a mirror for the fears of an era, horror films of the 1980s would continue to equate homosexuality with violence and evil as the press and investigators had done in the case of John Wayne Gacy, especially with regard to the HIV/AIDS epidemic.

AIDS, Family Values and Freddy's Revenge

With the presidential election of Republican conservative Ronald Reagan, the reality and cinema of the 1980s regressed to the conservative 1950s. Classic fifties science fiction and horror films such as *The Thing from Another World* (1951) and *The Blob* (1958) were reimagined for a new audience yet contained similar subtexts as their originals: fear of the unknown alien. Mark Jancovich, the editor of *Horror, the Film Reader*, acknowledges horror's conservative leanings, where "in science fiction, it is claimed, the unknown is viewed as positive and even potentially liberating, while in horror, the unknown can only be threatening. Horror is therefore said to be a conservative genre that works to justify and defend the status quo."[17] Though horror has evident queer roots and sentiments, its use of queer bodies *as* horror lends itself to pushing homophobic agendas, whether intentionally or not. Using a queer person or any Other as a villain causes straight audiences to subliminally take in homophobic ideas.

In a 1984 study of anti-homosexual attitudes, investigators broke heterosexuals' fears of gay and lesbian sexuality into three topic areas: (1) Homosexuality as a threat to the individual—that someone you know (or you yourself) might be homosexual. (2) Homosexuality as a threat to others—homosexuals have been frequently linked in the media to child molestation, rape, and violence. (3) Homosexuality as a threat to the community and other components of culture—homosexuals supposedly represent the destruction of the procreative nuclear family, traditional gender roles, and (to use a buzz phrase) "family values."[18]

The conservative agenda of the Reagan Administration included a War on Drugs, a decrease in federal government spending on education, and criticism of the gay rights movements, signifying a retreat to "traditional" American family values. While on the 1980 campaign trail, Ronald Reagan was vocal in his opposition to the gay rights movement, stating, "My criticism is that [the gay movement] isn't just asking for civil rights; it's asking for recognition and acceptance of an alternative lifestyle which I do not believe society can condone, nor can I."[19] His views on homosexuality remained largely the same since thirteen years prior when he was invited to speak at Yale University in 1967. Not only did Reagan assert that homosexuality was a mental illness but proclaimed that homosexuality should be illegal.[20] His attitude toward the queer community would soon be encapsulated in his response (or lack thereof) to the HIV/AIDS crisis which would strike America one year after Reagan's presidential win.

The narrative of the evil homosexual, as was insinuated during the trial of serial killer John Wayne Gacy, was showcased in *Fear No Evil* (1981). *Fear No Evil*'s protagonist Andrew is representative of Ronald Reagan's condemnation of the "alternative" homosexual lifestyle intertwined with the religious leanings of himself and the new Moral Majority-influenced Republican Party. Andrew Williams is a high school antichrist and loner. The film is "[a] conservative religious outing which pits the forces of good—a rather psychotic but ultimately justified Catholicism—against evil—in this case, as *The New York Times* described him, 'a conspicuously effeminate high-school senior who turns out to be the embodiment of Lucifer.'"[21] Andrew's antichrist character arc mimics that of parents fearing and shunning their queer child. Andrew's parents experience religious turmoil about their son, where his mother tries to save him through prayer. In addition, Andrew being the antichrist even scares himself, and he continues to hide the evil inside. Furthering the ideas of his evil being equated with his queerness is a homoerotic locker room shower scene. A bully tells Andrew to kiss him as a joke as the two boys are showering naked. Here, the bully is implying that Andrew's withdrawn personality and shyness, his effeminacy, equates to him being gay. As the bully kisses him, a strange power comes over Andrew, and after a minute of holding the kiss, accompanied by ominous music, the bully withdraws from him, fearful about what had just transpired. Andrew is also visibly shaken by the "power" of the kiss. This bizarre scene implies the wickedness of homosexuality by showing the boys struck with fear after they kiss, perhaps because it was a kiss enjoyed. Regardless, the fact of Andrew being the antichrist and having the homoerotic shower scene is unsettling. Having two scenes, along with tying in the fear his parents feel toward their son, the film signifies sinful homosexuality. This film was released in 1981, the same year *The New York Times* reported a "Rare Cancer Seen in 41 Homosexuals" that would be used as proof of God's wrath against sinful queer men.[22]

A rare film appeared in 1981 to limited release in Oregon and went to wider release in 1983: *Butcher, Baker, Nightmare Maker* (1981), later renamed *Night Warning* (1983). Unlike *Fear No Evil, Butcher, Baker, Nightmare Maker* includes an explicit gay male character, one whose storyline intersects with a homophobic detective whose vitriol for homosexuals elicits a sympathetic response from protagonist Billy and viewers alike. Somehow, this film, emerging during the early years of the HIV/AIDS epidemic, treated its gay character, Tom Landers, basketball coach to Billy, with compassion. Billy, raised by his over-protective and predatory aunt Cheryl, has a bond with his supportive coach who is helping him earn an athletic scholarship to the University of Denver. Landers' sexuality is discovered, however, when Aunt Cheryl murders a handyman whom she tried to seduce in her home. Detectives find a ring on the handyman's finger, engraved with Coach Landers' initials, indicating that the two were lovers. Detective Carlson proceeds to accost Landers, telling him he better quit his job or "be lynched." Det. Carlson later confronts Billy, who found his aunt with the bloody knife used to kill the handyman, asking him if he too is a "fag."[23] Billy does not turn on his coach and appears to support him whilst not judging him for his sexuality. Even when his aunt says homosexuals are sick, Billy responds, "Coach Landers is not sick!"[24] Aunt Cheryl, who supports the theory of homosexuality as a sickness, goes on to murder several people as well as fondle her teen nephew, while Coach Landers becomes a savior to Billy and his girlfriend Julia at the end of the film. *Butcher, Baker, Nightmare Maker* subverts the age-old stereotype of the villainous and predatory queer, while heterosexual villainy and bigotry run amok in the film. When asked about his role as Coach Landers in the Blu-ray commentary for Code Red's release of the film, Steve Easton states that "[Landers] is a gay man, but he's not a pervert. He just likes men, and he's got a boyfriend, and his boyfriend is murdered."[25] His gayness is not sinister like Andrew in *Fear No Evil*. The only people that have a problem with Coach Landers' sexuality are themselves ignorant and monstrous. Though *Butcher, Baker, Nightmare Maker* portrays a heroic and sympathetic queer character, the film came at the eve of the HIV/AIDS crisis. Any progress that this film spearheaded at the time is lost as conservative America scrambles to place the queer at the center of a world health crisis.

The outbreak of the plague of HIV/AIDS swelled in the first three years of the 1980s. In the beginning, the unknown disease was killing mainly gay men, resulting in names such as "gay cancer" and "gay plague." In 1982, an official name was given: Gay-Related Immune Deficiency, or GRID. Gay men, hemophiliacs, and Haitian immigrants were the first victims of GRID, though as the name connotated, the disease would be linked to gay men for decades. Auto-immune Deficiency Syndrome or AIDS was coined in September of 1982 by the Centers for Disease Control (CDC). Emaciated people, predominantly young men, wasted away in hospital beds with the disease. Many of the early AIDS-afflicted were left to suffer alone, abandoned by family members and even hospital personnel too afraid to go near a patient for fear of contamination. Families often did not claim the bodies of their children, even their ashes. During the early years of the epidemic, Ruth Coker Burks, a volunteer caregiver for hundreds of patients suffering from AIDS in Little Rock, Arkansas, recalls the heartbreaking reality of those abandoned by parents. After visiting an ailing young man in his hospital room, "I walked out and [the nurses] said, 'You didn't go in that room, did you?'... I said, 'Well, yeah. He wants his mother.' They laughed. They said, 'Honey, his mother's not coming. He's been here six weeks. Nobody's coming.'"[26] Burks took matters into her own hands and called the young man's mother, who promptly hung up on her.

> Her son was a sinner, the woman told Burks. She didn't know what was wrong with him and didn't care. She wouldn't come, as he was already dead to her as far as she was concerned. She said she wouldn't even claim his body when he died. It was a curse Burks would hear again and again over the next decade: sure judgment and yawning hellfire, abandonment on a platter of scripture. Burks estimates she worked with more than 1,000 people dying of AIDS over the years. Of those, she said, only a handful of families didn't turn their backs on their loved ones.[27]

The early years of AIDS were ones of a fear of the unknown: how was AIDS contracted? Could it be passed on through touch? Why are AIDS carriers predominantly homosexual and bisexual men? This last question resulted in the demonization of the gay community, specifically queer men.

Religious conservative propaganda and media outlets continued to slander the gay community, linking homosexuality to AIDS. Michael Bronski explains:

> AIDS was caused by a virus, not by homosexuality. It was, however, a "gay disease" in the important sense that because many of those affected were gay men, moral, social, political, and legal stigma attached to homosexuality shaped the country's response. As a result, hundreds of thousands of deaths occurred in circumstances that were unjust and a direct result of the behavior of the majority.[28]

The social correlation of AIDS to homosexuality, and the historical linking of homosexuality to sin, made it all the easier for heterosexual populations to literally demonize AIDS patients. Conservatives and religious zealots viewed AIDS patients as evidence of God's wrath upon the sinful lifestyle of gay men. Many looked on apathetically as thousands of people, an entire generation, wasted away.

Those who experienced the plague firsthand recall the horrors of the disease. The dark purple lesions and extreme weight loss were reminiscent of the bodies of zombies and contagion films. When attending a memorial for twenty-seven-year-old Ken Ramsauer in Central Park, New York City, Ian Hurst, friend of author David France of *How to Survive a Plague: The Inside Story of How Citizens and Science Tamed AIDS*, looked out at the sea of fellow mourners, many of whom were already severely afflicted by the disease: "It looks like a horror flick."[29] Mark Patton of *A Nightmare on Elm Street 2: Freddy's Revenge,* also experienced the horrors of AIDS during the 1980s:

> If you're not at the age to know what [the AIDS epidemic] was like—we don't watch *The Walking Dead* or any of those zombie movies because we saw it in real life. You'd see some guy who was the most beautiful boy in New York and six months later, he'd look like your grandfather. And then two months after that, he's dead.[30]

Mark Patton, born in Kansas City, Missouri, was a young closeted gay actor during the outbreak of the AIDS virus. After staring in a successful Broadway play and film adaptation of *Come Back to the Five and Dime, Jimmy Dean, Jimmy Dean* (1982), Patton landed the leading role in *A Nightmare on Elm Street 2: Freddy's Revenge* (1985). The film was in production during the height of the AIDS crisis. During filming, Patton's lover and actor on the hit television series *Dallas,* Timothy Patrick Murphy, was dying of the virus.[31]

Freddy's Revenge tells the story of high schooler Jesse Walsh, the new kid in town who has the hots for his neighbor, Lisa. In his new house on 1428 Elm Street in Springwood, Ohio—the same horror house from the first film—Jesse experiences vivid nightmares of a man in a red and green sweater with a burnt face: Freddy Krueger. This sequel to the widely popular first installment of the *Elm Street* franchise featured myriad homosexual-coded scenes, from a *Probe* board game in Jesse's closet to Jesse screaming that Freddy wants to "get inside" him, and a queer leather-bar scene where Jesse encounters his male gym coach Schneider in full-leather.[32] The queer bar is even explicitly mentioned in the film, "He hangs out at queer S&M joints downtown. He likes pretty boys like you," says Grady, Jesse's friend, about Coach Schneider.[33]

Unfortunately, these aspects of the film, including having Patton be regarded backhandedly as a Scream Queen earned *A Nightmare on Elm Street 2: Freddy's Revenge* the reputation of being the "gayest" horror film of all time, during one of the worst years of the AIDS crisis that villainized young homosexual men. The result was Patton's departure from Hollywood due to his perceived sexuality after the film was

Mark Patton as Jesse Walsh (left), arriving at the local S&M bar after a stormy midnight stroll in *A Nightmare on Elm Street 2: Freddy's Revenge* (New Line Cinema, 1985). He is greeted by the bartender, played by the film's producer Robert Shaye (right).

released, and due to fear of what was to become of his and other gay actors' careers:

> When the movie came out, my agent said to me, "We're going to have to find you different work. You can't be a leading man because you can't play straight." I got into showbusiness to be free, not climb into a prison cell. I quit, and that was pretty much it. I devoted my energy to saving my brothers. There were so many people to take care of and riots to go to. I got good and angry, [fueled by] the rage of a twelve-year-old who had been made fun of one too many times.[34]

The same year of *Freddy's Revenge*, Hollywood hosted a star-studded fundraising event, organized by Elizabeth Taylor in honor of her friend Rock Hudson, Hollywood icon who is often regarded as the first celebrity to bravely proclaim that he had AIDS. The event brought Hollywood stars together for the cause, including Shirley MacLaine who had three close friends already die of the virus: "The image is that Hollywood is panicky. Tonight shows most of us have made the choice of love rather than hate."[35] Unfortunately, Mark Patton did not feel this love from those behind-the-scenes in Hollywood. His dream of Hollywood stardom was cut short by his perceived homosexuality, due primarily to the overwhelming amount of gay subtext in *Freddy's Revenge*. The film was a financial success and received great reviews. However, Patton felt that his career was over because of the film, "I was out in my personal life [...] but you weren't allowed to be out publicly. Most specifically actors.... And there was a whole lot of people who gave you reasons to keep your mouth shut.... Casting directors especially."[36] Due to the gay subtext of *Freddy's Revenge*, after viewing the film for the first time, Patton felt that his cover was blown, "Everyone is going to know I'm gay."[37]

Throughout the 1980s, many actors like Patton, gay or perceived to be, were purged from Hollywood or felt the need to leave, as Patton chose to do, due to homophobia as a result of the AIDS crisis. "Conceived by screenwriter David Chaskin as a gay slasher spoof," states *Rue Morgue* writer Rocco Thompson, "*Freddy's Revenge* all but outed Patton to an industry that had begun to slam its doors in the faces of gay actors as the specter of AIDS and its ensuing hysteria reared its ugly head."[38] Chaskin was not shy about his attempts to use his script to make jokes at the expense of the gay community. Patton recalls the mood on set:

> [When we were shooting], they didn't notice that [Chaskin] was changing the script every day. He got away with one joke, so he thought he could get away with another, and another, and that nobody was catching on. Other gay crew members caught on, but everyone else was clueless. That's why it became so blatant—he just took his joke and ran with it, and he was a real creep about the whole situation for a long time.[39]

However, today Patton wants to set the story straight about how he handled the hurtful decisions by Chaskin: "[M]y dream was taken away from me by me. I quit [...] but by Chaskin robbing me of my confidence, I made a bunch of decisions that I otherwise would not have made."[40] In the documentary *Scream Queen! My Nightmare on Elm Street* (2019), Patton and the filmmakers confronted Chaskin who admitted that he used gay subtext with homophobic intent. The homophobia of American cinema was not relegated to the board rooms of studio executives but reared its ugly head in horror film scripts written by individuals like Chaskin, eager to jump in with homophobic jokes and proclaim America's new monster on screen: contagious homosexuals.

It is alleged by many scientists, though is continually reexamined, that the first person with the virus was a man named Gaetan Dugas, a French-Canadian flight attendant who was a key to the mystery as to how the disease rapidly spread from city to city around the world. Dugas was known as "Patient 0" among the medical community that studied AIDS in California:

> Although he wasn't named in the paper, researchers knew that "Patient 0" was, in fact, Dugas. Epidemiologists found that 8 of the first 248 gay men

who got AIDS had slept with "Patient o"; those men were subsequently linked, directly or not, to another 11 patients. This was a breakthrough study, proving for the first time that AIDS was passed sexually from person to person.[41]

Unfortunately, due to this breakthrough in the mystery of AIDS, Dugas became a scapegoat for the blame of its spread to the point of being villainized. People confused the "o" in "Patient o" as meaning "Patient Zero," forever linking him to the spread. The term actually stood for "Patient outside-of-California," where the study's population was focused.[42] After his death from the virus at age thirty-one on March 30, 1984, he was vilified for his promiscuity, charm, and attractiveness. He was the Dracula of AIDS, seducing and infecting scores of people all over the world, turning them into the same young men wasting away in hospital beds. If someone was to blame, the press aimed the garlic and crucifix at Dugas, "a hardened sociopath who did his best to spread the disease far and wide," as characterized by Randy Shilts, an openly gay reporter for the *San Francisco Chronicle* and author of *And the Band Played On* (1987). "You get a guy who has got unlimited sexual stamina," asserts Shilts, "who is very attractive, so he has unlimited opportunity to act out that sexual stamina." He called Dugas quite possibly "the person who brought AIDS to North America."[43] By naming Dugas as the enemy, there was ample fodder to blame the promiscuous homosexual, who was supposedly bent on recklessly spreading the infection far and wide. However, before his death, as his health began to fade, Dugas asked the scientific community about his condition, and they, like him, had no concrete evidence of how the virus was spread. Dugas had no idea that sexual contact was the culprit. On the day of his death, the CDC finally released the report that indicated sexual activity as the main means of the spread of HIV/AIDS. It would not be until 2016 that the allegation of Dugas being the first carrier and spreader of the AIDS virus was debunked. Nevertheless, the damage was done, and until 2016, Dugas was at the center of the AIDS virus mystery. In addition, Dugas never heard President Ronald Reagan mention the AIDS epidemic during his lifetime. Reagan's first AIDS-centered speech would not come until 1987, three years after Gaetan Dugas' death.

Creating such a narrative of villainy for Dugas allowed heterosexual people and some queer folks to blame the promiscuous lifestyles of gay men for the spread of disease, effectively villainizing an entire minority population. What was once a public expression of sexual freedom for a generation of young gay men had become a political and social curse. Two years after the death of Dugas, the American Family

Association released a funding letter, warning families of predatory homosexual men, and called for quarantine:

> Dear Family Member,
>   Since AIDS is transmitted primarily by perverse homosexuals, your name on my national petition to quarantine all homosexual establishments is crucial to your family's health and security. These disease carrying deviants wander the street unconcerned, possibly making you their next victim. What else can you expect from sex-crazed degenerates but selfishness?[44]

Villainization, as done in horror films to the movie monster, allows for a lack of empathy for the perpetrator of violence, and in the case of AIDS, the spread of disease. Gay men were being painted as sociopathic in-human creatures, which would result in viewing them as dispensable. This lack of empathy and image of "disease carrying deviants" looking for "their next victim" follows in the narratives of vampires in several horror films of the 1980s.

Vampirism and Pervasive Homophobia

Vampires before the 1980s had been known as predatory creatures of the night: seductive, androgynous, and often bisexual, especially female vampires. Author Marty Fink elaborates in a piece for the *Science Fiction Studies* journal that vampires have always been linked to the sexual and contagious, making the creatures perfect for representing the anxiety around HIV/AIDS:

> The vampire may connote a variety of fears attached to sexuality and disease, a symbol of all those perceived as "exotic, alien, unnatural, oral, anal, compulsive, violent, protean, polymorphic, polyvocal, polysemous, invisible, soulless, transient, superhumanly mobile, infectious, murderous, suicidal, and a threat to wife, children, home, and phallus."[45]

The bisexuality aspect of vampires stems from their feeding habits where victims are chosen regardless of their identity. Thus, vampires are a danger to just about anyone, which perfectly encapsulates the early fears about the mystery of AIDS, in that, anyone could contract the virus should they encounter a societal vampire.

The act of sucking blood, as started in sound film with Bela Lugosi's 1931 portrayal of Count Dracula, was a seductive dance that ended with fangs in the neck.[46] To get to a victim's neck, it indeed entails seduction, as kisses on the neck are prevalent in sexual foreplay. But with a vampire, they tend to seduce both sexes to get the blood they need. This may be viewed as being out of necessity, but the preamble

of seduction shows otherwise: vampires are not deterred from seducing either men or women, leaving them as bisexual. *Dracula's Daughter* shows this best, as Countess Zaleska seduces men and women for the
blood in their necks, as well as points to the androgyny of vampires in
general, especially female vampires. Promiscuity is another attribute of
vampires. They are sexual creatures, using the power of seduction to lull
their victims/partners into a false sense of security. They seduce often,
woo often, thus ultimately, they are considered promiscuous bisexuals,
a stereotype that will continue throughout the twentieth century and
beyond.

One of the clearest parallels between people with AIDS and vampires is the presence and contagion of fluids. The act of seduction for
the vampire is to suck the blood from their lover's and victim's neck.
This is sex for the vampire: gratification through receiving fluids, as
with sex between non-vampires. Once it was known that AIDS is transmitted through sexual activity involving bodily fluids (e.g., semen, vag-
inal fluid), gay men, the perceived villains of AIDS, were seen as not
dissimilar from vampires. Though queer men were not sucking blood
from each other's necks, semen contains blood cells with which these
men were coming into contact during sexual activity. Their homosexuality in relation to AIDS was also seen as similar to the life of a vampire with regards to religion. Vampires, affected by crucifies and holy
water, are demonic, sinful, as was seen by religious groups toward queer
folks. Jerry Falwell, a prominent religious zealot who demonized those
infected with the condemned virus, "welcomed the plague as proof of
God's will."[47] Just as the vampire hunters branded themselves with symbols of Christianity, the same was done by the Moral Majority of America upon queer men with their reactions to the AIDS epidemic.

Queer folks, like vampires, were seen as contagious malevolent
creatures when the AIDS epidemic advanced domestically and inter-
nationally. Both were/are viewed as promiscuous and sneaky, bent on
infection and indoctrination into a deviant lifestyle. "The AIDS crisis,"
asserts Benshoff in *Monsters in the Closet*, "which has spurred Christian compassion from some quarters, has also significantly fueled this
'homosexual as monster' rhetoric: now more than ever, gay men are
contagions—vampires—who, with a single mingling of blood, can infect
a pure and innocent victim, transforming him or her into the living
dead."[48] This sinister socially constructed connection is evident in how
queer folks had been portrayed in horror films during the rise of HIV/
AIDS. In folklore, vampires have a history of being equated with infectious disease and being allegories for illness. Since the introduction of
Count Dracula during the medieval age, the vampire has metaphorically

signified several illnesses, particularly tuberculosis, but including syphilis and cholera which were prevalent at the time of Stoker's publication of *Dracula* (1897).[49] Nicola Nixon, author of *When Hollywood Sucks, or, Hungry Girls, Lost Boys, and Vampirism in the Age of Reagan* discusses the illness-centered origin of the vampire and asks readers to "'consider its associations with wasting … with paleness, with the flow of blood from the mouth, night restlessness, alternate burning and chills, even with the victim's rumored sexual energy.'"[50] Fink elaborates: "In tracing the vampire's construction as a metaphor for illness preceding HIV/AIDS, we can begin to understand how our contemporary health crisis is connected to historical practices of blaming individuals for their own medical conditions through the racializing and sexualizing of disease."[51] As with the AIDS crisis, and the framing of gay men as the carriers and spreaders of the infectious disease, vampires were used again to become allegories for the rise of the AIDS epidemic. In film, the vampire has nearly always been linked to queer folks. With the epidemic, horror created a scapegoat for all villainy through the queer-coded vampire.

Otherness and evil surround the image of the vampire, as does the image of the AIDS-carrying-queer of the 1980s. Through othering a queer person, and the prevailing connotation of queer folks, specifically gay men, as rampant carriers of the disease, AIDS patients and sufferers were effectively othered by American society, producing a "non-identity and internalized abjection."[52] This was an effective tool for alienating, abandoning, and disregarding AIDS carriers, and can be seen through the abandonment of one's child once discovering their AIDS status. AIDS patients also faced flagrant neglect and abuse practiced by hospital staff during the early years of the epidemic. Apathy flourished, and the use of homosexual-villainy of the onscreen vampire furthered its production.

The vampires of 1980s horror films mark a return to the sexualization of their being, breaking from the 1970s made-for-television feature *Salem's Lot* (1979), a Stephen King tale of hideous vampires hidden in a small town, as well as the iconic blaxploitation flick *Blacula*. Though vampires like Blacula were sexual, they were not linked to queerness like the Countess in *Dracula's Daughter*. Roman Polanski's *The Fearless Vampire Killers* (1967), a horror-comedy, includes a rare glimpse of the not-so-subtextual flamboyant gay male vampire, Herbert Von Krolock. The 1970s American vampire, differing from the exploits of European horror vampires which were majorly queer for the sake of straight titillation, did not return to queerness until the 1980s. It was in the eighties where vampire films reigned again as big box-office draws. *The Hunger* (1983), *Fright Night* (1985), and *The Lost Boys* (1987) all display the

simultaneous queerness and villainy of the vampire, whether subtextual or outright. Importantly, all these films make sure that the vampire
can look "normal," and can be anyone from the new neighbor next door
to a gang of young California hooligans. The vampires depicted in these
films are extremely attractive, charming, and sexual. They also show
stereotypical characteristics of a queer person often speak in seductive
tones to their human male counterparts and live with same-sex vampires, implying that they too were seduced by their same-sex counterparts. They are plague-carrying killers who seduce unassuming
individuals to join them in carrying the infection of vampirism and
passing it along. All of this can be watched safely on-screen without
consequence for heterosexual audiences.

> Homosexual AIDS, like a distant curse, has all the teasing fright of horror
> flicks: the terror instigates and satisfies catharsis while no one (that is, any-
> one who matters) in the audience gets hurt. Or better—given the appar-
> ent lead time to the holocaust—straights are overcome by the convenience
> of this saving-face chance to stare at gays. Poke, probe, turn them on their
> backs to see their underbellies.[53]

In the final moments of these three films, all the vampires are vanquished with the exception of *The Hunger* where the antagonist vampire
is left to rot in a box in the protagonist's attic. The death of the vampires
represents a maintaining the heteronormative sexual status quo. The
queers are destroyed. This was the hope of many homophobic Americans during the AIDS crisis, and they received on-screen catharsis.

The vampiric-80s began with the avant-garde art-haus UK/US horror film *The Hunger*, starring Susan Sarandon as Dr. Sarah Roberts,
Catherine Deneuve as bisexual vampire Miriam, and queer icon David
Bowie as aging vampire John Blaylock. The film kicks off the eighties'
queer seductive vampire motif. John, an androgynous and sleek vampire in New York City, is deteriorating without the blood of another. His
deterioration mimics that of an AIDS patient with regards to his rapid
aging. Wrinkled and severely underweight, John asks Miriam, "How
old do you think I am? Yesterday, I was 30 years old."[54] He then pon-
ders if he has liver spots on his hands. Many AIDS patients suffer from
purple lesions, much like dark liver spots, and rapid weight loss. Often,
the young sufferers in the early years of AIDS would look thirty years
older than they were. The emphasis of the HIV/AIDS crisis is the suf-
ferer's body, and became highly politicized, especially upon gay men.
As Michel Foucault explains in *Discipline and Punish: The Birth of the
Prison* (1979), "the body is … directly involved in a political field; power
relations have an immediate hold upon it; they invest it, mark it, train
it, torture it, force it to carry out tasks, to perform ceremonies, to emit

signs."[55] When an audience gazes upon John's body, they now associate it with that of HIV/AIDS, despite the film's development before the widespread AIDS crisis. In May of 1983, one month after *The Hunger*'s theatrical release, news journalist/sensationalist Geraldo Rivera declared on television program *20/20* that the entire American population is in danger of contracting AIDS from the nation's blood supply. "From this time until Rock Hudson's death in October 1985," asserts Jan Zita Grover in her essay "Visible Lesions: Images of the PWA," "mainstream media found an image for [HIV/AIDS]: the moribund *AIDS victim*, who was also (magically) a demon of sexuality, actively transmitting his condition to the 'general population' even as he lay dying offstage."[56] The blood-sucking vampire, a mythical *demon of sexuality,* is the perfect villain for the American 1980s. John Blaylock's withering body is therefore fitting.

Once a socialite among the NYC nightclub scene, John is now wasting away. His journey correlates with that of a young vibrant gay man in electric New York City prior to the epidemic, as casual sex and parties light aflame by the Gay Rights Movement and the Sexual Revolution swelled in queer city enclaves. Nicola Nixon posits that

> although chronologically [*The Hunger*] cannot be an allegory for AIDS [though the film is based on a novel published in 1981, the first year "gay

Catherine Deneuve and David Bowie as lovers Miriam and John Blaylock. John is seen wasting away from a lack of blood to drink in *The Hunger* (MGM/UA Entertainment Co., 1983).

cancer" was written about in news articles], such an analysis is nevertheless tempting because its cinematic elements so heavily signify the narrative
tropes we have come to associate with the pandemic: "New York nightclubs
and leather bars, anonymous sex with ambiguously-infected strangers,
transmitted and undiagnosable blood diseases ... and same-sex sexuality
add up, now, to only one thing."[57]

The film also reflects on the parasitic nature of the vampire: Miriam,
when seducing human John, promised eternal life, but did not mention that he will continue to age. This motif follows that of the narrative conjured up by many conservative Americans who saw gay men
as vessels of disease, giving it knowingly to other gay men through sex
without regard for their sex partner's health, much like how news media
depicted "Patient 0," Gaetan Dugas.

    Aside from John's narrative that, intentional or not, correlates to
the reality of many young men stricken with HIV and AIDS, *The Hunger* also highlights queer women. John's lover and partner Miriam, still
young and seductive unlike John, seeks out a new lover and fresh blood
supply through Dr. Sarah Roberts. During Miriam's seduction to get the
doctor into her inner vampiric circle, Sarah becomes "very drunk under
[Miriam's] spell" and proceeds to have passionate sex with her, intermingled with violent imagery.[58] This sex scene, unlike many female sex
scenes that lean toward male exhibitionism, produces an artistic sensual
seduction between two beautiful women. The film concludes with Sarah
rejecting the vampiric lifestyle and locking the now deteriorating Miriam in a box in the attic, as Miriam had done with John, disposing of the
queer vampiric body. Yet, it is alluded that Sarah will follow in the steps
of Miriam, catching the vampiric itch for blood and seduction.

    In the years following *The Hunger,* the American media partook
in the demonization of AIDS carriers through othering, mainly with
the help of horror film tropes. A film that has been examined time and
again for possible queer panic in the era of AIDS is *The Hitcher* (1986).
The film is about Jim Halsey, a young man on his way to California who
after falling asleep behind the wheel wakes abruptly to dodge an oncom-
ing truck and subsequently picks up a hitchhiker. "My mother told me
never to do this!" exclaims Jim enthusiastically as the hitchhiker, John
Ryder, hops in the car.[59] After Ryder looks Jim over to his discomfort,
he holds Jim at knife-point and threatens him to keep driving. Eventually, Jim finds a way to shove Ryder out of the moving car. Sadly, for Jim,
Ryder begins to stalk him along the long stretch of highway, at gas sta-
tions, and to a police department, killing everyone in his path except
for Jim. When Ryder tracks Jim down at a diner, Jim asks Ryder desperately, "Why are you doing this to me?" "You're a smart kid," replies

Ryder. "Figure it out."[60] The audience never truly does, which allows for myriad interpretations of Ryder's motive.

The year the film was released, one reviewer described *The Hitcher* as a "slasher movie about gay panic, a nasty piece of homophobic angst for the age of AIDS," conjuring discourse for the relationship between Jim and Ryder, despite the non-existence of any clear indications of queer desire. Decades later, viewers still feel there is more to the film than meets the eye, especially the character of Ryder, who Scott Drebit of horror news site *Daily Dead* feels signifies Jim's fear of his homosexuality in an era plagued with HIV/AIDS. This subtext is supported by the ambiguity of Ryder's very existence, where Drebit posits that Ryder is but a dream, citing Jim's nodding-off behind the wheel at the beginning of the film.[61] Whatever the case may be, if there is even a true motive to Ryder's relentless stalking of Jim, *The Hitcher* relies on ambiguity in which subtext can be placed.

During a 1986 news show segment (the same year as *The Hitcher*'s release) on the growing AIDS epidemic, American news journalist Tom Brokaw referred to AIDS patients/gay men as "silent carriers, much like vampires that live in the shadows ready to strike. [...] These silent carriers [...] possibly are legion—one or two million; it is among us like *The Invasion of the Body Snatchers*."[62] Hadleigh continues an analysis of Brokaw's words in *The Lavender Screen*,

> With such horrific facts established, Brokaw makes the central and the glibbest statement of the show. "There is small danger of AIDS spreading into the heterosexual community." The "science" he's advancing mollifies straight fears of AIDS and sex, while stealing every option from gay men. The worse homosexuality is made to look, the more heterosexuality appears to be anointed.[63]

Brokaw and many of his journalist colleagues were calling upon the fears of the past, specifically the Red and Lavender Scares of the 1950s, of infectious and sinister queers living among straights. An op-ed piece in *The New York Times*, from the same year as Brokaw's news report, advocated for tattooing AIDS carriers. Writer William F. Buckley, Jr., asserted that "[e]veryone detected with AIDS should be tattooed in the upper forearm to protect common needle users and on the buttocks to prevent the victimization of other homosexuals."[64] The idea that perceived homosexual AIDS carriers were so hidden among straight society led an individual, in this case, a high-profile conservative author, to blatantly channel Nazi Germany's tattooing of the European Jewish, Romani, and homosexual population in identifying both queer folks and AIDS carriers. This idea of hidden infection is key to understanding the prominence of vampire films during the age of AIDS.

The theme of the infiltrating vampire on straight society is portrayed in *Fright Night* (1985). The film follows boy-next-door Brewster and his friends as they try to convince their town's police force that a vampire has just moved into the neighborhood. Jerry Dandrige is a suave yet blood-thirsty vampire, living with a male partner in an antique-dealing business, not unlike the gay couple in *Blacula*. "I hear he's got a live-in carpenter," states Brewster's mother, referring to Dandrige's male roommate. "With my luck, he's probably gay."[65] Though this dialogue is not intended to be derogatory as the mother is not actually making a joke at the expense of Dandrige, the film perpetuates the gays-among-us fear, since Dandrige is revealed later to be a violent vampire. What the film does succeed in, however, is the humanization of creatures and vampires, specifically in the storyline of "Evil" Ed, Brewster's pal. Ed becomes a vampire at the hands of Dandrige in a misty dark alleyway. Albeit through indoctrination into the vampire lifestyle, Dandrige acknowledges Ed's already outsider status: the goofy kid next door who does not fit in with any known crowd, much like a bullied young queer person struggling to fit in. "You don't have to be afraid of me," states Dandrige. "I know what it's like being different. But they won't pick on you anymore. Or beat you up. I'll see to that. All you have to do is take my hand."[66] Ed takes his hand and becomes a member of Dandrige's vampire entourage. At the film's climax, Ed turns into a werewolf-like vampire creature. He is impaled by a wooden stake and lies dying on the ground. His intense and emotional death allows for audience empathy, a humanization of poor Evil Ed who yearns only for acceptance. However, audiences can also blame his death on the evil head vampire Dandrige, thus solidifying the anti-gay AIDS stereotype of the infectious queer spreading disease to others, effectively killing them.

The type of indoctrination Evil Ed experienced by a vampire is the central theme of the MTV-infused teen scream *The Lost Boys* (1987). After moving to California with his younger brother and single mother, teenage Michael seeks to find acceptance in his new city. On the bustling boardwalk teeming with young hip children run-amok, he encounters an enticing girl who surrounds herself with several punk boys on motorcycles. The mysterious pack convinces Michael to join their escapades, from dangling from a bridge above a foggy precipice to munching on some Chinese food in their cave lair. The leader of the gang, David, continuously asks Michael, in seductive tones no less, to join them, "Join us, Michael."[67] Eventually, Michael gives in to peer pressure and "joins" the crew by drinking blood from a chalice. Unbeknownst to him, this will transform him into a vampire. Director Joel Schumacher, an openly

Evil Ed, played by Stephen Geoffreys (left), being called upon by head vampire Jerry Dandrige, played by Chris Sarandon, in a dark alley to join him as a vampire in *Fright Night* (TriStar Pictures, 1985).

gay man, discusses in an interview with *Vulture* in 2020 that he lost many friends during the HIV/AIDS crisis, with one friend being diagnosed with the disease in 1983. He feared for his health during that time, as he was very involved with the sexual culture of the period and created an action plan for his death. It is hard to imagine Schumacher not having the threat of HIV/AIDS in mind when directing a film so fixated on blood and contamination.[68]

As Michael turns into a creature of the night, he realizes he had been trapped by the vampire gang into murdering people for blood. He confronts his younger brother Sam for help. Sam becomes livid at the thought of his brother being a "god damned shit sucking vampire!"[69] Sam's reaction to his brother's turning drips with disdain for the different, for the societal threat of infection, even though Sam himself does not conform to traditional gender stereotypes in the way he dresses, often adorning himself in flashy blouses and blazers. He even has a nearly shirtless poster of then-teen heartthrob Rob Lowe on his bedroom wall. Sam eventually receives help from the angsty Frog Brothers who warn him that the city is crawling with disgusting predatory vampires. Armed with Rambo-style headbands and a strong knowledge of the undead, the Frog Brothers, Sam, and Michael defeat the vampire gang and kill the head vampire, Max. Though the film has subtle queer themes throughout, the film ends with the destruction of the predatory vampire, the queer. Such queer subtext and vampires as villainous AIDS carriers continued in American films into the twenty-first century. *The Forsaken* (2001), a film about a young man named Sean who picks up a hitchhiker who reveals that he is a vampire hunter, not only has queer subtext cultivated by the vampire films of the 1980s, but directly equates the treatment of the "infection" of vampirism with the drug concoctions of the HIV/AIDS virus during the 1980s. Nick, the hitchhiker, gives Sean a mix of pills after Sean is bitten by a vampire:

> SEAN: "What are these?"
>
> NICK: "Antigens, aminos, proteins. Back in the late '80s when they were getting into drug cocktails for HIV, some doctor that had been bitten mixed one that slowed the virus. Now, everybody's different, but usually, it takes about a week to turn. If you get on the cocktail, you'll buy yourself some time."[70]

Likewise, *Blade* (1998), a film about a human-vampire hybrid who kills vampires, includes a line of dialogue from hematologist Karen Jenson referring to evil vampire Deacon Frost as a "sexually-transmitted disease."[71] Not only had vampire films of the 1980s villainized queer people, especially queer men, but the films succeeded with regards to longevity: vampire films, from then on, had strong correlations to the HIV/AIDS virus, as evidenced by these two films.

The vampire films of the 1980s all share common characteristics for their vampires: coded queerness, predatory indoctrination of "normal" people, and their violent on-screen destructions by each film's end. Vampires are non-human creatures, making their destruction on screen easy to digest and even enjoyable—good triumphs over evil. When one ties in the vampire's linkage to queerness, their victorious destruction becomes more sinister. If vampires are queer, then queer destruction can be viewed as victorious as well. The destruction of the queer vampire echoed the real-life violence inflicted upon queers by a society that deemed them similar, if not the same, as the vampires they saw in horror films: predatory monsters bent on seducing vulnerable youths to join them in a life of violence and perversion. Due to the blazing homophobia during the AIDS crisis and the continuous news coverage on the epidemic that often correlated the virus to gay men, waves of anti-gay violence surged. Often, heterosexual Americans invested little concern in bringing the assailants to justice. Author David France was present during the epidemic, and acknowledges such violence toward his queer friends and the subsequent invention of the "gay panic defense":

> [I]t seemed that every minor advance in public attention [of AIDS] brought sickening waves of violence. Everybody knew a victim. My friend Andy Mosso was stabbed nine times. Nobody took his wallet; this was no robbery. They left him gasping in his vomit, his pain and death being the whole point. Convalescing in the hospital, he was interviewed once by police, but no arrests were made. [T]hese crimes were carried out mostly by young white men in their teens and twenties who if caught might say they acted out in self-defense in response to unwanted sexual advances, importunings that disgusted them to the point of temporary madness. Lawyers called it the "gay panic defense."[72]

Ultimately, stories of predatory queer vampires mingling with the real threat of HIV/AIDS resulted in the further demonization of queer folks and those struggling to survive the epidemic. The horror genre was a participant, whether intentionally or not, with this demonization. Without uplifting narratives in the era of AIDS, as advocated by Arthur Bressan at the beginning of this chapter, viewers would continue to see queer characters as punchlines and villains.

Anti-gay sentiments in '80s horror films were made casual through adolescent dialogue. Anti-gay slurs and homophobic attitudes were seemingly welcome additions to myriad horror film scripts. *The Monster Squad* (1987) follows a group of horror-loving boys on the run from Count Dracula and his band of other horror creatures, including Frankenstein's Monster, the Mummy, Gillman from *The Creature of the Black Lagoon* (1954), and the Wolfman. Unlike other vampires of the 1980s, Count Dracula in *The Monster Squad* is not coded queer, but is simply evil for evil's sake, on the hunt for an enchanted amulet that will allow him to rule the world. The film's heroes are the young horror-obsessed boys. It is easy for a horror audience to relate to this nerdy precocious bunch, but unfortunately, the boys' dialogues are riddled with anti-gay slurs. The young boys use "fag" and "faggot" three times early in the film, and their dialogue even infers gay men are similar to pedophiles when a male teacher, scolding two of the boys for not paying attention in class, was "homo-ing out" when he allegedly touched one of their shoulders.[73] This sort of anti-gay prejudice in popular films flourished during the AIDS era, with heterosexual audiences barely batting an eye to the anti-gay propaganda.

The vampire horror-sex-comedy *Once Bitten* (1985) includes a sissy gay manservant Sebastian who assists his vampire Countess in finding virgin male blood for her to remain young and beautiful. Jim Carrey plays the protagonist Mark who is lured into a sexual encounter with the Countess after his girlfriend refuses to have sex with him. During oral sex, the Countess bites Mark on his inner thigh, causing him to slowly turn into a creature of the night in the days that follow. Mark's girlfriend, concerned with her boyfriend's behavior and fearing him a vampire, asks Mark's two close male friends to find the two puncture marks on his inner thigh. Though apprehensive, the friends agree to the task and ambush him in the high school locker room showers. As the friends tackle him naked to find the puncture marks, a classmate showering nearby hollers "Fags in the shower! Fag alert!" several times.[74] All the surrounding boys sprint from the showers. Later, one of Mark's friends worries that he enjoyed looking for the puncture marks. "We're homos!" he cries, resigning to the idea that he is now gay.[75] While examining the trends of teen sex comedies of the 1980s, film historian Vito Russo asserts that scenes such as this vile homophobic shower sequence are "undeniably homoerotic."[76] As seen four years earlier in *Fear No Evil* and *A Nightmare on Elm Street 2: Freddy's Revenge*, the homophobic yet homoeroticism of teen boys in locker room showers is where young homophobic male fears come to life: gay boys watching you bathe and the frightening possibility of enjoying the gaze.

Adolescent homophobia rears its ugly head throughout the 1980s,

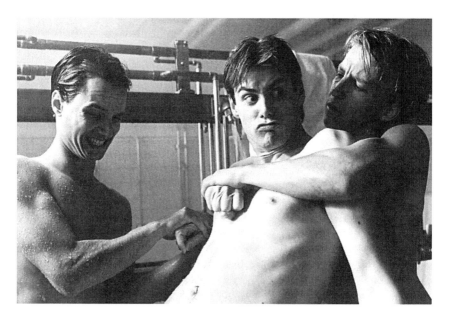

Friends Jamie (left) and Russ, played by Thomas Balatore and Skip Lackey, corner their friend Mark (Jim Carrey, center) in the locker room showers to find the vampire fang wounds on Mark's naked body in *Once Bitten* (The Samuel Goldwyn Company, 1985).

most shockingly portrayed in horror films. Child characters, written by adults, were given homophobic rhetoric to spread, ultimately to young viewers. The same children who will identify with the young film heroes of films like *The Monster Squad* would feel that it is acceptable to say anti-gay words, and perhaps later, feel that it is acceptable to treat queer folks with apathy or disdain.[77] This sentiment is clear with the use of children to further homophobic jargon among their age group, fostering an environment of homophobia from a young, impressionable age, nearing homophobic propaganda. Cited in Eric Marcus' *Making History: The Struggle for Gay and Lesbian Equal Rights, 1945–1990, An Oral History*, Russo elaborates on his personal experiences as a gay man watching a film: "when you're a politicized gay person and you love the movies, you spend your life sitting through movies waiting for the shoe to drop."[78] The shoe drops when a character that a queer person finds likable utters a homophobic slur casually or a moment of homophobic vitriol appears on screen. The likeability immediately vanishes, and a queer viewer is left to feel alone. It is even worse when young children in films use harmful language, seeing that they were taught to hate queer folks at a young age but do not know the harm their words truly cause. This was the case in *The Monster Squad* when the shoe dropped no less than ten minutes into the film.

A film that famously uses the dialogue of children to further homophobic sentiments is *Sleepaway Camp* (1983). Angela Baker, both protagonist and antagonist, orphaned when her father and twin brother were killed in a boating accident, is sent to summer camp by her wacky aunt Martha. There, Angela is quiet and reserved, and becomes the butt of jokes for bullies. Somehow, Judy, a nasty camper who taunts Angela incessantly, equates her withdrawn personality with being queer: "Why don't you shower with the rest of us? What are you, queer or something?"[79] In addition, flashbacks surface toward the middle of the film to reveal that Angela's father was in fact queer. He is seen in bed with a man, kissing and holding one another. Angela and her brother look on from afar, pointing and giggling. Felissa Rose, who stars as protagonist Angela, later asserted in an interview that, despite film director Robert Hiltzik's denial of homoeroticism in the film, Rose believes that "it absolutely was a major player in the game."[80]

Angela's father's homosexuality is key, as implied by the film, to comprehending Angela's introverted personality and ultimate serial killer status.[81] *Sleepaway Camp* is an extremely complicated horror franchise, with two more films released straight to video in the eighties, for its polarizing dialogue and plot for protagonist/antagonist Angela Baker.[82] To understand the franchise and the infamous character of

Angela, revealed to be someone that she does not appear to be, a discussion of the root of transgender bodies in horror must be had. The roots of trans and non-binary bodies in horror films are problematic and polarizing. Often lumped in with homosexuality, transgender folks in horror are often mislabeled, as well as *used* as the horror displayed on screen.

In Memorium: The following names are of those who passed away due to complications of HIV/AIDS. They are actors, writers, and directors of American horror films. Vito Russo, who is heavily cited in this book, succumbed to illness brought on by AIDS within a decade of the publication of his groundbreaking work *The Celluloid Closet*.

ROCK HUDSON
November 17, 1925–October 2, 1985
Actor
Embryo (1976)

MERRITT BUTRICK
September 3, 1959–March 17, 1989
Actor
Fright Night Part 2 (1988), *Death Spa* (1989)

JACK SMITH
November 14, 1932–September 25, 1989
Actor
Silent Night, Bloody Night (1972)

COOKIE MUELLER
March 2, 1949–November 10, 1989
Actor
Multiple Maniacs (1970)

VITO RUSSO
July 11, 1946–November 7, 1990
Writer
The Celluloid Closet (1981)

KEVIN PETER HALL
May 9, 1955–April 10, 1991
Actor
Prophecy (1979), *Without Warning* (1980), *One Dark Night* (1982),
Monster in the Closet (1986), *Predator* (1987), *Predator 2* (1990),
Highway to Hell (1991)

ANDY MILLIGAN
February 12, 1929–June 3, 1991

Director
The Ghastly Ones/Blood Rites (1968)

Robert Reed
October 19, 1932–May 12, 1992
Actor
Bloodlust! (1961)

Anthony Perkins
April 4, 1932–September 12, 1992
Actor/Director
Psycho (1960), *Psycho II* (1983), *Psycho III* (1986), *Destroyer* (1988),
Edge of Sanity (1989), *Daughter of Darkness* (1990),
I'm Dangerous Tonight (1990), *Psycho IV: The Beginning* (1990)

Keith Prentice
February 21, 1940–September 27, 1992
Actor
Cruising (1980)

David Oliver
January 31, 1962–November 12, 1992
Actor
Night of the Creeps (1986), *The Horror Show* (1989)

Howard Gruber
November 28, 1941–February 23, 1993
Actor
Multiple Maniacs (1970)

Ray Sharkey, Jr.
November 14, 1952–June 11, 1993
Actor
Hellhole (1985)

Tom Villard
November 19, 1953–November 14, 1994
Actor
Parasite 3-D (1982), *Popcorn* (1991)

Anthony Hamilton
May 4, 1952–March 29, 1995
Actor
Howling IV: The Original Nightmare (1988)

John Megna
November 9, 1952–September 4, 1995

Actor
Hush.... Hush, Sweet Charlotte (1964)

TOM MCBRIDE
October 7, 1952–September 24, 1995
Actor
Friday the 13th Part II (1981)

ALEXIS ARQUETTE
July 28, 1969–September 11, 2016
Actor
Bride of Chucky (1998)

PAUL LANDIS
Dates Unknown
Actor
Multiple Maniacs (1970)

The following are names of horror actors who are living and surviving with HIV/AIDS (and have publicly disclosed their status). Mark
Patton, who plays Jesse Walsh in *A Nightmare on Elm Street 2: Freddy's
Revenge*, is a passionate HIV/AIDS activist who continues his activism
today.

MARK PATTON
Actor
A Nightmare on Elm Street 2: Freddy's Revenge (1985),
Family Possessions (2016), *Amityville: Evil Never Dies* (2017)

DANNY PINTAURO
Actor
Cujo (1983), *Timestalkers* (1987)

CHARLIE SHEEN
Actor
Grizzly II: The Predator (1983), *The Arrival* (1996),
Scary Movie 3 (2003), *Scary Movie 4* (2006), *Scary Movie 5* (2013)

Chapter 4

Manifesting Monstrous Bodies

The Use of the Transgender, Intersex, and/or Non-Binary Body as Horror (1932–2001)

Origins and Media Influence

1932	Josephine Joseph, *Freaks*
1952	Christine Jorgensen undergoes gender affirmation surgery
1953	Glen/Glenda, *Glen or Glenda?*
1960	Norman Bates, *Psycho*
1961	Warren, *Homicidal*
1974	Leatherface, *The Texas Chainsaw Massacre*
1983	Angela Baker, *Sleepaway Camp*
1986	Joan Lambert, *Aliens*
1988	Angela Baker, *Sleepaway Camp II: Unhappy Campers* — Lawrence, *Curse of the Queerwolf*
1989	Angela Baker, *Sleepaway Camp III: Teenage Wasteland*
1991	Buffalo Bill/Jame Gumb, *The Silence of the Lambs*
1993	Brandon Teena is murdered
2000	Leonard Marliston, *Cherry Falls*
2001	Raven, *Soul Survivors*

Figure 6

Josephine Waas (she/her pronouns) was a circus and carnival performer in the early twentieth century. She is best known for her portrayal of Josephine-Joseph in Tod Browning's *Freaks* (1932). Waas practically played herself in the film, for in real life she had advocated her physiology as a true "hermaphrodite," the proper term today being intersex.[1] Intersex is an umbrella term used for the myriad differences in reproductive anatomy and/or sex traits that go beyond the typical two ways of human body development. In the film, Josephine-Joseph is a freak due to her split anatomy and gender expression: one half showcased stereotypical masculine characteristics, while the other displayed stereotypical feminine traits. Unlike a majority of the other freaks, Josephine-Joseph is routinely mocked by other circus members, particularly the cisgender able-bodied men, having been socked in the eye by Hercules, the strongman. She also, despite frequent screen appearances, rarely receives any dialogue, her body being the main focal point. Josephine-Joseph's body is her freakishness; her body was used to shock the 1932 audience. Body horror would continue in twentieth-century films, where non-binary, intersex, and transgender individuals would be used *as* shock and horror through their bodies.

Negative portrayals of transgender folks have been commonplace in horror films, as well as mainstream media. Trans women are depicted as violent men in women's clothing, often confused and psychotic. As with the othering of queer folks in horror films, portraying them as villains and monsters, transgender folks, particularly women, have been othered through their queer bodies. Because the transgender body

Josephine-Joseph (Josephine Waas, center) being ridiculed by fellow circus performers The Rollo Brothers, Edward Brophy (left) and Matt McHugh, in *Freaks* (Metro-Goldwyn-Mayer, 1932).

does not fit into American society's idea of "normal," the trans body in film defies perceived normality and therefore becomes and is used in the abject sense. Jenni Holtz explains in their essay "Blood, Bodies and Binaries: Trans Women in Horror":

> Trans women in horror are presented as abject beings—or anything that is considered gross because it is outside of the self. Think of all the bodily fluids that suddenly become grotesque when they're no longer part of the body: blood, vomit, hair, etc. These things cross the boundary of self and not-self because they are not human, only pieces of it. Trans bodies—not unlike intersex bodies, Black and Brown bodies and disabled bodies—are abject due to their transgression of social boundaries. At their core, they are in opposition to the white, able-bodied, cisgender, heterosexual man who is the image of the default, normative person in Western societies.[2]

Due to the trans, intersex, and non-binary body's defiance of ingrained social norms, they are the perfect villains in a horror movie because they have already been othered for the past several centuries of American history and society. The abjection placed upon these queer bodies not only rears its ugly head in media but can be attributed to the real-life violence and negative attitudes of trans, intersex, and non-binary people perpetrated by cisgender folks.

Films with murderous transgender characters like Angela Baker in *Sleepaway Camp* and Jame Gumb in *The Silence of the Lambs* (1991), though their transgender status is continually up for debate, have been explicitly cited in studies examining the effects of negative trans portrayals in film. A 2018 study published in *Sexuality Research and Social Policy* concluded that negative representations of trans women in visual media led to more negative attitudes by the subjects of their study.[3] The authors of this study, Haley E. Solomon and Beth Kurtz-Costes, discuss the fact that since transgender folks make up a small number of the population, most cisgender people receive their first images of transgender individuals through media. Film can reach millions of viewers on myriad platforms, including the internet, physical copy via VHS and DVD, and in-theater viewing. Thus, the images created for transgender characters in films are seen by diverse populations across the world. This study, citing a 2002 analysis of film theory and character perception by an audience, also states that people perceive fictional characters "similarly to how they perceive real people, and therefore watching a television character onscreen produces the same psychological effects as if the character had had a personal interaction with the viewer."[4] Based on these theories, what would happen should a viewer meet a violent trans character?

According to a study from the Gay & Lesbian Alliance Against

Defamation (GLAAD) documented in the Netflix feature *Disclosure*, approximately eighty percent of Americans have never met, or do not think they have met, a transgender person in their lifetime. Thus, when these same Americans see a violent transgender character in film, their attitudes toward transgender people in real life could be fearful and linked to these negative images on film. "For decades," explains Nick Adams, GLAAD Director of Trans Media & Representation, "Hollywood has taught audiences how to react to trans people. And sometimes, they're being taught that the way to react to [transgender people] is fear, that we're dangerous, that we're psychopaths, that we're serial killers."[5] This fear that has been fed to horror audiences for decades becomes fuel for transphobia, including self-hatred among those who identify as transgender, and often anti-transgender violence.

Haley E. Solomon and Beth Kurtz-Costes' study begins by analyzing the violence transgender women face, the level of which is disproportionately higher than that of the rest of the population. Furthermore, their research reports that forty percent of trans folks reported being physically assaulted in their lifetime, and approximately fifty percent of transgender folks have been said to have been sexually assaulted or raped.[6] In 2017 alone, at least twenty-nine transgender people were murdered, and these are just the murders that were reported.[7] From seeing all the violence inflicted upon transgender bodies, one cannot help but ask why. One of the reasons for this violence is media representations of confused and mentally ill transgender women. This stereotype is repeatedly used in horror films, and specifically, for horror film villains.

Solomon and Kurtz-Costes concluded that when their study participants were shown negative representations of transgender women, a viewer's negative attitudes were confirmed or developed. According to Dolf Zillman's exemplification theory, audiences are more likely to generalize an entire minority population from an evocative portrayal than a less stimulating one.[8] Horror films are extremely evocative. Therefore, negative portrayals of minority groups in horror are more likely to cause viewers from majority groups, such as cisgender heterosexual ones, to negatively generalize minority populations.

Cold War Emergence

For most of the twentieth century, homosexuality was equated with transgender identity. A man who was viewed as *wanting* to be a woman was portrayed as gay, and vice versa for women who *wanted* to be men.

To be transgender is to have been born in the wrong body and identify as the opposite gender to the one assigned at birth, or even non-binary. To be non-binary is to have no identification with any assigned sex or gender identity. In the 1950s, it was acknowledged that if a person identified as transgender, they were mentally ill. For a biological male who identified as a woman, that person was viewed as a confused male. Such was the case, with much intrigue, with Christine Jorgensen, a Bronx native and Army veteran, who achieved her true gender identity through a surgical transition in 1952. She had been a soldier during World War II and went through her transition a few years after being discharged. With the help of a doctor in Denmark, Jorgenson returned to her home in Bronx, New York, as her true self. "Nature made a mistake which I have had corrected," Jorgensen wrote to her parents after her surgery. "[N]ow I am your daughter."[9] Jorgensen was a media sensation and made the front page of the *New York Daily News* in 1952, the headline reading "Ex-GI Becomes Blonde Beauty."[10] Though many saw Jorgensen as confused, she used her platform as a media magnet to preach acceptance. She appeared on radio programs, television, and became "a tireless lecturer on the subject of transsexuality, pleading for understanding from a public that all too often wanted to see transsexuals as freaks or perverts. Ms. Jorgensen's poise, charm, and wit won the hearts of millions."[11] While Jorgensen was helping to transform the discussion and perception of trans folks, an independent filmmaker attempted to add to the conversation through his art.

One year after Christine Jorgensen's transition, Ed Wood, a low-budget B-movie director, released *Glen or Glenda* (1953), a story about transgender protagonists and the struggles they face internally. Wood, who was "(by most accounts) ... a heterosexual male transvestite," largely created *Glen or Glenda* as an autobiography of his internal struggles with gender identity.[12] The film begins with the suicide of a transgender woman whose experiences were those of many transgender folks in the early twentieth century. Her suicide note went accordingly:

> I was put in jail recently. Why? Because I, a man, was caught on the street wearing women's clothing. This was my fourth arrest for the same act. In life, I must continue wearing them. Therefore, it would only be a matter of time until my next arrest. This is the only way. Let my body rest in death forever in the things I cannot wear in life.[13]

In an empathetic gesture, the investigating officer of the woman's suicide reaches out to a psychiatrist, Dr. Alton, in an attempt to understand the lives of "transvestites" and how to help them lead lives devoid of suicide. *Glen or Glenda* defines "transvestite," a term used for those who cross-dressed and/or transgender folks during that time, as a man dressing in women's clothing, yet still implies that nature is at fault for the compulsion these men have to wear stereotypically women's clothes. In an analogy used by the film's narrator, people have said the invention of airplanes and cars is sacrilege because if humans were meant to fly and drive, they would have been born with wings and wheels. However, humans corrected nature's mistake by inventing airplanes and cars. The narrator explains this to be the case with trans folks: when a woman is born in the body of a man, this mistake of nature can be corrected through what was then called a sex change operation, "We've corrected that which nature has not given us.... [Yet] the world is shocked about a sex change."[14] The movie continues with the story of Glen/Glenda, played by Ed Wood himself. Ed lives with his sister and is engaged to a woman named Barbara. Before Barbara knows of Glen's affinity for wearing his sister's clothing, they have a sincere discussion about a news story involving a transgender medical operation:

> BARBARA: "I wonder how some people's mind works."
> GLEN: "Well some people aren't happy the way they are."
> BARBARA: "I suppose so. But to change someone's sex, that's a pretty drastic step to take."
> GLEN: "If it's the only way, I'm for it."
> BARBARA: "I wonder what I would do in a case like that. If I was in the mental turmoil that person went through [...] Here we are, two perfectly normal people, about to be married and lead a normal life together. And there's this poor fellow who never could've been happy if it wasn't for modern medical science."[15]

Here, Barbara seems to grasp the emotional elements involved in undergoing gender affirmation surgery and is more inquisitive than judgmental. Later, when Glen comes clean to Barbara of his desire to wear women's clothing, after a minute of contemplation, Barbara exclaims that although she does not fully understand, she is willing to work together with Glen to better grasp his identity. The scene concludes with Barbara removing the soft white sweater Glen had been admiring and handing it to him as a sign of goodwill. However, ultimately, Glen is "cured" of his desires by Dr. Alton and no longer has the urge to wear women's clothing. The final twenty minutes of *Glen or Glenda* is mainly dedicated to the story of Alan, who, like Christine Jorgensen, undergoes gender affirmation surgery after serving in World War II to become their true self, Anne: "a very happy, lovely young lady that modern medicine and science has created almost as a Frankenstein Monster."[16]

     Despite sympathetic dialogue throughout, Ed Wood infuses horror tropes into Glen's and Anne's stories, resulting in a menagerie of gender and sex misinterpretations mingling with staples of the horror genre, such as Bela Lugosi of *Dracula* (1931) who plays the role of a scientist/God, and the correlation of Anne's transition to the creation of Frankenstein's Monster. Although the film discusses taboo subjects and was progressive in some of its ideas for the 1950s, *Glen or Glenda* still, unfortunately, links the monstrous to the homosexual and transgender identity, as well as makes confusing the correlations between transgender people and cisgender folks who enjoy dressing in drag. The film also asserts that such inclinations as dressing in drag are curable. All these factors contributed to the overall rejection by trans folks to be in the film, as propositioned by the producers. George Weiss, a producer for *Glen or Glenda*, recalls that the production had trouble convincing transgender folks to appear in the film or promote it due to the linking of horror with transgender folks. By Bela Lugosi's presence in the film, his horror status meant to trans folks that "any sex change, therefore, was horror."[17] Despite the usage of pro-equality slogans such as "Love is the only answer," the film persisted with 1950s gender stereotypes and even disregarded the possibility of a transgender or cross-dressing person being homosexual.[18]

Though *Glen or Glenda* was a low-budget B-movie release, it had a true impact on how transgender folks were portrayed on screen. The movie would even spawn a key genderfluid character, Glen/Glenda, in a film within the *Child's Play* franchise in 2004 (this will be discussed later in Chapter 5). Until then, transgender and genderfluid folks would continue being used as horror. Seven years after Ed Wood's *Glen or Glenda*, the world was introduced to one of the most iconic horror villains in cinematic history.

Bates, Bobbi, Baker, and Buffalo Bill

Alfred Hitchcock's *Psycho* (1960) has shocked audiences for decades and is one of the most memorable and revered horror films. *Psycho* antagonist Norman Bates provides an example of a horror icon that has dominated pop culture and the horror world beyond 1960. The infamous and cinematically celebrated shower scene where Bates, as his mother, stabs Marion Crane to death has become an essential reference in popular culture. It has been used in comedic movies and television shows for children and adults alike, such as *The Simpsons, National Lampoon's Vacation* (1983), and *Looney Tunes: Back in Action* (2003), where even if one had never seen *Psycho*, they have seen the iconic shower scene at some point in their lives.[19]

Norman Bates has been cemented in popular culture as a gender-confused, maniacal, cross-dressing murderer who is often confused for transgender. Although Bates is not considered transgender by definition, his presentation as a cross-dressing man while speaking in the voice of his mother would be viewed by an audience in 1960 as an abnormal male who weaves in and out of traditional ideas of femininity and masculinity. While a person is transgender when their gender identity does not correspond to the sex assigned to them at birth, cross-dressing is when a man wears conventional/stereotypical women's attire and vice versa. John Phillips in *Transgender on Screen* suggests that *Psycho*'s use of cross-dressing is a representation of "perverse symptoms" of a psychological disorder, "[h]ence, by association if not by definition, transgender is negatively coded, associated with castration, madness, murder and monstrosity."[20] The film's ending even tries to reason with its audience that Bates is not transgender, but rather mentally ill, through explicit dialogue by the arresting officer: "He was simply doing everything possible to keep alive the illusion of his mother being alive. He tried to be his mother."[21]

The motif of monstrosity surrounds Bates, the knife-wielding maniac wearing his mother's dress and wig, slashing women in the shower, and having a female inner-voice (that of his mother). At the end of *Psycho*, after being caught in the act of attempted murder and arrested, Bates' inner voice utters that he "never hurt a fly" followed by a devilish grin.[22] Bates is a man with no remorse, and it is assumed that he has the ability to kill again. Importantly, it must be noted that Bates only murders when he is wearing his mother's dress. This would imply that as a man dressed in women's clothing, he is extremely violent and mentally ill as Philips suggests, while Bates in plain masculine clothes is meant to signify a lonely man, assumed to be heterosexual and cisgender, therefore benign. Semiotics theorist Roland Barthes discusses in his 1964 essay "The Rhetoric of the Image" that an image can hold three meanings, as well as carry an ideology. Analyzing an image involves seeing the linguistic message (words, captions), the symbolic message (non-linguistic aspects of the image), and the literal message. For the sake of analyzing film, a viewer would adjust the view of the word for dialogue, as well as a film score, and thus analyze a character's speech, dress, and a larger message of what the directors and writers intended: ideology.[23] There are two levels of meaning for an image: denotation, which is the direct, real image, and connotation, which is the interpreted image that is culturally and contextually dependent and/or a symbol for an ideology. Using Barthes' semiotics, the literal image of Norman Bates in the final scenes of his capture is one of a man wearing a dress, wielding a knife with a crazed look in his eye, his screams indicating madness, and thus an ideology: the monstrosity lies in the man wearing a dress. The twists in his face as he is captured, his dress being torn off, and the grey wig falling to the floor, depict a man who is mentally unstable, confused about his identity, and violent. These images have followed the cultural ideas of what a transgender person is—Bates, despite not being transgender explicitly or by definition, has given popular culture a monster to be shocked by: a man wearing women's clothes. Similarly, William Castle's *Homicidal* (1961), written by Robb White, would echo the representations of trans people as violent with the character of Warren. Warren is revealed to be the murderous Emily, a girl who had been disguised since childhood to be a male to be safe from her misogynistic father. The theme of adults forcing gender upon a child would follow transgender and non-binary characters into the eighties and beyond.

The same cross-dressing murderous male motif of Norman Bates in *Psycho* would be on display forty years later in the rape-revenge film *Cherry Falls* (2000), where the antagonist Leonard Marliston, on a path of bloody revenge for his mother who was raped twenty-seven years ago by a group of drunk high school jocks, goes on a murderous rampage wearing fishnet stockings and a long black wig, reminiscent of the style of his mother. It is alleged by his backstory of being the product of the rape and the receiving end of his troubled young mother's vicious abuse that his mental state became warped, thus he became a cross-dressing killer. Similarly, the legendary character of Leatherface in *The Texas Chainsaw Massacre* (1974), who makes his own masks using the faces of humans he and his demented family have murdered, cross-dresses as a woman, even adorning his human face mask with eye shadow, blush, and lipstick for the climactic chainsaw-waving finale. A film as intensely popular and iconic as *Psycho* has permeated American culture, as well as the images it has painted of the cross-dressing maniac for decades.

Dressed to Kill (1980), released twenty years after *Psycho*, echoes the sentiments expressed in the pivotal 1960 gender-bending slasher. Written and directed by Brian De Palma, *Dressed to Kill* mimics Hitchcock's murder mystery where the killer, apparently a woman, is a male in drag. The film shifts from *Psycho*'s narrative by stating that the murderous Bobbi, who dresses as a woman, identifies as not a cross-dresser like Norman Bates, but rather, as a woman, expressing to her psychiatrist via answering machine message that she is unhappy in her male body, "I'm a woman trapped inside a man's body. And you're not helping me to get out! So, I got a new shrink [Dr. Levy] ... he's gonna sign the papers so I can get my operation."[24] Bobbi is revealed to be the therapist she had been calling throughout the film, Dr. Elliott. After Dr. Elliott's murder spree, psychiatrist Dr. Levy explains that Bobbi takes over Dr. Elliott's body whenever he becomes aroused by a woman. Bobbi, donned in a blonde wig, then stalks and kills these women for reasons which are illuminated by Dr. Levy in a long-winded monologue:

> [Dr. Elliott] was a transexual ... about to make the final step, but, his male side couldn't let him do it.... There was Dr. Elliott, and there was Bobbi. Bobbi came to me to get psychiatric approval for a sex-reassignment operation. I thought he was unstable, and Elliott confirmed my diagnosis. Opposite sexes inhabiting the same body. The sex-change operation was to resolve the conflict. But as much as Bobbi tried to get it, Elliott blocked it. So, Bobbi got even [by killing Kate Miller, the film's first protagonist] ... she aroused Elliott.... Elliott's penis became erect, and Bobbi took control, trying to kill anyone that made Elliott masculinely sexual.[25]

Dressed to Kill equates transsexuality (to use the film's term) with personality disorders and mental disturbance, linking trans folks to psychopathic tendencies. De Palma's film is the 1980s version of *Psycho*, marking the beginning of a new violent trans narrative for the silver screen. However, De Palma's trans narrative goes beyond Norman Bates. Where Hitchcock assures audiences that Bates was not transgender when the arresting officers discuss his murderous mother persona, De Palma asserts the opposite: Dr. Elliott/Bobbi murders *because* they are trans and has been denied physical transition surgery. Additionally, both *Psycho* and *Dressed to Kill* paint an image of a trans person as rather two warring entities/personalities in a single body. This internal turmoil culminates in the harm of those around them, spreading their toxicity to the cisgender majority. The idea that cross-dressing people and transgender folks are mentally ill and vicious (as well as synonymous) saturates political, religious, and social thoughts on gender and LGBTQ+ issues. Movies do not have to have critical acclaim to successfully perpetuate stigma for minority groups.

If a film has shock value, like most horror films, there is a strong chance an insidious ideology can be passed on. This is the case with the slasher-cult classic *Sleepaway Camp* (1983), whose shocking twist-ending has become a staple in horror fandom. *Sleepaway Camp* follows twelve-year-old Angela Baker and her cousin in a New York summer camp, Camp Arawak. Angela is very shy and mysterious, causing her to be ridiculed by her fellow campers. She hardly speaks and often stares like a deer in headlights rather than open her mouth. It is assumed that this is due to her traumatic past: years before she arrives at Camp Arawak, Angela witnessed the murder of her father and brother in a boating accident, where she was the sole survivor. After her father's death, she was sent to live with her wacky aunt Martha and cousin Ricky. Upon stepping foot in Camp Arawak, the camp became plagued with death after death of camp staff and Angela's fellow campers, with no one knowing the killer's identity until the film's harrowing conclusion.

Angela is revealed as having been the mysterious killer all along, who knocked off one by one those who ridiculed her. However, as if this is not enough of a twist, the final minutes reveal that Angela is in fact her rumored-dead brother Peter: it was his sister Angela who died along with her father years before. Peter's aunt had always wanted a daughter and decided to have Peter live as female, with hair and clothing to match. The investigating camp counselors find Angela naked at the lakeside, holding the severed head of her camp love interest, Paul. She whips her body back toward the counselors. As they look at her body, the camera pans out to show Angela (Peter) with a blood-splattered muscular upper body and a fully formed penis. This shocking film finale is reminiscent of campy classic *Beyond the Valley of the Dolls* (1970). At the film's end, key character Ronnie "Z-Man" Barzell, a flamboyant music producer, reveals that he has breasts. The film's score becomes hectic, ominous, as Z-Man begins to ruthlessly murder anyone in his path in a psychotic episode that is uncharacteristic of anything that came from his character prior. It is unclear whether Z-Man is a transgender man or woman, but rather, his final-act body is used for shock value. Upon seeing Angela's exposed penis, a camp counselor utters in terror "How can it be? She's a boy!"[26] As they stare, Angela is wide-eyed, crazed, growling and moaning, staying completely still. This is a haunting image of a crazed transgender woman, and it is assumed by the end that Peter being forced to live as Angela is the source of the animalistic rage and violence she inflicted upon unsuspecting campers.

Sleepaway Camp was not a blockbuster film, nor does it even have an exciting or eventful beginning and middle. The film's popularity lies in the final moments of Angela's big reveal as Peter, which acts as the film's climax. The image of growling, naked Angela is what makes *Sleepaway Camp* iconic in the horror genre. Feminist film critic Willow Maclay writes: "*Sleepaway Camp* is a curtain-yanking picture with a reveal that works only to make a woman with a penis a vessel for horror."[27] The spectacle of Angela's biologically-male body keeps horror fans coming back to the film again and again. Felissa Rose, who starred as Angela while a young girl, feels that her character's reveal as a boy is not linked to Angela's murder spree. She says, "In *Sleepaway Camp*, [Angela's] not transgender—she's a transvestite. She's figuring out her sexuality. And there are homoerotic undertones to that—her figuring out who she is, thinking about her dad and his lover. She's going through puberty. And I don't think the killing had anything to do with that."[28] Though Rose's comments are empathetic to the trans and queer community, the primal reveal of Angela's penis remains as a reminder of the lack of understanding from cisgender writers, such as Robert Hiltzik who wrote, produced, and directed the film. *Sleepaway Camp* is a time capsule for a world that did not know how to grasp the transgender body and used it shamelessly to elicit shock and awe. Maclay states that "[t]he real-life implications of creating a scene where a woman is shown to have a penis to the disgust of others cosigns the idea that transgender bodies are freakish."[29] Angela's body is a spectacle. Her body is the draw to this film for fans and those who have heard of the twist ending. The creators of *Sleepaway Camp* created such a grotesque, frightening image of this body that viewers cannot help but be shocked and gawk at Angela as the screen turns to a sickly green as the credits begin to roll.

Film theorist Laura Mulvey examines the fascination with the human form in "Visual Pleasure and Narrative Cinema" (1999). Visual pleasure is achieved when we see the human form, usually the female form, since, in a patriarchal society, the male gaze towers over others. Mulvey reflects on Freud's analysis of scopophilia, where an onlooker would take "other people as objects, subjecting them to a controlling and curious gaze."[30] This curiosity often turns toward the naked body, as Freud relates scopophilia to "the activities of children, their desire to see and make sure of the private and the forbidden (curiosity about other people's genitals and bodily functions, about the presence or the absence of the penis and, retrospectively, about the primal scene)." Freud's ideas of scopophilia directly correlate to both the visual shock of Angela's body and the fascination many cisgender folks have with the transgender body.

Regrettably, many films that attempt to portray transgender folks, or use them shamelessly, follow this path toward a climactic reveal of trans-ness, with the central focus being on the discovery of one's genitalia. Prior to the reveal, the audience considers the character they see before them to be the sex that is representative of their physical and often stereotypical gender expression and presentation. As described by Jack Halberstam in their book *In a Queer Time & Place: Transgender Bodies, Subcultural Lives* (2005), a reveal of a transgender character, and particularly their genitalia, is the climactic centerpiece of many transgender-themed films, some of which include *Dressed to Kill, Ace Ventura: Pet Detective* (1994), *Boys Don't Cry* (1999), and of course *Sleepaway Camp*. The reveal acts as the character's decline and, as Halberstam explains, a rewind in cinematic time:

> The transgender character is presented at first as "properly" gendered, as passing in other words, and as properly located within a linear narrative; [their] exposure as transgender constitutes the film's narrative climax, and spells out both [their] own decline and the unraveling of cinematic time. The viewer literally has to rewind the film after the character's exposure in order to reorganize the narrative logic in terms of the pass.[31]

Here lies the thrill of the trans-reveal plot devise—one can rewind the film and watch again to identify scenes in which partially indicate the character's trans-ness. Enjoyment is conjured when one can skillfully identify the times in which a trans character has passed, making light of their humanity, exposing them over and over again in an environment that is not safe for them in their respective films. We find the instances with Angela: her refusal to put on a bathing suit to go swimming, her not showering with the other girls in her cabin, and the fear after kissing a boy as he reaches for her blouse. The audience can actively participate in outing Angela with every viewing.

As with *Sleepaway Camp*, the outing of a trans person, particularly with the "discovery" of genitalia that does not match their stereotypical gender expression, has embedded itself within American culture and politics. For the latter half of the 2010s, America's various government-sponsored bathroom bills helped to corroborate Freud's ideas by showing that cisgender folks feel they need to confirm a person's genitals in order to use a public, gendered restroom. Jack Halberstam inspects the public bathroom in his book *Female Masculinity* (1998). He describes the public restroom as an extension of our own gender identities to the point of parody and the enforcement of gender conformity. "Public sex," states Halberstam, "versus private gender, openly sexual versus discreetly repressive, bathrooms beyond the home take on the proportions of a gender factory."[32] He goes on to explain the danger transgender folks face when they enter this factory if their gender presentation deviates from the social norm:

> [I]f caught [in the men's room], the [trans man] may face some version of gender panic from the man who discovers him, and it is quite reasonable to expect and fear violence in the wake of such a discovery. The [trans woman], by comparison, will be more scrutinized in the women's room but possibly less open to punishment if caught. Because the [trans man] ventures into male territory with the threat of violence hanging over his head, it is crucial to recognize that the bathroom problem is more than a glitch in the machinery of gender segregation and is better described in terms of the violent enforcement of our current gender system.[33]

Most bathroom bills have stressed the idea that cisgender women and children are in danger of the predatory male, *posing* as female, in public women's restrooms. As a result, as indicated by Halberstam of the violence looming over a trans woman's head, the bathroom bills conjured up by political leaders have reinforced the stereotype of violent transgender folks and people willing to take advantage of gender fluidity to enter a bathroom and harm someone of the restroom's designated gender.

Bathroom bills based around the myth of violence perpetrated by transgender folks toward children in restrooms sprang up across the United States in the 2010s, primarily in southern and conservative states. The Public Facilities Privacy & Security Act, also known as House Bill 2 (HB2) was introduced in March 2016. This bill called to restrict the use of bathrooms and other sex-segregated facilities based on sex assigned at birth, specifically targeting those that do not identify with the gender assigned to them at birth, transgender Americans. The transgender body became a topic of national attention, bringing with it discrimination, harmful stereotypes of confusion and predatory violence, and transphobia. According to a study examined by Dr. Edith Bracho-Sanchez of CNN in 2018 that researched bathroom and locker room assaults on transgender and cisgender youth, results indicated that despite the assumption by conservative lawmakers that transgender folks are the perpetrators of violence or "transgender intruders or predators posing as transgender" in public restrooms, it is transgender youth most at risk in these spaces.[34] As Halberstam indicates in *Female Masculinity*, violent responses to the discovery of a transgender person in a public restroom are sadly common. The anonymous 2016 web-based study, the LGBTQ Teen Study, analyzed data from 3,673 adolescents from age thirteen to seventeen:

> Just over 1 out of every 4 students in the study, or 25.9%, reported being a victim of sexual assault in the past 12 months. Transgender and gender-nonbinary teens who were subject to restroom or locker room restrictions had an even higher prevalence of sexual assault, at 36%, according to the findings, published [2016] in the journal Pediatrics. The rates of sexual assault for non-trans US teens, those whose gender identity matches their sex assigned at birth, is 15% for girls and 4% for boys, according to the Youth Risk Behavior Surveillance Survey administered by the US Centers for Disease Control and Prevention.[35]

The myth of transgender folks causing violence, including sexual violence, spread with bills such as HB2. Fascination with a person's genitalia and the need for confirmation on genitalia assumptions is the true cause of violence with regards to transgender bodies. Sexual violence upon the discovery of genitalia for a non-binary or transgender person is often the case with many horrific attacks. Such violence was inflicted upon Brandon Teena (see Chapter 5), a trans man who was raped when his "friends" exposed and discovered his biologically female genitalia in 1993. Teena was later murdered by these same friends. The horrific event was the subject of the film *Boys Don't Cry* (1999). Bathroom bills like HB2 are steeped in the history of how transgender folks have been typecast in media and film, especially in horror films.

The basis of fascination and fear of the physical transgender body as exhibited in the era of the bathroom bill is embedded in and facilitated by horror films such as *Sleepaway Camp*. The confirmation of Angela's genitals, with the accompanied flashbacks of Peter's deranged aunt forcing him to *become* a girl, is the pivotal "shocking" scene of the majorly slow film. Within *Sleepaway Camp*, the shock of the "primal scene" itself provides visual pleasure for the audience.[36] A horror film's ultimate goal is to scare, and an audience expects that the film will succeed in enacting this visual pleasure. Viewers are then confronted with the reveal of the villain and a frightening naked transgender body. Angela is the object of curiosity and fulfills an audience's desire for a primal scene of said body growling. The entire film relies heavily on this reveal, subjecting a voyeuristic gaze upon the naked body of a transgender person. In the real world, this is a huge invasion of privacy if consent is not granted. This is where *Sleepaway Camp*'s popularity rests.

Angela Baker from *Sleepaway Camp* is left at the end of the film exposed as being a boy who was raised as female by an unhinged aunt. *Sleepaway Camp II: Unhappy Campers* (1988), however, is outright about Angela being transgender. This is still problematic, in that Angela is not by definition transgender because her aunt forced Peter, Angela's true identity, to *be* Angela. Because of this complicated storyline, *Sleepaway Camp II: Unhappy Campers* makes Angela transgender, as in, Angela identifies as female. She identifies *as Angela* rather than Peter. At the beginning of the film, an older Angela is now a camp counselor at the newly renovated Camp Arawak, rebranded as Camp Rolling Hills. She announces that she officially transitioned while in a mental hospital after she was arrested for her murder spree at Camp Arawak a few years earlier. Thinking herself cured, Angela is a beacon of politeness and good in a camp full of mean counselors. Throughout, Angela's admission of being transgender is used for the sake of jokes by other counselors, though they equate Angela being transgender with her being a lesbian. She is often referred to as a "dyke" by bully Ally who makes comments like "Maybe if I'm lucky, the dyke will send me home!"[37]

Although *Sleepaway Camp II: Unhappy Campers*, like the first film, does not give any justice to trans audiences, there is something to be said about using Angela's character as a symbol of a queer protagonist/

Pamela Springsteen as exemplary camp counsellor Angela Baker, seen lounging with her dismembered and bloody victims in a publicity still for *Sleepaway Camp II: Unhappy Campers* (Nelson Entertainment, 1988).

antagonist rising above the bullies. There is catharsis in seeing Angela, still as homicidal as in the first film though more outgoing, murdering homophobic counselors and those who continue to ridicule her.

This is brought full circle in *Sleepaway Camp III: Teenage Wasteland* (1989). Again, Angela returns to the again-renewed camp, now Camp New Horizons, to murder the mix of underprivileged and affluent campers, sent there to mingle with one another. Angela returns as a fellow camper once again and aims her violent energy toward racists, homophobes, and fornicators. As she is about to murder an openly racist cheerleader, Angela scolds her, as she does with all her victims this time around: "You're a cheerleader, a fornicator, a drug-taker, and a nasty snotty bigot!"[38] It is cathartic to see Angela rise above the verbal abuse she once endured as a young girl and the homophobic remarks as a counselor at Camp Rolling Hills, and hack away at bullies who seek to harm her and others. Angela Baker is a murderer, but her hatred for bigots gives her status as a hero of sorts for a queer audience who had also been treated unfairly by society. Like Carrie White in *Carrie* (1976), who wreaked havoc on a prom full of her peers who treated her like dirt all her life, the rise of Angela Baker as an anti-hero works for many queer horror lovers.

Unfortunately, not every transgender character can be easily reclaimed as with the case of Angela Baker. Fellow 1980s low-budget horror-comedy *Curse of the Queerwolf* (1988) took an unabashed approach to their film's villain: the Queerwolf, a transgender woman who spreads a "venereal disease" through saliva to unknowing male sexual partners. This new venereal disease, as asserted by doctors over a radio program, "possesses men to dress in women's clothing" and develop a limp wrist.[39] When protagonist Lawrence, a cisgender heterosexual male, and his friend take home two women from a bar, Lawrence discovers mid-make out (and post-ass bite) that his date, Paula, stuffs her bra with tissues and has a penis. "He's a fuckin' dude!" he screams, "I'm gonna be sick!"[40] Lawrence pushes Paula against the wall and proceeds to try and choke her. This reaction from cisgender straight males is sadly frequent in American society. Far too often, trans women are murdered after a man, often during a sexual encounter, discovers that the woman he is sleeping with has biologically male genitalia. The toxic male response has been one of violence toward the woman, resulting in physical injury or death. And recurrently, the attacker and/or murderer will plead the trans panic defense. As explained by Cynthia Lee of George Washington University Law School, the trans panic defense is a non-traditional defense strategy "associated with the provocation or heat of passion defense. A murder defendant asserting trans panic will claim that the discovery that the victim was a transgender female [...] provoked him into a heat of passion, causing him to lose his self-control."[41] This loss of self-control tends to be linked to the perception that the man who pursued the transgender woman is somehow gay, striking the man's inner toxic masculinity and homophobia. Upon seeing Paula's penis, Lawrence quickly goes from shock to disgust to anger, then straight to violence with his hands around Paula's neck.

When an angry mob and a priest knock on the door and demand to enter, Paula pleads with Lawrence, "They're gonna kill me!" "Good!" Lawrence shouts.[42] The angry mob tells Lawrence that they have tracked the "Queerwolf" to this address. "He used to be my son before he was bitten by one of *them*," one of the men explains. "I thought it was just a phase he was going through. He started wearing his mother's perfume, reading *Playgirl* ... he was no longer my son. His soul is in torment and he must be destroyed."[43] Paula soon escapes out a window with the mob hot on her trail. When Lawrence's friend tells him he is a "spoiled sport" after letting the incident ruin his night, Lawrence replies, "a goddamn fag bites me in the ass and you call me a spoiled sport!" He exclaims that he is going home to his girlfriend, "a real woman."[44] Similar dialogue between men occurs eight years later in the fourth installment of the *Hellraiser* series, *Hellraiser: Bloodline* (1996). A scene begins mid-conversation with two twin security guards discussing sex with a transgender woman: "So she starts asking me all these weird questions … like, would I do it with a woman who used to be a man." "Like, with a guy who had it cut off?" the other twin asks. "Yeah. Hormones, the whole bit." "So, what'd you say?" "I mean, I guess so. If she was cut and all."[45] Though crude at points, the twins' dialogue does not include any slurs toward trans folks and uses correct pronouns when referring to the woman in question. For a 1996 film, this dialogue is quite progressive and does not turn into a toxic masculine tirade unlike the many films before and after.

Unfortunately, *Hellraiser: Bloodline* is an outlier in the horror genre and more horror films that involve transgender dialogue lean more toward the extreme *Curse of the Queerwolf*. The next day, Lawrence begins to change. A Romani fortune teller, whom he accidentally hit with his car, notices a "pansy-gram" symbol on his palm, echoing the pentagram symbol found in the palm of the original Wolf Man of 1941. That night, in the full moon, Lawrence physically becomes a Queerwolf: his wrists go limp, lipstick appears on his face, a red handkerchief grows from the back right pocket of his jeans, and a flower grows from his hair. The act of placing a handkerchief in the back pocket of your pants was an early signal to and of gay men. The Handkerchief Code was popular in gay circles across America from the 1970s into the 1990s, with a wide variety of colors and patterns indicating certain fetishes in the gay community. Lawrence's hanky, if intentional by the film's writers, signifies the enjoyment of being anally fisted.[46] Lawrence wakes up the following morning naked in a gay bathhouse sauna surrounded by half-naked men.

Ultimately, at the core of this incredibly transphobic film is the equation of being transgender as also being gay and vice versa. Although transgender folks can be anywhere on the sexuality spectrum, popular media has often linked sexuality and gender, especially gender stereotypes, together. Lawrence, when transforming into a Queerwolf, exhibited stereotypical female gender characteristics (lipstick, long painted fingernails) while additionally adopting gay male cultural codes (handkerchief in the back pocket, waking up in a gay bathhouse). Susan Stryker, author of *Transgender History: The Roots of Today's Revolution* (2017) explains:

In practice, the distinctions between what we now call "transgender" and "gay" or "lesbian" were not always as meaningful [in the past] as they have since become. Throughout the second half of the nineteenth century and the first half of the twentieth century, homosexual desire and gender variance were often closely associated. One common way of thinking about homosexuality back then was as gender "inversion," in which a man who was attracted to men was thought to be acting like a woman, and a woman who desired women was considered to be acting like a man.[47]

It is no coincidence then that this way of thinking had become so permeated in American culture that the writers of *Curse of the Queerwolf* created a character that not only transformed into a female during a full moon but also became gay in the process.

Curse of the Queerwolf reflects the major misunderstandings, prejudices, and real-life violence toward transgender people. Even well-meaning films have a disconnect when trying to navigate transgender experience in certain film characters, often relegating them, like the Queerwolf, to villains and monsters, using their bodies for horror. One such character is Jame Gumb, also known as Buffalo Bill, from *The Silence of the Lambs* (1991). The film presented Hannibal Lecter to the world: a cannibal psychiatrist jailed for his numerous murders and attacks of the flesh. Despite Anthony Hopkins' iconic sinister role as Hannibal Lecter, it is Buffalo Bill who is the villain of the Academy Award-winning film. Jame Gumb, nicknamed Buffalo Bill by the press for his multiple skinnings of young women, was once a patient of Dr. Lecter. Dr. Lecter, interviewed for the ongoing investigation by FBI agent-in-training Clarice Starling, the film's protagonist, gave insight into the madness of Gumb, and why he skins young, plump women. It is revealed that Gumb aims to create a female skinsuit to transform himself into a true woman. Although freakish and evil, this process is assumed to represent Gumb's desire to be female, making him transgender. However, Dr. Lecter asserts that this is not the true psychological reason for Gumb's suit:

> LECTER: "The significance of the moth is change. Caterpillar into chrysalis, or pupa, from thence into beauty. Our Billy wants to change too."
> CLARICE: "There's no correlation in the literature between transsexualism and violence. Transsexuals are very passive...."
> LECTER: "Clever girl! ... Billy is not a real transsexual, but he thinks he is, he tries to be. He's tried to be a lot of things, I expect."[48]

To have this type of dialogue in this film is to assert that it is Jame Gumb's mental instability that causes him to "think" he wants to be a woman. This perpetuates the idea that trans men and women are simply confused about their gender identity, and do not actually wish to be the opposite sex (or somewhere in between). They are thought to have a mental illness that is causing the desire to feel transgender. The dialogue then doubles down on this pervasive theory:

> LECTER: "There are three major centers for transsexual surgery: Johns Hopkins, the University of Minnesota, and Columbus Medical Center. I wouldn't be surprised if Billy had applied for sex reassignment at one or all of them, and been rejected."
> CLARICE: "On what basis would they reject him?"
> LECTER: "Look for severe childhood disturbances associated with violence. Our Billy wasn't born a criminal, Clarice. He was made one through years of systematic abuse. Billy hates his own identity, you see, and he thinks that makes him a transsexual. But his pathology is a thousand times more savage and more terrifying."[49]

Lecter's dialogue and theories for the sadistic nature of Jame Gumb/ Buffalo Bill correlate Gumb's violence with being rejected by hospitals conducting gender affirmation surgeries. After years of systemic abuse Lecter asserts Gumb endured throughout his life, the rejection by medical institutions for surgery was the straw that broke the camel's back, causing Bill to snap and go on a murder spree in an attempt to create a body, a skin, of his own. Despite Clarice's urging that transgender folks are not inherently violent, Lecter's psychiatric "insight" and pseudo-science (built by author Thomas Harris) equates Gumb's alleged and/or imagined transgender identity with his depravity. Director Jonathan Demme has also stated that Jame Gumb does not want to be a woman, but rather loathes himself so much that he wishes to start a-new, and the way Gumb would do so would be to murder and slice women for a skin suit.[50]

In a provocative scene involving penis-tucking, audiences get a chance to see Gumb "perform" his desired gender in an ominous and (intended) grotesque dance. Like the shower scene in *Psycho* that elicits countless parodies, Buffalo Bill's performance to Q Lazarus' "Goodbye Horses" is frequently referenced in popular culture. Gumb, dressed in a flowing kimono, wearing the scalp of a blonde woman, applies lipstick and eyeliner as his captive Katherine screams from the bottom of a well inside the house. As he dances into a recording camera, he backs up to reveal himself nude with his penis tucked between his legs, visually transforming his penis into a vagina.[51] Gumb sees himself as the woman he longs to be, or as Dr. Lecter asserts, may not exactly desire to be, but "covets" nonetheless. This scene is haunting and grants the audience an opportunity to see Jame Gumb as female-presenting while wearing a skinned scalp from one of his victims. The dance becomes a curiosity, a performance. Mulvey would proclaim this scene to be a spectacle, a

Jame Gumb/Buffalo Bill (Ted Levine) nude at his sewing machine amid creating his female skin suit in *The Silence of the Lambs* (Orion Pictures, 1991).

controversial and titillating addition to a mainstream horror film: it is meant to shock. Although this scene could signify the triumph a trans person may feel seeing themselves as the gender they truly are, Katherine screaming in the background and Gumb wearing a woman's scalp turns Gumb's body into a horror show. In addition, Gumb focuses only on the cosmetic details of being a woman, as he brutalizes his victims for their skin. Phillips, author of *Transgender on Screen*, elaborates:

> At the same time, Gumb is undeniably transsexual in his orientation and not simply transvestite or homosexual. However, his understanding of transsexuality is a superficial one that undermines the claims of transsexuality to be taken seriously. [Jack] Halberstam describes the film as a "skinflick," drawing attention to the way in which, by representing the transsexual murderer as motivated by the desire to wear the skins of his girl-victims, it demonizes the feeling, common to the transsexual, of being

"in the wrong skin" and wishing to replace it with the skin of the opposite sex.[52]

Using Jame Gumb through Buffalo Bill, the murderer, makes the real desire of transgender folks to have different skin appear extremely sinister.

Buffalo Bill is a sadistic murderer. The problem is that his transgender expression is tethered to his being a murderer. All that is tied to him, the desire to be anatomically female and the skinning of women, is linked to his murders. These links can cement themselves in the minds of the audience as well, even those who do not outwardly express transphobia, and permeate the social and cultural subconscious. Actress Jen Richards describes this very experience in Netflix's *Disclosure* (2020), a documentary dedicated to media representation of transgender folks, "I was about to go through transition, and I worked up the courage to tell one of my colleagues [...]. She's a very smart woman [...] and she looked at me and she goes, 'You mean like Buffalo Bill?' Like her only point of reference was this disgusting, psychotic serial killer."[53] As with the case of Buffalo Bill, horror films use the transgender narrative as a character device for the villain resulting in a cultural misconception of a correlation between being transgender and being violent.

Although writers and the director of *The Silence of the Lambs* make it clear that they had no intention of painting the transgender community as violent, connecting Gumb's desire to be female into his murderous nature has caused discord between cisgender audiences and the ideas of what it means to be transgender. On-screen, audiences see a violent unhinged criminal whose acts directly correlate to his desire to be physically female-presenting. As established by the study conducted by Solomon and Kurtz-Costes, this type of representation does indeed contribute to transphobia. Even the best of intentions cause harm to minority groups, and *The Silence of the Lambs*' Buffalo Bill proves this. Trans voices are disregarded for their outrage over the character due to the assertion that "it is just a movie." Yet it is clear the writers and directors ignored trans voices as well, and perhaps if trans folks were included, Buffalo Bill's desire to be female would not dominate his murder narrative.

It would not be until ten years after the release of *The Silence of the Lambs* that audiences would see a neutral genderfluid and/or possibly transgender character in the commercial horror/thriller flop *Soul Survivors* (2001). Neither villain nor hero, Raven, played by cisgender actress Angela Featherstone, is a clairvoyant person with explicit he/him pronouns. His aesthetic is exclusively butch lesbian, evoking k.d. lang in her iconic 1993 Vanity Fair cover where she donned a sharp pantsuit and short hair while getting a face shave by model Cindy Crawford. His screen time is limited and cloaked with intrigue, though he engages in sexual acts with the protagonist's best friend Annie. Three years later in 2004, trans and/or non-binary audiences would see an unexpectedly positive portrayal in a mainstream horror film that lingers in popular culture consciousness and proves to have been incredibly ahead of its time.

A Source of Unexpected Light (and Darkness)

It is not until the advent of home video could horror and sci-fi fans find an unexpected truth about a character of one of the most celebrated films, and its sequel, of all time. *Alien* (1979), directed by Ridley Scott and written by Dan O'Bannon, follows a crew of seven aboard the spaceship *Nostromo* in the distant future. Of the seven crew members, two are women: Navigator Joan Lambert (Veronica Cartwright) and Warrant Officer Ellen Ripley (Sigourney Weaver). Lambert is a more passive character than Ripley, who becomes the central character of the *Alien* franchise. Unlike sole survivor Ripley, Lambert suffers a

Joan Lambert (Veronica Cartwright, left) sitting with her only other female crewmate Ellen Ripley (Sigourney Weaver) aboard the Nostromo in *Alien* (20th Century–Fox, 1979).

gruesome death by the Xenomorph alien creature along with her other shipmates.

In *Aliens* (1986), written and directed by James Cameron, though Lambert is already dead, dossiers on the crewmembers of the *Nostromo* are revealed, albeit out-of-focus. The first sentences of Lambert's file, shown too brief to read without an at-home video system, state, "Subject is Despin Convert at birth (male to female). So far, no indication of suppressed traumas related to gender alteration."[54] The gender politics of *Alien* from the onset were neutral, as all actors auditioning for the roles in Scott's feature were chosen not based on already gendered characters. In this regard, it is not shocking then that a character would be possibly non-binary or gender non-conforming. Such gender-non-conforming is evident in Ripley's character, whose androgynous attributes have been a part of gender discourse in film since *Alien*'s 1979 release. What remains surprising is the transgender inclusion, however quick, in a major blockbuster film released in 1986.

When a fan, who is swift enough to pause their copy of *Aliens* to inspect Lambert's out-of-focus dossier, watches *Alien* within the context of Lambert as a trans woman, her death is all the more upsetting. As the Xenomorph slides its tail up between Lambert's legs and she subsequently screams in pain, her death can be interpreted as following her rape. The scene becomes sinister when one reflects on the statistics of rape and death of trans women in America. Director Scott offered some credibility to the long-standing fan theory that Lambert was indeed raped in the Alien Anthology commentary. He posits, "Was that some dreadful ending? Was that some terrible invasion of her body? A rape?"[55]

Due to the *Alien* franchise's fixation with Ellen Ripley and her gender presentation, Joan Lambert is frequently forgotten within the discourse. However, she reappears ever so often in the internet age when screenshots of her dossier can be posted and discussed on sites such as Twitter, Reddit, and Instagram. LGBTQ+ visibility has increased thanks to the wide breadth of the internet as well as dedicated fans eager to share their queer findings from the horror archives. The reemergence of Lambert's gender identity time and time again signifies the combing of the horror genre by fans for even the most minute pieces of queer representation, confirming a desire by queer folks to see themselves on screen, especially vulnerable groups such as transgender individuals.

CHAPTER 5

Exposure

Queers and the Millennium
(1990–2009)

The Clinton Era: Hate Crimes and Queer Infusion (1990–1999)

1990	Jerry Falwell proclaims AIDS as punishment for gay lifestyle	*Def by Temptation*	*Nightbreed*
1991	*The Silence of the Lambs*	*Poison*	Jeffrey Dahmer arrested
1992	Protests erupt at Academy Awards for negative queer portrayal in films	Los Angeles County reports record hate crimes	
1993	Brandon Teena is murdered	"Don't Ask, Don't Tell" enacted	Hate Crimes Sentencing Enhancement Act amendment
1994	*Interview with a Vampire*	*Tammy & the T-Rex*	
1996	Defense of Marriage Act (DOMA)	*Scream*	
1997	*Scream 2*		
1998	Matthew Shepard dies of injuries sustained from beating	*The Faculty* — *Bride of Chucky* — *Psycho*	Westboro Baptist Church pickets Shepard's funeral
1999	*The Rage: Carrie 2*	*The Haunting*	

Figure 7

Due to the mainstream perpetuation of queer stereotypes, independent filmmakers have created their own narratives of queer characters. As queer cult film director John Waters had spearheaded with his gang of misfit absurd queers in films like *Multiple Maniacs*, independent filmmakers of the millennium began crafting their own films on low-budgets and limited-time releases, some of which went straight to home video. This trend continued into the 1990s with the rise of New Queer Cinema, a movement comprised of queer filmmakers creating movies of all genres centered around queer lives and stories. Todd Haynes was one of the earliest proponents of the New Queer Cinema movement with his debut feature-length film *Poison* (1991). Of *Poison*'s three interconnected stories "Hero," "Horror," and "Homo," "Horror" was modeled after 1950s' era science fiction horror with scientist Dr. Thomas Graves isolating the sex drive gene. After accidentally ingesting the solution, Graves starts to sprout sores on his face that spread to anyone his face touches. A newspaper headline read, "Leper Sex Killer on the Loose."[1] Haynes' "Horror" is an artistic dramatization and science fiction adaptation of the AIDS crisis that was still gutting the queer community and the world at large. *Philadelphia* (1993), directed by Jonathan Demme (*The Silence of the Lambs*) and starring Tom Hanks as a young successful lawyer who is discriminated against for having AIDS, brought the HIV/AIDS epidemic to a wider audience, yet queer visibility in mainstream cinema remained either jocular or tragic.

By 1990, major religious personalities and congress members related the HIV/AIDS epidemic to God's Will. "AIDS is not just God's punishment for homosexuals," proclaimed Jerry Falwell, a popular televangelist, in 1990. "It is God's punishment for the society that tolerates homosexuals."[2] Films like *Def by Temptation* (1990) followed such an ideology by framing queer folks, especially gay men, as sinful. Produced by Troma Entertainment, a low-budget company that creates mainly absurd comedic films, *Def by Temptation* focuses on a demon spirit named Temptation who appears in the form of an attractive seductress. Temptation is labeled as an "it" who "uses sexuality to hold morality hostage ... seducing sinners," by picking up men and killing them.[3] The most graphic violence in the film is aimed at a gay man named Jonathan whom Temptation lures in by saying he should try having sex with a woman. Jonathan shows up at Temptation's apartment the following day, perhaps to try and convince himself that he can be straight, only to be ripped to bloody shreds by Temptation during their sexual encounter. At the time of this movie's release, anti-gay violence was on the rise. As indicated by author Robin Means Coleman,

> The most ferocious scene in the film, it is a startling depiction of anti-gay violence aligning with, and giving tacit approval for, the real-life violence gays and lesbians experience, For example, a 1989 report, issued one year before *Temptation*, revealed that 5 percent of gay men and 10 percent of lesbians polled reported being the victim of anti-gay violence, while 47 percent of all gays polled reported some form of (non-violent) discrimination based on their sexual orientation.[4]

As anti-gay violence was on the rise by the late 1980s, the early 1990s were wrought with normalized anti-gay and anti-transgender sentiments. This violence was not eased by films such as *The Silence of the Lambs* whose main antagonist was a homosexual and gender-confused male (as indicated in Chapter 4, Buffalo Bill does not truly identify as transgender but is rather confused mentally about his gender identity). The 1992 Academy Awards, in which *The Silence of the Lambs* was nominated for several big awards, was protested by queer activist groups for its perpetuation of the stereotype of the villainous queer.

> Across the street from the Dorothy Chandler Pavilion in Los Angeles, several hundred protesters, loosely organized by the gay-rights activist group Queer Nation, marched and chanted behind a police barricade. Celebrities exiting onto the red carpet faced signs like "Hollywood Stop Censoring Our True Queer Lives" and "Worst Picture: *Silence of the Lambs*."[5]

The protesters at the Academy Awards were demanding more empathetic portrayals of queer folks in cinema. This was also during a time when Los Angeles County reported a "record high" in hate crimes in 1992: of the 161 incidents that targeted gay men and women, only seven arrests were made.[6] Based on the fact that so few hate crimes were solved, it is clear that the culture among police officers of the 1980s and 1990s was one of indifference to the lives of queer Americans. The pattern exhibited in the Los Angeles hate crime statistics of police indifference to the murders of queer folks was similar to a high-profile case that occurred in 1991 regarding one of the most notorious serial killers of the twentieth century.

The Silence of the Lambs was released on Valentine's Day of 1991. Coincidentally, another gay serial killer like Buffalo Bill would be arrested five months later on July 22 and brought to media attention for the first time: Jeffrey Dahmer. Like Gacy before him, Dahmer was a sadistic pedophile killer who happened to be a homosexual man. Often, Dahmer would pick up young gay men and boys from gay bars, later raping and murdering them to conduct brutal science experiments on their corpses. He would reveal that his mutilation and experimentation on the corpses of his victims was an attempt to create "sex zombies," who would satisfy his sick sexual desires and never leave his side:

> [Dahmer] explained that he was taking the men, drugging and raping them, before drilling holes into their frontal lobes and pouring in chemicals to create silent, zombie (sex) slaves. When his victims died, he would variously keep their body parts around, engage in necrophilia, or eat them.[7]

Dahmer murdered seventeen men and boys, most of whom were gay young men of color, and unfortunately, as was the case with John Wayne Gacy's victims, the police often disregarded the testimony of gay survivors and their families. One victim, a fourteen-year-old boy named Konerak Sinthasomphone who escaped Dahmer's apartment in May of 1991, was found by police wandering the streets naked, still dazed from Dahmer drugging him.[8] Dahmer spoke with the police and explained that the boy was his lover who should be returned to his care. The police obliged, and Dahmer soon murdered the boy. A "successful lawsuit filed against [Milwaukee, WI] by Sinthasomphone's family argued that police had to go to great racist and homophobic lengths to fail to see Dahmer as the monster he was."[9]

In 1991, with Dahmer in the news and Buffalo Bill on the silver screen, the American public was receiving myriad messages saying that homosexual serial killers were running rampant in American society and were frequently linked to pedophilia. The infamy of men like Dahmer and Gacy, and their continuous press coverage, perpetuated the idea that gay men were pedophiles and extremely violent, while killers like Richard Ramirez and Ted Bundy who were heterosexual seemed to not be labeled as heterosexual serial killers, and their sexuality was not the forefront of their murderous identity. The labeling of queer folks as being prone to violent acts because of their "malicious" sexuality would be a root cause of violence toward queer people. In addition, it was toxic masculinity that was perpetuated by films such as *Def by Temptation* and casual homophobia of films from the 1980s that would result in the violence inflicted upon queer bodies in the 1990s and well into the twenty-first century.

A film whose subtext examines the creation of queer families for protection from outside violence culminates in Clive Barker's *Nightbreed* (1990). Clive Barker, the boundary-pushing openly gay writer, has coded nearly all his stories with his queerness. Barker's directorial debut was his film adaptation of his novella *The Hellbound Heart* (1986) titled *Hellraiser* (1987). Produced and released in the United Kingdom, *Hellraiser* introduced the leather-clad, demonic BDSM clan, the Cenobites, and their to-be infamous leader, Pinhead. Barker's cenobites were inspired by punk, Catholicism, and his frequent visits to sadomasochistic nightclubs in New York City.[10] *Hellraiser*'s blend of queer BSDM culture and hellscape imagery would become a fixture in the horror genre. Following the film's success, the *Hellraiser* series continued without Barker, spawning the sequel *Hellbound: Hellraiser 2* (1988) which continued with the cenobites' antagonistic fury. Barker returns to the director's chair with American-produced *Nightbreed*. Protagonist Aaron, after being manipulated by his doctor into believing he is a serial killer, finds refuge among the Nightbreed, a band of misfit creatures that live in an abandoned cemetery to hide from society for fear of violence. "Can anyone watch *Nightbreed* and not automatically associate the titular creatures with queer people?" asks Trace Thurman, co-host of the *Horror Queers* podcast. "They've been outcast by society and are deemed as dangerous by the 'normal' people. The climax of the film culminates in an assault on the Nightbreed's home base of Midian as the 'normies' would rather kill all of them as opposed to understand them. Sound familiar?"[11] *Nightbreed* thrives on queer subtext. The monsters of the film formed their own community outside of polite society to protect themselves from the wrath of said society. "Normies" wish to hurt and kill those different from them: the monsters, Othered by their appearance, formed Midian and their own Other/queer family for both protection and support.

The creatures of *Nightbreed*'s Midian were very much present in the 1990s American reality. The monsters knew they had to stay together, away from the violence perpetrated by "normal" people, and protect one another, should one of their own be targeted. The 1990s were not free from anti-queer and trans violence, and sadly, two of the highest-profile homophobic and transphobic murders occurred during the decade, those of Brandon Teena in 1993 and Matthew Shepard in 1998. Brandon was a transgender man from the midwestern United States. After moving from Lincoln to Falls City, Nebraska, Brandon made a new group of friends. Two of these friends, John Lotter and Tom Nissen, discovered and exposed Brandon as transgender after seeing that he had not undergone genitalia surgery. The men viciously raped and beat Brandon, leaving him with jagged knife wounds on his body, a bullet wound under his chin, and a fractured skull. Brandon went to the authorities but was faced with dehumanizing questioning. The police waited too long to investigate, leaving the assailants free to search for Brandon in revenge for going to the authorities. Brandon was murdered six days later on New Year's Eve by the same men that assaulted him. He was twenty-one years old. Lotter and Nissen were arrested and tried for murder in 1996, for which they were convicted, with Lotter receiving a death sentence and Nissen with life in prison.

Matthew Shepard's case would be at the forefront of the conversation of justice for victims and survivors of hate crimes under the Clinton Administration. The Clinton Administration (1993–2001) was a time of contradiction with regards to queer rights. Clinton was on the receiving end of one of the first documented gay voting blocs. At a campaign event in Los Angeles dedicated to LGBTQ issues, Clinton advocated for gay acceptance and an end to a ban against LGBTQ folks in the military if elected president. After the event that included an address by activist and gay advisor to Clinton's campaign David Mixner, queer Americans contributed three million dollars to Clinton's campaign, helping him to win the presidency in the 1992 election.[12] Unfortunately for queer Americans, Clinton was bluffing and his promises on ending the military ban went unkept. In 1993, President Bill Clinton signed a military policy directive, Don't Ask, Don't Tell, that prohibited openly gay and lesbian Americans from serving in the military. However, it also prohibited the harassment of those perceived to be gay, lesbian, or bisexual. In 1997, this policy was referenced in *Scream 2* by the bodyguard that was designated as gay in the film. When protagonist Sidney and her friend are taken by Sidney's bodyguards, they ask, "Where are you taking us?" After his fellow bodyguard answers with "If we tell you, we'll have to kill you," the gay bodyguard states "don't ask, don't tell." No doubt this was a cheeky line added by openly gay writer Kevin Williamson.[13]

Despite failing on his promise of ending the military ban against queer Americans, the Clinton administration was proactive in its efforts toward queer acceptance, beginning with protections for queer victims and survivors of hate crimes. The Hate Crimes Sentencing Enhancement Act was also introduced in 1993 as an amendment to the Violent Crime and Law Enforcement Act of 1994, allowing a judge to place a harsher sentence on a person if it is clear that they chose their victim because of their "actual or perceived race, color, religion, national origin, ethnicity, gender, disability, or sexual orientation."[14] This was directly used in the case of twenty-one-year-old Matthew Shepard, who in early October of 1998, was tied to a fence in the freezing cold, severely beaten, set on fire, and left to die near Laramie, Wyoming. He was later found by a passing cyclist and taken to the hospital. There, he died from his injuries. The perpetrators, Russell Henderson and Aaron McKinney, were arrested for attempted murder and given two life sentences. In response to Matthew Shepard's brutal murder, the infamous Westboro Baptist Church of Topeka, Kansas, whose anti–LGBTQ+ philosophy resulted in a hate group designation by the Southern Poverty Law Center (SPLC), picketed Shepard's funeral on October 16, 1998, with signs reading "God Hates Fags."[15] The church's homophobic rhetoric and actions would continue into the 2000s. Director Kevin Smith's horror-thriller *Red State* (2011) is inspired by Westboro Baptist Church's homophobia, complete with the zealot Five Points Trinity Church picketing young gay Jacob Harlow's funeral in the film's opening scene. It is revealed later, after capturing and murdering three teenage boys and a gay man, that the church tortured and murdered Harlow themselves. Smith provides his explanation for the religious extremists of America at the end of the film. After a bloody armed battle with the church members on their rural compound, ATF special agent Joe Keenan, played by John Goodman, solemnly explicates why Five Point Trinity Church vehemently believes that queer folks are Satan's instrument on Earth, and why they are willing to die for the cause: "People just do the strangest things when they believe they're entitled. But they do even stranger things when they just plain believe."[16]

President Clinton, despite the successes with hate crimes amendments and laws, signed the Defense of Marriage Act (DOMA) in 1996. This law would ensure that same-sex marriage would be federally banned, and legal marriage was defined as a legal union between one man and one woman as husband and wife. For many queer folks and activists like Larry Kramer, a co-founder of AIDS activist organization ACT UP, the election of Bill Clinton started hopeful but resulted in frustration: "We fell for his [progressive] pitch hook, line and sinker."[17]

Two years earlier, the film adaptation of Anne Rice's *Interview with a Vampire* introduced the first queer horror family: two male vampires, and a vampire child. The two protagonists, Louis and Lestat, played by Hollywood hunks Brad Pitt and Tom Cruise, had a homoerotic relationship. When a child, played by Kirsten Dunst, is turned and ages within her child body, Lestat and Louis take her in and care of her.[18] *Interview with a Vampire* brought a different image of the vampire into the new millennium. Here were two vampire men cohabitating and looking after a child. There was still strong sexuality present between both men, and that homoeroticism, as stated by horror fan Alice Collins for *Gayly Dreadful*, "just existed. No need to explain."[19] There was no ominous subtext as with the vampire films of the 1980s, but rather a return to 1931 romanticized Dracula, though with more homoeroticism and an Addams-Family-like queer family. Chosen families are often how queer people survive if their biological families reject them. *Interview with a Vampire* was an intimate look into how families, bonded by Otherness rather than with blood, like Barker's Nightbreed, try to survive in a world that fears and rejects them. Queer families and couples like in *Interview with a Vampire* would have to wait until the repeal of DOMA under the Obama Administration (2015) to be official in the eyes of the law.

The Use of Alternative Girls and Sissy Boys by Queer Writers and Directors

In the late 1990s, alternative teenage girls, often gothic in attitude and already Othered, were portrayed as closeted lesbians. Such is the case with two female characters in the horror films *The Faculty* (1998) and *The Rage: Carrie 2* (1999). Both Clea DuVall's character Stokely from *The Faculty* and Emily Bergl's Rachel from *The Rage: Carrie 2* are written as social outcasts dressed in goth teen clothes and with somewhat butch attitudes. Additionally, both are written to be seen as queer by their classmates, often the butt of lesbian jokes and at the receiving end of the slur "dyke."

Stokely and Rachel's fashion and attitude perpetuate the idea that lesbians are not feminine in the realm of the teen horror film. Though neither girl is lesbian, their characters exude and conjure lesbianism in the stereotypical sense. As was with the dominant characterizations in early Hollywood of sissy gay men, writing Stokely and Rachel as "alternative" or butch registers with broad audiences and says that these girls are meant to be lesbian presenting. Jack Halberstam explains in *Female Masculinity* (1998), "the butch stereotype [...] both makes lesbianism visible yet seems to make it visible in nonlesbian terms: that is to say, the butch makes lesbianism readable in the register of masculinity, and it actually collaborates with the mainstream notion that lesbians cannot be feminine."[20]

Miraculously, Stokely and Rachel begin dressing more feminine when being pursued by a male love interest. Their clothes become a rejection of their lesbian veils. Stokely veils herself with lesbianism and explicitly says so. She tells Marybeth, an alien creature hiding within the body of the new girl who is surprisingly supportive of Stokely's rumored lesbianism, that she likes that her peers view her as a lesbian, though she is straight. After the mean popular girl mocks Stokely's alleged sexuality by accusing Stokely of trying to seduce Marybeth, Marybeth approaches Stokely openly:

> MARYBETH: "I didn't know you were a lesbian. I don't think I've ever met one before. Have you been out long? Now I think it's very impressive how evolved...."
> STOKELY: "I'm not a lesbian, alright?"
> MARYBETH: "Be one. Fly free!"
> STOKELY: "You were right about me: I don't have any friends and I like it that way. Being a lesbian is just my security."[21]

Queer audiences were so close to being seen by this film, only to have it be ultimately revealed that Stokely isn't actually queer. She likes to be considered lesbian because it allows her to remain on the outskirts of high school society—protection from the disappointment of having no friends, of being different. However, the fact that Kevin Williamson, the openly gay writer for *The Faculty*, included such a considerate and accepting character in secret-alien Marybeth is quite transgressive: the only person in the film who openly embraces a queer person is herself

Clea DuVall as Stokely, reading a pulp science fiction novel alone in the high school quad in *The Faculty* (Miramax Films, 1998).

just as alien. There is more representation and visibility for a queer person in Marybeth's dialogue than in Stokely's. Later, Marybeth leaves her human body and is killed by the group of teens; Stokely falls for a jock turned academic, and all possible queer representation from her is lost. Rachel of *The Rage: Carrie 2*, on the other hand, is a bit more ambiguous: her extremely close best friendship with Lisa, made concrete by matching heart-in-barbed-wire tattoos, is heartfelt and nearly queer. Rachel even sarcastically tells a jerk football player trying to bribe her with a date that she won't accept because "I'm a dyke."[22] Later, this same jock would refer to her with that label.[23] After Lisa's suicide at school, Rachel is wooed by male jock Jesse. Coincidentally, Stokely and Rachel's sexualities are "saved" by male jocks, giving the audience closure by the end of both films that these women are straight. At the end of *The Faculty*, it is acknowledged through a pastel purple cardigan that Stokely will go on to live a straight life with her new jock boyfriend, Stan. Unlike Stokely, Rachel dies during the climax of *The Rage: Carrie 2*. Her jock boyfriend Jesse goes off to college and brings along her orphaned dog in a gesture that would have one believe that if Rachel survived, she and Jesse would have lived happily ever after. Due to both scripts being written by non-lesbians, the films stereotype these girls, and it is up to the audience to decide if the representation given is offensive or salutatory.

Queer writers and directors have spearheaded the horror genre since the 1930s. This does not always mean, however, that they will have the best interests of queer audiences in mind. Kevin Williamson, who came out as gay to family and friends in 1992, wrote *The Faculty*, as well as the mega slasher hit *Scream* (1996).[24] Unfortunately, his character Stokely is a stereotype of a butch queer girl who just needs to find "the right boy" in order to embrace femininity. Queer writers and directors have a responsibility to deplete the amount of negative queer representations in films by the inclusion of queer characters while being careful as to not perpetuate harmful stereotypes. "There is no question," Judith Butler explains in "Imitation and Gender Insubordination" (1991),

> that gays and lesbians are threatened by the violence of public erasure, but the decision to counter that violence must be careful not to reinstall another in its place. Which version of lesbian or gay ought to be rendered visible, and which internal exclusions will that rendering visible institute? [...] And this is not a call to return to silence or invisibility, but, rather, to make use of a category that can be called into question, made to account for what it excludes.[25]

Unfortunately, as queerness has been censored or rendered villainous for decades, queer filmmakers, particularly queer writers, will have their work incessantly culled for indicators of queer sexuality. Such was the case with openly lesbian feminist Rita Mae Brown's script for *The Slumber Party Massacre* (1982). Originally meant to parody the sexist and heteronormative slasher films of the 1980s, Brown's screenplay was ultimately shot like a typical horror film of the era nearly indetectable as a criticism of mainstream horror. She acquiesces, "to assume that a screenwriter has any power over the process of filming is naive in the extreme."[26] However, a few feminist and lesbian themes remain, such as the girls of the film saving themselves from the power-drill killer without the help of a male character, a young girl reads *Playgirl* magazine while in bed, and, for an attuned queer viewer, a copy of the lesbian coming-of-age novel *Rubyfruit Jungle* (1971), written by Brown herself, can be seen sitting atop one of the girls' nightstands.

Perhaps it can be viewed as unfair to put so much responsibility for the queer image on the shoulders of gay artists when just as much should be placed on the shoulders of their straight and cisgender peers. However, given the unique perspective which queer folks have on their communities that straight and cisgender folks do not, queer writers and directors of the genre have an opportunity to give audiences a look into and through the queer lens and create characters that are not odes to the perpetuated stereotypes that have plagued queer characters for decades. The fact that Stokely of *The Faculty* and Rachel from *The*

Rage: Carrie 2 have storylines that intertwine with queer existence, or even bring up queer sexuality at all, is a step in a good direction, considering the extreme lack of queer characters in Hollywood films. But high-profile horror film writers like Kevin Williamson must be careful with what they deliver to mainstream audiences.

David from *Bride of Chucky* (1998) signified both a return to the sissies of the 1930s and 1940s but with a twist: he is out and proud about who he is. As Thomas Waugh explains in his piece "The Third Body: Patterns in the Construction of the Subject in Gay Male Narrative Film," the gay male characters of the 1980s and particularly the 1990s become no longer a tragic subject, as in films such as *Suddenly, Last Summer,* but as comic, "through parodic quotation or through reversals (and with the rise of the comic queer comes their relegation to the role of side character since horror leads are seldom the comedic relief)."[27] David, sissy and proud, is both a parody of sissy characters of horror films' past (*Bride of Frankenstein, Savage Weekend*) and a reversal, for he is complex and sympathetic. This is similarly the case with Byron of *Tammy and the T-Rex* (1994), a mad-scientist horror/teenage romantic comedy/mid–90s gorefest. Byron, like David, is a sissy gay character infused with cliché. However, the only anti-gay sentiments aimed toward Byron are from police officers, except for Bryon's father, the sheriff. What is notable about this film's treatment of its sole queer character are his interactions with his father: there was no disdain for his son, which is usually not the case in film narratives of parents with a queer child. As with David in *Bride of Chucky*, Byron has agency throughout the film.[28]

In David's case, however, he would be seen as a response by a queer filmmaker, Don Mancini, to the stereotypes that have circled Hollywood for decades, a reclamation of the sissy, but one who now speaks for himself.[29] *Bride of Chucky* is Mancini's fourth *Child's Play* franchise film, centering around Chucky, the evil Good Guy doll who murders and wreaks havoc on the human world. Following his death in *Child's Play 3* (1991), Tiffany, Chucky's former lover when he was the human serial killer Charles Lee Ray, takes his remains from an FBI evidence locker, stitches him together, and revives him via voodoo ritual. Chucky, reborn, goes after Tiffany during a lover's spat, turning her into a doll like him. The two dolls are taken by lovers Jesse and Jade to be brought to Chucky's human body in a cemetery in New Jersey, for Chucky to be human again. Jade and Jesse's friend, David, is the voice of reason for the couple, yet he does harbor sissy stereotypes that plagued Hollywood in its early days. While posing as Jade's prom date to please her cruel uncle Warren, David discusses how he grows orchids and wants to go into figure skating.[30] It is made clear early on by this dialogue that he is not Jade's true boyfriend, but rather the gay best friend. Though David is sissified, he is given an honest storyline by openly gay writer Mancini: David discusses his heartbreak of being caught with his boyfriend by his parents, effectively losing him, and is a true friend and supporter of Jade and Jesse. He is a side character, but he is not used for comic relief, nor is his sexuality a punchline. David, unlike many gay characters in horror and cinema, was created by a gay man. Just as James Whale created the sissy character of Dr. Pretorius for *Bride of Frankenstein* not for laughs but as simply a character, Don Mancini treats David the same. "Whale ... used the sissy character in far more empowering ways," advocates William J. Mann. "In the post-studio era, it would not be until the late 1980s that gay directors would emerge who would directly challenge the prevailing homophobia and change the depiction of homosexuality on screen."[31] Mancini is one of these gay directors that emerged and included true queer representation in his films.

Mancini's understanding of queer codes in cinema is evident in *Bride of Chucky* regarding his frequent references to Whale's *Bride of Frankenstein* throughout the film, either through actual film clips or dialogue, and not to mention, the film's title.[32] Mancini's choices to include queer signifiers and characters are deliberate, as they are nods to queer audiences, letting them know that he is speaking to them.[33] Mancini also includes out queer actress Alexis Arquette as Damien, Tiffany's boyfriend at the beginning of the film. As audiences would see again in *Seed of Chucky* (2004), Mancini continues to bring in queer actors and characters to his films, showing that he is truly dedicated to inclusion. Queer filmmakers often let their queerness seep into their art. The results are films that are either outright queer or create a narrative to which only queer folks would respond and understand. Such is the case with Mancini's art and his *Child's Play* franchise: he is creating art for all horror fans while winking to his fellow queers. He is a queer artist who intentionally infuses his queerness into his art, and *Bride of Chucky* was just the beginning.

Unfortunately, some out gay directors and writers whitewash film narratives. Gus Van Sant's *Psycho* (1998) reboot straight washes the acknowledged queer character of Norman Bates. Played by Vince Vaughn, Bates defied what made Anthony Perkin's original Bates' sexuality more ambiguous.[34] Van Sant practically shot his film word for word, scene by scene as Hitchcock's original. As Bates watches his female hotel guest Marion, played by Anne Heche, he masturbates, "thus leaving nothing to the audience's imagination, and rendering Norman Bates heterosexual."[35] This addition to the scene is not included in Hitchcock's original film (then again, something this scandalous would in no way be featured in a major motion picture in 1960). It is never indicated in the original that Bates is watching Marion for sexual pleasure, yet Van Sant decided to include this in his reboot. Additionally, in the final scene in which Bates is taken into custody, there is no mention of his alleged "transsexualism," as is indicated by a police officer in *Psycho* (1960). The Bates of 1960 is problematic to the transgender community—could this reboot's omission be an attempt to erase that painful portrayal? This question is hard to answer. Van Sant still includes Vaughn in drag for the role but does not label Bates as transgender. Perhaps this could be a reversal of the 1960 problematic portrayal, but it is odd especially since Van Sant made his film almost identical to the original, but without these details.

The end of the 1990s was optimistic for the future of queer representation in horror. Unfortunately, this hope for horror would be sidetracked by queer characters meant solely for comedic purposes in horror spoofs that flooded the 2000s box office. The rise of the horror-comedy would be accompanied by often-misogynistic torture-porn films, a subgenre that focuses on body horror mixed with sexuality, as a result of the mass media footage of falling and broken bodies from the devastating attacks on the World Trade Center in 2001, as well as internet footage depicting suspected terrorists being subjected to gruesome torture techniques including waterboarding and bodily stress positions by American CIA agents.[36] The beginning of the new millennium would bring just as much frustration on account of negative queer representation as decades past. It would take some time before positive queer representation hit the bloody silver screen, mainly through the art of independent filmmakers.

Toxicity, Comic Relief, and the Seeds of a New Era: The Turbulent 2000s

On April 14, 2000, Republican presidential nominee George W. Bush met with openly gay Republicans to discuss national issues. At the news press conference, Bush stated that he wants his conservative colleagues "to understand we judge people based upon their heart and soul."[37] This attempt to reverse bad press resulting from not meeting with gay republicans when fellow Republican candidate John McCain did was nothing more than a photo opportunity for the self-proclaimed Compassionate Conservative. Throughout his presidency, from 2000 to 2008, Bush made clear his stance on gay marriage, calling for a constitutional amendment to ban same-sex marriage in 2004, and

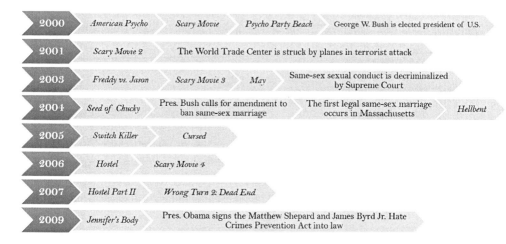

Figure 8

openly proclaiming in 2006 that the sacred union of marriage should be reserved for heterosexual couples. His philosophy on the matter was criticized and at odds with his vice president Dick Cheney, whose daughter is openly lesbian. At a campaign rally in Davenport, Iowa, in August of 2004, Cheney spoke of his daughter and the issues of which his family has been involved: "With the respect to the question of relationships, my general view is freedom means freedom for everyone. [...] People ought to be free to enter into any kind of relationship they want to."[38] His initial vague support for gay marriage was muddied by his additional remarks on state determination of the definition of marriage rather than federal government-sanctioned marriage rights for queer couples. Nevertheless, this state determination of marriage rights was beneficial for queer Massachusetts couples months earlier, with the state holding the first legal gay marriage of the United States in May of 2004. Moreover, despite the conservative agenda of the Bush Administration, the U.S. Supreme Court decided on the decriminalization of same-sex sexual conduct in June 2003.

Media representation of LGBTQ+ folks, especially in the horror genre, continued to be marred by tired homophobic tropes, jokes, and slurs. A major motion picture, and a much-anticipated horror titan battle royale, *Freddy vs Jason* (2003), even had the audacity to include a gay slur aimed at horror legend Freddy Krueger, hurled at him by real-life pop group Destiny's Child member Kelly Rowland, who plays the character of Kia: "What kind of faggot wears a Christmas sweater?" (If this doesn't act as a time capsule for early 2000s pop culture, it would be an opportunity missed.)[39] Chris Eggertsen asserts in *Uproxx* (2016) that

Kia Waterson, played by Kelly Rowland (right), insults Freddy Krueger's (Robert Englund) wardrobe in *Freddy vs Jason* (New Line Cinema, 2003).

"[Kia] uses it as a term of denigration and emasculation; it is lobbed in an effort to diminish his power, just as it has been against LGBT individuals throughout history. 'You're not even scary,' she follows up. Freddy goes on to semi-refute this by having Jason brutally murder her. If only he could have murdered that line, too."[40]

Millennium horror tends to echo the casual homophobia of the 1980s. While some films of the decade used queer folks as punchlines, films like *American Psycho* (2000), set in 1980s Wall Street, expose that use for what it was: homophobia based on fear of the Other. The film's antagonist Patrick Bateman is a successful and homicidal man who dresses in sharp Wall Street suits and is obsessed with the design of his business card. He frequently uses gay slurs like his friends for the sake of fitting in, and recoils from his sissy coworker Luis who tries to seduce him in the men's bathroom, where Bateman aggressively washes his gloved hands after Luis touches him.[41] This sort of toxic masculinity was ingrained in 1980s wealth culture, as well as permeated boy's locker-room talk for decades, including the 2000s.[42] Director Mary Harron states how the film dialogue is "a quite brilliant attack on male behavior, as much anti-male as anything else. The focus is on the satire of this kind of corporate male behavior, elite male behavior."[43] The male behavior Harron is extrapolating in *American Psycho* is the toxic, anti-gay sentiments by elite straight white males. It is safe to say that the world of Bateman was not far off from the actual toxic male environment of a 1980s corporate office. Peter Staley, a closeted gay man in the 1980s who worked in a similar stocks-and-bonds environment as character Patrick Bateman, and whose story is told in David France's *How to Survive a Plague: The Story of How Activists and Scientists Tamed AIDS*, often heard the "locker room" spill into the board room:

> Several times a week, some hideous and costly outcome gave cause for a trader to slam his telephone against his cubicle or a salesman's chair or one of the room's many pillars, with such force that plastic shards shot across several tiers. Almost without variation, the targets of rage were "fags," "pansies," "sissies," "fairies," "cocksuckers," or "queers."[44]

The verbal homophobia Staley could hear throughout his office would continue into the new century. Casual homophobia endured and would take decades to die out from casual conversation. This locker room talk would be the excuse for Eli Roth's homophobic dialogue in his film *Hostel* (2006).

Eli Roth is the man at the helm of torture-porn horror flick *Hostel* (2006). Written and directed by Roth, the film follows three male friends Josh, Paxton, and Oli traveling through Europe in search of girls, drugs, and good times, but they soon find themselves at the mercy of psychopathic brutalizers who pay an elite "hunting" team to torture people. Blood, gore, and bro dialogue flood the film, and this bro dialogue consists heavily of calling each other "fag" or "gay" as insult and humor.[45] In addition, Josh has an encounter with a man on a train who touches his leg and asks, "What is your nature?"[46] Josh screams at the man and he kicks him out of their train car. Later, Josh bumps into this same man behind a bar and tries to make amends. His friends call him a faggot for doing so. As it turns out, this man, who admits to Josh that he is gay, will be Josh's killer. Ennio Chialo, a horror fan who wrote to *Fangoria* magazine about the film in 2006, felt that this storyline was highly homophobic: "The lesson learned? 'No matter how nice they seem, never be nice to a homosexual, because in the end they'll get you!'"[47] Many queer folks who have seen this film, whether upon its release or years later, are left with a bad taste in their mouth—movies are supposed to be an escape, but there is no reprieve for queer viewers from Roth's homophobic dialogue.

Most concerning was Roth's reaction to critiques from queer folks and their allies. In *Fangoria*'s "Postal Zone," a section that allows people to write into the publication about all things horror, Chialo protested the film's use of gay slurs and blatant homophobia:

> The characters continuously refer to each other as "fag" or "you're gay," and everyone laughs and everything is jolly. But not for a lot of queer rights

supporters.... I understand that this is just a horror film and that it probably won't impact much of society, but as long as movies like this continue to target an audience of teens to late-twenties heterosexual males, issues of anti-gay prejudice will never be satiated.[48]

Roth met this respectful criticism of his film with "mansplanation," the act of disregarding critiques made by non-white, female, or other minority groups for the sake of considering your own opinion more sophisticated because you are male. Roth blames political correctness in his rebuttal to Chialo's concerns and affirms that "boys will be boys":

> Letters like this one reflect a very disturbing trend happening in cinema today: political correctness. This person is clearly out of touch with how young people in America speak. [...] I am trying to write characters who are real and speak the way young American people talk to each other. When someone is acting like a pussy, they call that person a "fag." It does not mean that the person using it is homophobic or is saying that someone afraid to do something is homosexual. [...] Does this person honestly believe that this movie will make people think homosexuals are killers? Come on. Grow up. Get over yourself.[49]

Roth continues by saying this reader should not even be watching horror if they don't want to be offended. Yet, if we do not hold filmmakers responsible for their art, then it is left to be interpreted in whichever way an audience member sees fit. For many, films with dialogue like *Hostel*'s embolden their homophobic ideas and actions. Roth would submit one last response to the criticism against his film to *Fangoria*, furthering his position of indifference for offending others, "I will never sanitize my films or make them safe for fear of offending someone."[50]

The following year, horror metal musician turned director Rob Zombie releases his remake of John Carpenter's *Halloween* (2007). As with Roth's *Hostel*, homophobia rears its ugly head with slurs littered throughout the film. However, while Roth's use of homophobia is more gratuitous, chalked up to young peoples' vernacular, Zombie's frequent uses of homophobic slurs, particularly the f-slur, are hurled by characters the audience is not supposed to empathize with but rather revile, unlike Roth's protagonist trio.

In Roth's second installment of the franchise, *Hostel Part II* (2007), the protagonist is a queer-coded woman, though there is no verbal label confirmation, named Beth. Additionally, the main cast is nearly all women as opposed to the first film's male group of friends. Unlike her friends, Beth has no intention of flirting with men while on vacation in Prague but is open to flirtations from Axelle, a woman who modeled nude for her college art class.[51] Though still misogynistic with respect to how the males of the film, dripping with toxicity, treat Beth and her friends, the film is less xenophobic and the only mention of the word "gay" is in the context of saying a place is lame rather than using it and its offensive slang variations for homophobic purposes. *Hostel Part II* is an example of how Roth had grown in his thinking based on the heavy critiques, such as those from Chialo in *Fangoria*, he faced from *Hostel*. This film is still tethered to the torture-porn trend of post–9/11 horror, so no character is safe from mutilation. One critique that Roth received from countless horror fans and critics was the extreme deaths of his female characters, most of whom were naked during their tortures, as well as having one of the villains, Axelle, be a queer woman, as was the villain from *Hostel* a gay man. Roth's decision to have a queer woman protagonist, though she is level-headed and not fetishized by Roth's writing, does not save Roth from his poor narrative decisions in *Hostel*. A film that has a similar straight misogynistic male arc is *Wrong Turn 2: Dead End* (2007). Queer character Amber is a Latina ex-marine who is continuously sexually pursued by male character Jonesy to the point of viewer nausea. Eventually, Amber verbally affirms that she is queer, "You don't get it, do you? I'm not into men," to which Jonesy replies, "You're a lesbian? How hot is that!" Despite his misogyny and annoying banter about queer women, such as "We are on the same team!" Jonesy accepts Amber for the tough, smart queer woman she is. However, as is the case with Josh of *Hostel*, once the obnoxious male redeems himself as an honest friend to the queer that he had once offended, he is killed, albeit with Amber by his side.[52]

Despite Roth's seemingly evolved mindset and the changes which he made to his second *Hostel* film, his first installment has stood the test of time for what it was in 2006: a graphic, misogynistic, xenophobic, and homophobic film. Filmmakers have a responsibility to not embolden those who wish to harm others either physically or verbally based on their sexuality. It is also important that filmmakers are open to a dialogue of how their privilege can result in a platform on which they help promote homophobic slurs. Homophobic sentiments are in numerous millennia films, whether allegedly harmless or purposeful. In most cases, these sentiments are meant to entertain and be a source of comedy within the film.

The early 2000s gave birth to the blockbuster horror-parody, via the Wayans Brothers: Keenan Ivory, Marlon, and Shawn of *In Living Color* fame. In the *Scary Movie* franchise, the comedian brothers created many gay male characters, yet these characters often leaned towards problematic and were deeply stereotyped. Before the *Scary Movie* films, the wildly popular television program *In Living Color* (1990–1994), created and written by Keenan Ivory Wayans, included a running skit titled "Men on ...," hosted by campy flamboyant black gay film critics Blaine Edwards and Antoine Merriweather, played by heterosexual men Damon Wayans and David Alan Grier, complete with swishy-ness.[53] Both fans and critics of the show have debated whether the portrayal and creation of Edwards and Merriweather are offensive or grant mainstream audiences an opportunity to see queer black male sexuality on screen. Marlon Riggs, an openly gay black independent filmmaker, weighed in on the discussion for a piece by Essex Hemphill in 1990:

> I feel very ambivalent about Men on.... It plays into the stereotypes the dominant culture has of us, but that's not my concern, not that their queens—they're camp queens—but rather it's an image of queens who function in a way that justifies all of the very traditional beliefs about black gay sexuality [...] it plays into a notion of black *gay* sexuality held by the black community. A notion that black gay men are sissies, ineffectual, ineffective, womanish in a way that signifies inferiority rather than empowerment.[54]

The Wayans Brothers' first film, *Scary Movie* (2000) perhaps learned from the mistakes of "Men on..." while sadly still retaining key personality features when creating the character of Ray (Shawn Wayans), a masculine football player with a girlfriend who is not-so-secretly gay. His queer antics throughout the film and its sequel, however, are reminiscent of homophobic tropes sustained by Hollywood and the queer comedic characters of *In Living Color*. Ray continuously alludes to his homosexuality in the forms of consistently coming on to his peers in inappropriate ways, playing the iconic gay club hit "It's Raining Men" by the Pointer Sisters in the car, and excitingly running to the locker room showers as he hits his male teammates on their asses with a wet towel. The horror parody even includes Ray tucking his penis between his legs in front of his friends—such a gesture has great cultural weight thanks to the identical tucking motion by Buffalo Bill in *The Silence of the Lambs*.[55] The Wayans Brothers write Ray's death in the film as being punctured in the brain by a penis through a Gloryhole in the men's room.

Scary Movie parodies Wes Craven's *Scream* (1996), with Ray and antagonist Bobby revealed to be the killers, as were Stu and Billy in Craven's film. Bobby announces during the film's climax that he is gay, even though he spent most of the film trying to have sex with his girlfriend Cindy, and "so is Ray." This storyline reflects on the unspoken alleged queer relationship of Stu and Billy in *Scream* (in *Scream 2*, the character of Randy reflects on the original killers from *Scream*, stating that Billy was a "homo-repressed mama's boy").[56] Ray denies this, even though Bobby informs everyone that Ray "made love to him." *Scary Movie* also has the incredibly transphobic character of Ms. Mann, a girl's gym coach played by female bodybuilder Jayne Trcka. Mann makes several sexual comments toward the girls, even going so far as to sniff girls' underwear in her office. Mann also tells Cindy, *Scary Movie*'s protagonist, that she wanted to get an edge up on the competition in athletic sports, indicating that she made a male-to-female physical transition purely for athletic gain. Despite this inclination, Mann's testicles are exposed to Cindy, later brushing Cindy's shoulder, as Mann tells her, "We all have our little secrets."[57] Mann's predatory, yet meant to be comedic, actions become all the more cynical for an observant viewer when a Nazi SS uniform hangs behind her desk.[58] There has been significant scholarship on the mythical correlation between homosexuality/overall queerness and Nazism. Books such as Richard Plant's *The Pink Triangle* discuss Hollywood's creation of queer Nazis, and ultimately, the erasure of Nazi crimes against homosexuals. Ms. Mann's SS uniform is evidence of the enduring myth of the predatory queer Nazi. Similarly, *The Silence of the Lambs*' Buffalo Bill has Nazi paraphernalia around his house. A swastika-emblazoned bedspread can be seen in the final fifteen minutes of the film.[59] Despite the seriousness behind the legacy of Ms. Mann's casual Nazi SS uniform, Mann, along with Bobby and Ray, was created for comedy. Their queerness in this horror-comedy spoof is both comical and predatory, culminating in the classic homophobic horror tropes of films past. *Scary Movie* parodies twentieth-century horror films, as well as the genre's homophobic history.

Though killed by *Scary Movie*'s end, Ray returns in *Scary Movie 2* (2001), in which, his predatory flirting with his male friends becomes his main storyline, including sodomizing a possessed clown for a laugh.[60] His queerness, however, remains very masculine presenting. This trend of masculine characters being secretly yet not-so-secretly gay continues for two more films with two new characters, Mahalik and CJ, though the franchise had taken a different direction with new writers and a new director using the same characters developed by the Wayans Brothers. Mahalik eyes his male friends' bodies on many occasions and alludes to gay sex in *Scary Movie 3* (2003).[61] Mahalik and CJ are not as stereotyped as Ray is, but they still present subtle problematic stereotypes with their cliché gay behavior. In *Scary Movie 4* (2006), the two men, while parodying the transgressive film *Brokeback Mountain* (2005), finally have sex, and the final scenes of the film show them retreating to the mountain on which they made love to be happy together.[62] It is never explicitly said that they are gay, but rather, their relationship was indeed meant for a comedic side-story as it was in *Scary Movie 3*. Although the comedic-side story, at least Mahalik and CJ survive the film and confirm their love for one another. In addition, while parodying M. Night Shyamalan's *The Village* (2004), the film has a brief side-story of a gay male couple. Upon looking at the couple kissing over-zealously, a village elder states, "This village isn't what it used to be."[63]

On the other end of the horror parody spectrum is camp satire slasher *Psycho Beach Party* (2000) based on the 1987 play by drag legend Charles Busch. The Wayans Brothers' horror spoofs of the *Scary Movie* franchise make no attempt at examining the homophobia embedded in the genre and instead, crank it up to ten. Busch's *Psycho Beach Party*, both an homage and examination of 1960s camp, pokes fun at campy B-movies while acknowledging just how queer the genre really is and subverting queer expectations. Busch himself dresses in drag for his role as Captain Monica Stark, the lead investigator into the murders that seem to follow protagonist Florence "Chicklet" Forrest.

Chicklet is a painfully ordinary girl who just wants to surf and be one of the guys. Within the first ten minutes of Busch's script, Chicklet's less-than hyper-feminine attitude unlike the other 1960s hip girls leads to jibes at her gender identity by the unassuming bully Rhonda. In an exchange with Chicklet at the drive-in snack bar, Rhonda says she heard Chicklet was off to Denmark for the summer, "I heard you were going there to have some sort of operation.... I heard you're having your dick cut off and turning into a girl!"[64] This is an explicit reference to the life of Christine Jorgensen who underwent gender affirmation surgery in Denmark in 1952 to much publicity throughout the world. This is brilliantly placed in a script that uses both subtle historical references and explicit psychoanalysis jargon amongst bright bouncing bikini tops and campy computer-generated wave-shredding. *Psycho Beach Party* additionally makes a clear reference to Alfred Hitchcock's *Psycho* through Chicklet's ominous split personality that alludes to her being the murderer plaguing the beach hopping teens. Horror audiences had been trained since *Psycho* to keep an eye on the mentally unstable character. However, Busch refuses to go where the likes of the *Scary Movie* franchise would: by the end of the film, the killer is revealed to be the Swedish foreign exchange student, not troubled Chicklet. Though, the film ultimately turns out to *be* a film, with a group of teens at the drive-in watching Chicklet wake up in a mental institution, having dreamt the whole thing. There seems to be no malicious intent by Busch with this ending, but rather just a quirky unexpected way to cap it off.

Busch's script analyses the toxic yet homoerotic machismo of early '60s horror B-films as well as the romantic elements in a female best friend relationship. With regards to the male characters, the perfectly sculpted male body is on full display in most beach scenes, along with the cocky surfer bravado, yet something is clear when surfer buds Yo-Yo and Provolony wrestle half-naked not once but twice in the sand. Homo-erotic tones, complete with sultry music and the spraying of tanning oil on the chests and backs of the pair, envelop the scenes. Busch ensures that their forbidden love will be dealt with throughout the film, ending with a big kiss at the tiki-lit luau party. Even Chicklet's best friend Berdine, a geeky independent girl who prefers examining horror film subtext over boys, tries to make her move on "best friend and soulmate" Chicklet but is interrupted.[65]

Though *Psycho Beach Party* made abysmal box office dough and is oft forgotten in the vast catalog of B-movie horror-comedies, the film was a sign of trends to come in the horror genre. Independent filmmakers and studios began producing content not meant to be *Scream*-like blockbusters.[66] Instead, these films would go beyond the usual cookie-cutter formula for horror films and showcase more stories and characters with queer folks in mind.

The Dawn of a New Queer Age

Queer visibility prior to the 2000s is riddled with offensive comedic roles and storylines, as well as stereotypical indicators of queerness. Despite the numerous historical and historical-fiction films regarding the queer experience, most had been about tragedy rather than triumph. Films like *Boys Don't Cry* (1999), about the real brutal death of young transgender man Brandon Teena, and *Philadelphia*, are important and powerful, but they continue a narrative of death and grief for queer folks. Nonetheless, visibility was present, but in many ways to the detriment of the queer community. Film historian Vito Russo explains that

[g]ay visibility has never really been an issue in the movies. It's *how* they have been visible that has remained offensive for almost a century. So no more films about homosexuality. Instead, more films that explore people who happen to be gay in America and how their lives intersect with the dominant culture.[67]

There was a need for new queer stories in the 2000s. Rather than tales that focused on the negatives of being queer in America, now was the time for a new narrative: Americans who just *happen* to be queer, and their queerness not being their main character arc. "Queers do not experience only shame, guilt, or grief," advocate authors Castiglia and Reed of "Queer Theory Is Burning: Sexual Revolution and Traumatic Unremembering" (2012). "[W]e also experience exuberance, defiance, pride, pleasure, giddiness, enthusiastic innocence, outrageous optimism, loyalty, and love [...] as wonderfully and complexly queer as were those in our social and rhetorical pasts."[68] Queer everyday life is bursting with a range of emotions, occupations, families, and friends. Queers with pets, queers enjoying sex, queers participating in holiday celebrations. The queer on film in the 2000s is not only relegated to comedic relief or a victim of murder. If the film is helmed by responsible and conscientious filmmakers, queer characters are multifaceted.

May (2002), directed by Lucky McKee, follows a young woman who was bullied as a child for her lazy eye. May is odd, shy, and has trouble relating to those around her. She falls for a local mechanic named Adam but is also intrigued by her outgoing co-worker at the veterinary clinic, Polly. Polly is infatuated by May and continually tries to seduce her. She helps May get out of her shell and even gives her a cat so May isn't lonely in her apartment. She doesn't know that May has an unorthodox friend, a doll to whom she speaks in the privacy of her home. Despite May's descent into a sadistic killer later in the film, sparked by Adam dumping her and calling her strange, the viewer empathizes with this strange girl just wanting affection. After Adam tries to avoid May, she goes to the arms of Polly, who tells her, "I've

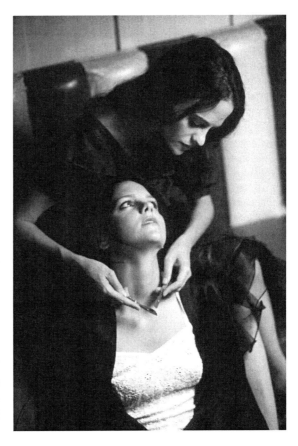

Angela Bettis as May, with two surgical scalpels, seconds away from murdering her flirtatious coworker Polly, played by Anna Faris, in *May* (Lions Gate Films, 2002).

wanted to kiss you since I first saw you." She starts to kiss May. At first, May is unsure, but she slowly begins to realize she enjoys it. Polly asks shy May, "Do you feel weird doing this?" May replies, "I am weird," to which Polly exclaims, "I love weird," and begins to orally pleasure May.[69]

Though Polly and her other lover Ambrosia become victims of May's desire to create a doll out of human parts, much like a modern Frankenstein's Monster, Polly's, as well as May's sexualities, are not to blame for their demise or villainy. They simply are queer women in a horror film, subjected to the fate of many a horror character.

Hellbent (2004), written and directed by openly queer Paul Etheredge-Ouzts, is another horror story where the characters just happen to be queer. The film takes place during the West Hollywood Halloween Carnival, a key gay event and celebration.[70] Eddie, the film's protagonist, is a gay man who works at the police station.[71] He and his friends are preparing for a wild Halloween night in West Hollywood. The entirety of the main cast is queer—across the spectrum are Chaz, a "hedonist and ultra-sexual bisexual"; Joey, toeing the waters of the leather subculture; and Tobey, "a male semi-supermodel doing drag [a tradition at the Santa Monica Boulevard parade] for the first time as a lark."[72] According to producer Steven Wolfe,

> [w]hat is lacking right now are gay films that are just entertainment. We've seen enough coming-out stories and suffering people, and it's time to move into the next phase and portray characters who are just out there in every-day normal life like a lot of us are, and don't have a problem with being gay.[73]

The characters of *Hellbent* are just average men who happen to be gay, enjoying Halloween. But of course, this is a horror movie, so most do not survive. The group of friends is stalked on Halloween night by a Devil-masked serial murderer. Throughout the film, The Devil, as he is referred to by the film writers, kills multiple men, including a gay male couple at the beginning of the film. The Devil, though, does not seem to be targeting queer men specifically, but rather murdering those around him. As it is Halloween night on Santa Monica Boulevard, those around him are predominantly queer men. Etheridge-Outzs assures viewers that these men are not murdered because they are gay, and the villain in the Devil mask is not a gay-basher.[74]

The filmmakers of *Hellbent* were not blind to the fact that their film is majorly a gay film. Film officials even wanted queer participation in the naming process of the film; the poll to decide the film's title was featured on Gay.com.[75] They acknowledged, still, that although their film has cross-over potential to diverse audiences, based on the little positive representation of queer folks in horror films, they felt their film would particularly be a nod to horror queers: "'There is an untold secret out there that plenty of gay people like horror films. We aren't going to hide the fact that this is a gay film.'"[76] The filmmakers of *Hellbent* catered to the cravings of horror queers everywhere: the desire to be represented as human beings who happen to be gay and to be painted as multi-faceted characters in a horror film. The film would be an inspiration for future independent queer horror films centering around gay men including *Kissing Darkness* (2014) and *Killer Unicorn* (2019).

Simply because a film is independent does not mean it will be progressive in its representation of queer life, like *Hellbent*. Some independent films took a different route, opting for the problematic clichés of horror films past. This, of course, involves using queer bodies as props for villainy and victimhood. One such film is the reviled *Switch Killer* (2005), released directly to DVD. Originally titled *Transamerican Killer*, the film follows Jamie, a young woman who escapes from a physically and emotionally abusive relationship with her boyfriend Bobby. Upon announcing that she is leaving him for a woman, Bobby attacks her, "You're breaking up with me for a dyke?"[77] "Dyke" is used throughout the film to refer to both unavailable or queer women by Bobby, who grows a hatred for queer women after Jamie leaves him. Nevertheless, in the first few minutes of the film, Bobby pronounces that he will "change" for Jamie.[78] Ultimately, Bobby becomes a woman through gender affirmation surgery, but for Bobby's motives, to call it such would be an offense to all transgender folks. He only seeks revenge on Jamie, and any woman whom Jamie encounters, by stalking and hiding in the shadows, watching their every move. For the sake of Bobby's insidious motives and not actually identifying as a woman, he/him pronouns will be used for Bobby going forward.

The film is, majorly, girl-on-girl sex scenes and female-centered nudity, as Jamie becomes a stripper in Las Vegas after leaving Bobby. But this nudity is strictly for the heterosexual male audience. In *Switch Killer*, if a woman loves a woman emotionally, she is hurled with "dyke," yet their physical bodies are well on display for the titillation of the male gaze. This film was made by and for this gaze. Having lesbian-identified characters is the extent to which *Switch Killer* shows any sort of queer representation, and it is supremely mishandled. Near the film's climax, Jamie tells her controlling butch girlfriend Brooke that she is not gay, but rather wanted to "switch" to women based on her negative past with Bobby. Hence, the only queer character in the film is essentially a lesbian villain, Brooke, who is controlling of Jamie. Bobby only surgically transitions to a woman in the first place because he wants his girlfriend back, whom he assumes is now a lesbian.

There is no reprieve from bigotry, specifically homophobia and transphobia, in *Switch Killer*. Bobby's transgender persona is reminiscent of Norman Bates in *Psycho*. The film was even mentioned in character dialogue, and Bobby's main weapon while in women's clothes is a butcher knife, like Bates. The ending shows Bobby, after revealing his new post-surgery body to Jamie, murdered by his ex-girlfriend. *Switch Killer* continues the stereotype of transgender folks being confused and their bodies as being monstrous. Bobby exclaims to Jamie, "Look at what you've done to me. Turned me into a fucking freak!"[79] Jamie is revolted by what she sees when Bobby exposes himself to her. Additionally, Bobby as a transgender woman, though to give him that declaration is false because he just changed his external body and does not view himself as a woman internally, is given glowing sinister red eyes that flair when he kills. *Switch Killer* is a film that aims to affirm transphobic stereotypes.

There are ways in which film writers and directors can combat stigmatizing transgender and non-binary folks, and that is through open dialogue with these folks as well as hiring more LGBTQ+ people for film productions. Don Mancini, with his *Child's Play* franchise, develops queer characters and hires LGBTQ+ actors for many of his films. Mancini is gay himself and continues through the decades of *Child's Play* films to include queer characters. In 1998, the franchise's fourth installment *Bride of Chucky* includes a gay character and openly queer actress, Alexis Arquette. Arquette would come out as transgender a few years after the film and undergo gender affirmation surgery in 2006. Mancini's next film would feature, in doll-form, a non-binary and/or transgender character: *Seed of Chucky* (2004).

Glen/Glenda (they/them pronouns), child of Chucky and his doll bride Tiffany, was separated at birth from their parents in the final scene of *Bride of Chucky*. Mancini's use of the names Glen and Glenda for the character is directly invoking the incredibly queer Ed Wood film *Glen or Glenda*. The 1953 film even has a quick excerpt from Glen/Glenda's childhood indicating that his mother was supportive of her (then) son's decision to wear a dress to a grade-school costume ball, while his father disapproved. This would mimic the parental actions of Tiffany and Chucky later in the film.

Six years after their birth in a New Jersey cemetery, "Shitface," named by the cruel puppet master who found them as a baby and took them to the UK, travels to Hollywood to search for their parents after seeing television commercials for a film featuring two dolls with the same "Made in Japan" markings on their wrists.[80] Due to their haircut and how their puppet-master referred to them, Glen/Glenda is initially treated as male. However, upon meeting their parents for the first time, Chucky and Tiffany argue over Glen/Glenda's gender. Tiffany wants to call them "Glenda" while Chucky wants his child to be "Glen." They pull down Glen/Glenda's pants to reveal the genitalia all dolls possess: none. Yet both Chucky and Tiffany assert that Glen/Glenda is the gender that they wish Glen/Glenda to be.

This genitalia scene points out the absurdity of choosing a child's gender, and how parents' expectations and desires get in the way of the child's. In a rather progressive scene, Tiffany and Chucky have a dialogue with Glen/Glenda about who they want to be:

> TIFFANY: "I want a girl!"
> CHUCKY: "I want a boy!"
> GLEN/GLENDA: "You're tearing me apart! What about what I want!"[81]
> TIFFANY & CHUCKY: "What?"
> GLEN/GLENDA: "Doesn't what I want mean anything at all?"
> TIFFANY: "Oh.'"
> CHUCKY: "Okay, tell us."
> TIFFANY: "What do you want, sweet face?"
> GLEN/GLENDA: "I think.... I want to be a boy.... But, being a girl would be nice too."
> CHUCKY: "Well, which is it?"
> GLEN/GLENDA: "I'm not sure. Sometimes I feel like a boy, sometimes I feel like a girl. Can I be both?"
> TIFFANY: "Well, some people."[82]

As a piece of Glen/Glenda's dialogue, "You're tearing me apart!" is a direct reference by Mancini to James Dean's iconic line from *Rebel Without a Cause* (1955). Since his untimely death in 1955, speculation has circled over Dean's sexuality, and he is often considered to have been bisexual. The famous line has become a queer signifier in films and is a conscious addition by Mancini. Following this dialogue, it is ultimately Tiffany who approves of her child's gender identity and/or lack thereof. In the film's final moments, Glen/Glenda's soul is transferred into a set of human twins, with one expressing Glenda's murderous side like her father, and one representing the gentler side as Glen. This allowed Glen/Glenda to exist as both male and female in human form.

"Although neither depiction is an ideal representation of being gender-queer," states writer Vincent Bec for *Gayly Dreadful*, "it is interesting, and even uplifting, to see these characters created in a time before non-binary genders were widely acknowledged in western culture."[83] The prior scene of gender discussion shows two parents genuinely listening to their child talk about who they are. Noreen Giffney and Myra J. Hird in *Queering the Non/Human* discuss just how imperative this

Supportive mother Tiffany gazes at her child Glen/Glenda as distracted father Chucky contemplates a future murderous episode in *Seed of Chucky* (Rogue Pictures, 2004).

scene is. It demonstrates just how absurd it is to argue about your child's gender expression without including them and/or having them lead the conversation:

> In this brilliant intersexual thematic, gender legibility is shown to be important for the parents, not the child, and the film foregrounds the ways in which normative identity requires stable gender. In refusing to be either Glen or Glenda and insisting on being both, Chucky and Tiffany's kid focuses our attention on the horrific effects of heteronormativity and turns attention away from the monstrosity of the ambiguously gendered body.[84]

Glen/Glenda presents a queer possibility for the future of horror, one that will focus more on the harmful social constructs of gender, and the reality that queer folks (and dolls) exist not to be a spectacle, but to have honest storylines. Glen/Glenda's body is not monstrous, but rather, how their parents argue about their gender is what is monstrous. Instead of using Glen/Glenda's body as horror, Mancini uses Glen/Glenda to express to audiences that a person who is non-binary is valid and they must be able to examine their gender identity and sexuality without input from others. Bodies belong to those who inhabit them.

Glen/Glenda is forced to live as a boy for most of their childhood in England as part of a ventriloquist act where they were referred to as male. When given the opportunity to finally be heard, Glen/Glenda expresses a desire to be both male and female, non-binary. In an interview from *Fangoria* magazine, Mancini reflects on Glen/Glenda's question "Can I be both?" by saying he believes Glen/Glenda to be a third sex, or non-binary: "[Glen/Glenda] embodies both the stereotypical traits: femininity is thought of as soft and passive. He has that. And masculinity is defined as harder and more assertive. And he asks, 'Why can't I be both?' And that's a very modern question."[85] Transgender and non-binary folks are not to be confined to heteronormative gender and sexuality boundaries; they live across the LGBTQ+ sexuality and gender spectrum. Glen/Glenda is an example of a child who feels they exist in such a spectrum. Although Mancini is not transgender or non-binary, he has clearly shown that he values having queer characters in his stories. He is willing to analyze heteronormativity and gender fluidity through a horror lens, which allows him to examine the subject in the realm of absurdity.

Jennifer Tilly, star of *Seed of Chucky* as both herself and Tiffany, acknowledges how ahead of its time this film was with regards to its queer inclusions in an interview with *Pride Source*. She did not understand the significance of *Seed of Chucky* in the queer community until fans started having conversations about Glen/Glenda in the context of representation in queer pride parades. Tilly explains that Universal Pictures took notice of the film's queerness, calling *Seed of Chucky* "too funny" and "too gay," a term which Universal thought of as negative.[86] Tilly is referring to the film's gayness attributable to its inclusion of queer camp hero John Waters, who is murdered by acid at the hands of Chucky, and the film's reference to Tilly's lesbian love story from her film *Bound* (1996).[87] In a brief interview with horror queer podcast *Attack of the Queerwolf!*, Mancini elaborates on his queer inclusion, saying he was inspired by films like *Psycho* and states that he infused the film with his own gay sensibility. "Well," he states, "you know what they say: write what you know. I just couldn't resist going full fag with *Seed*. It was also driven simply by a desire to create an interesting character with Glen/Glenda. The movie was a parody of domestic family dramas [...] so Glen/Glenda's gender non-binary status provided the basis for all the conflict."[88] Under Mancini's authority, *Seed of Chucky* is gloriously queer and refuses to paint trans and non-binary bodies as violent and grotesque, despite their physical scary-doll appearance.

The 2000s concluded on an unlikely optimistic note for the future of queer characters in horror with *Jennifer's Body* (2009). *Jennifer's Body* is a story about an intense female friendship that goes through the downs associated with jealousy, insecurity, and demonic possession. Jennifer, played by Megan Fox, is a gorgeous teen girl who is best friends with nerdy Needy, played by Amanda Seyfried. Best friends since childhood, popular Jennifer and meek Needy share a bond that seems uncommon from the outside because of the often-strict social structures of high school. They share tender moments of affection to the point of peers alleging that they are "lesbigay," but also harbor deep competitive feelings toward one another.[89] They reside in the fictional small town of Devil's Kettle, Minnesota, and frequent the town's only bar. There, Needy and Jennifer go to a late-night gig from a visiting emo band called Low Shoulder. Jennifer becomes transfixed by the lead singer who before their set discusses with his band of needing a virgin, their motive soon to be revealed. Suddenly, the bar begins to burn down, and Jennifer and Needy escape the wreckage. Outside, Low Shoulder waits and abducts an in-shock Jennifer in their van, and Needy looks on helplessly. Jennifer appears at Needy's house hours later covered in blood and vomiting up a black mixture of "roadkill and sewing needles."[90] Jennifer has changed—she was used in a sacrifice by Low Shoulder to become a world-famous band. They meant to kill a virgin, however, Jennifer lied thinking virginity would save her. It is a common horror trope that virgins survive at the end of a horror film, therefore such an idea would be on Jennifer's mind when confronted with possible violence. *Scream* character Randy explains this to his peers in the 1996 film as to why Jamie Lee Curtis of *Halloween* is *the* Scream Queen, stating "You can never have sex."[91] The result of the occult ritual is a demon infestation of Jennifer, and she begins to kill her male peers.

What sets *Jennifer's Body* apart from other demonic films is the fixation on Jennifer and Needy's relationship. Jennifer's demonic tendencies are not the main narrative. Throughout the film, Needy and Jennifer share moments of seduction, love, and even lust. After Jennifer devours one of her victims, she goes to Needy's house to sleep in her bed. Needy is startled, and Jennifer begins to slowly kiss her. Needy is confused at first but then reciprocates, laying Jennifer down on the bed for a passionate make-out session. The scene is not exploitive, though, and Megan Fox in an interview with *InStyle* magazine concurs, "That was a real thing that goes on with teenage girls that are discovering their sexuality, and sometimes that's discovering that they love other girls. It's not like that [kissing] scene was even particularly sexual for men. It was more so for any woman who's ever thought, 'I really love my best friend, and I don't necessarily know what that means, but I'm going to figure it out.'"[92] The seduction is brief and ends with Needy confronting Jennifer about her weird behavior, not even mentioning the seduction seconds earlier. Everything moves on as if it never happened.

Jennifer (Megan Fox) plays with best friend Needy's hair (Amanda Seyfried) in the high school hallway in *Jennifer's Body* (20th Century–Fox, 2009). A photograph of them together is in Needy's locker.

Subsequently, Jennifer tells Needy what happened to her after the failed blood sacrifice by Low Shoulder, and Needy asks her to leave. Jennifer does not want to go and asks Needy to "play boyfriend-girlfriend" like they used to as kids.[93] It is in lines like this where, as stated by writer Jossalyn Holbert for *Gayly Dreadful*, "Jennifer and Needy could be more than friends, and that Jennifer could be resisting the urge to *eat* the living hell out of her."[94]

Fox, who is openly bisexual and was so by the film's 2009 release, frequently speaks on the importance of *Jennifer's Body* and how fans of the film have personally told her how much the film contributed to the discovery about their own sexuality. "It's constant a girl will come up to me and be like, 'You had a lot to do with me identifying and understanding that I was gay or understanding that I was bisexual,'" Fox explains in a video segment called "Let's Unpack That" for *InStyle* magazine. "And that is of course, by far, the most moving, rewarding thing that I have experienced in my life: to be a part of something that helped people figure that out, people deal with that, or people feel better about that."[95]

Queer codes are evident in the film's script and direction, both headed by women with director Karyn Kusama and writer Diablo Cody. In the DVD commentary for *Jennifer's Body*, Kusama and Cody confirm that Needy and Jennifer are clearly more than friends, and their complicated relationship borders on toxic. At the film's climax, as Needy is trying to save her boyfriend Chip from Jennifer's wrath, Needy inquires, "I thought you only murdered boys." "I go both ways," proclaims Jennifer as she charges at Needy.[96] This one line alone is Jennifer's tongue-in-cheek sexuality reveal, courtesy of Cody's snarky comedic writing style.

The film was a flop upon release, barely earning its money back. However, *Jennifer's Body* has become somewhat of a cult classic due primarily to its feminist undertones, dark cheeky dialogue, and queer signifiers. The intense love, hate, and friendship of Needy and Jennifer would be similarly shown in *Black Swan* (2010). *Jennifer's Body*, a film with two queer protagonists, would be followed by myriad horror films with queer representation. The film set off a 2010s trend of more queer folks in horror that are written to be multi-faceted leads or endearing side characters without having their stories revolve around their sexual orientation.

CHAPTER 6

Queer Resistance

*Representation and Trump's America
(2010–2021)*

Burgeoning Queer Representation and Politics in the Obama and Trump Eras

2010	*Black Swan*	*Hatchet*			
2011	*Scream 4*				
2012	*Jack & Diane*				
2013	Same-sex marriage is officially legal in the U.S.	*All Cheerleaders Die*	*Curse of Chucky*		
2014	*The Taking of Deborah Logan*				
2015	*The Final Girls*	*You're Killing Me*			
2016	Pulse nightclub is targeted by homophobic shooter	Donald Trump is elected president of the U.S.			
2017	Trump announces plan to ban trans people from serving in the military	*Happy Death Day*	*Cult of Chucky*	*Jigsaw* Blood Donation Campaign Ads	
2018	*Hell Fest*	*Puppet Master: The Littlest Reich*	*Birdbox*	*Truth or Dare*	*Annihilation*	*Unfriended: Dark Web*
2019	*Happy Death Day 2 U*	*It Chapter Two*	*Velvet Buzzsaw*	*The Perfection*	The first Straight Pride parade is held in Boston, MA

Figure 9

At the 1984 Democratic National Convention, Bobbi Campbell, a prominent AIDS activist, advocated for a candidate who would address the AIDS crisis. In his speech, he discussed the need for diverse representation of queer folks in media:

> I have a message for the nation. Very often lesbians and gay men are portrayed as isolated, alienated, and alone or else in a pathetic search for desperate sexuality. I don't think that that's true. And I think that it's important

for people to understand that lesbians and gay men do not exist outside of a context. We exist in the context of the people we love and those that love us.[1]

Campbell's demand for more stories that truly represent the queer experience *as* human experience permeates the 2010s bloody silver screen. An unprecedented amount of 2010s horror stories placed queer folks front and center as protagonists, with films such as *Black Swan* (2010), *Jack & Diane* (2012), and *All Cheerleaders Die* (2013), to name a few. In fact, *Black Swan* was nominated for several film awards, and Natalie Portman won the Academy Award for Best Actress for her role as Nina, a struggling but passionate ballerina who explores her sexuality with both men and women, particularly her antagonist Odile, on screen.[2] The characters in these films follow the guidelines of a horror Final Girl and/or monster. They all experience isolation, alienation, and loneliness—the feelings of which AIDS activist Bobbi Campbell felt in 1984 left the queer community in a pitiful state. However, these same queer characters are given romantic storylines where they yearn for autonomy and are given moments of elation, frustration, curiosity, and struggle.

Openly gay screenwriter Adam Robitel had his directorial debut with *The Taking of Deborah Logan* (2014). Deborah Logan, an elderly woman who is battling early-onset Alzheimer's, becomes the subject of a Ph.D. student documentary in order for her daughter, Sarah, to pay for and keep her mother's house. What begins as a film about a woman in the thralls of a neurological disease, the story becomes one of demonic possession. The freshness of *The Taking of Deborah Logan* is the mother-daughter storyline. Despite being a possession film, the story does not shy away from the complexity of mother-daughter/mother-queer-daughter relationships. Sarah's storyline illustrates the density of the mother-daughter relationship, as well as how her mother reacts to her daughter's sexual orientation which includes nitpicking at her daughter's masculine-presenting clothes and a brief conversation of Deborah catching her ten-year-old daughter kissing another girl.[3] Sarah is a compassionate, frustrated, and loving daughter struggling to take care of her ailing mother. Her character is representative of many queer children who as adults must take care of their elderly parents and the tension that exists between heterosexual parents and queer children.

Sarah's sexuality is not her main narrative, rather, the focus lies in how a daughter pulls together the strength to care for her mother who has not shown great support for her sexuality. Initially, it is revealed that after catching ten-year-old Sarah in their gardening shed kissing another girl, Deborah ships her off to boarding school. However, in a touching turn of events, it was not Sarah's sexuality that led Deborah to send her away, but rather, Deborah was protecting her daughter from child-kidnapper Desjardin, whose soul is now inhabiting Deborah's ailing body and mind. Thus, the story moves back into the horror realm, free from becoming a passé story about a mother finally accepting a queer daughter or a coming-out narrative. In an interview with Waylon Jordan of *iHorror*, director Robitel stresses his desire to tell stories of the human condition: "I've always wanted to be a filmmaker who tells human stories first, filled with all kinds of characters: straight, gay, trans, etc. [*The Taking of Deborah Logan*] centered around a lesbian protagonist. I just wanted the work to speak for itself."[4] The success of *The Taking of Deborah Logan* is Robitel's ability to reject the cliché queer stories that have been told for decades. Robitel successfully ties horror and queer experience together without relying on outdated modes of queer representation. Sarah is nuanced, subtle, and relatable.

A character's queerness not being their main narrative is a relatively modern idea. It allows the complexity of a character to be expressed, even negative sides, to showcase the true diversity of a queer community. Egocentricity, self-delusion, and vanity are on full display in Jim Hansen's independently released *You're Killing Me* (2015) about internet star wannabe George who falls for Joe, a handsome, creepy stranger just released from a mental institution for his murderous impulses.[5] Unlike films past that would surely equate Joe's sinister urges with his queerness, Joe's queer sexuality is inconsequential to the overall plot. Hansen explains in an interview with internet blog *The Binge* that *You're Killing Me* is, rather, Joe's coming out story as a psychopath: "he's basically coming to terms with the idea that he's a serial killer. He's always been gay; I think he dealt with coming out as gay a long time ago, so that isn't the issue in the movie. It's that he's actually coming out as a serial killer."[6]

Like *Hellbent* (2004), *You're Killing Me* is purely a comedy-slasher film starring a nearly all queer cast, both in story and reality, along with being written and directed by openly gay Hansen. While queerness is at the core of the film, queerness is not being analyzed, used, or exploited. Queerness merely *is*, just as heterosexuality *is* and has been a part of a wide variety of film genres since motion picture inception. It is simply background noise.

2010s America teemed with new-found representation in popular culture and within society at large. Often, however, this new representation and recognition of myriad diverse queer stories, experiences, and milestones receives heavy backlash from homophobic and

Joe, played by Matthew McKelligon, covered in blood in one of his many imaginative psychotic regressions throughout *You're Killing Me* (Wolfe Video, 2015).

transphobic Americans. While marriage equality was passed under the Obama administration in 2013, the election of Donald Trump in 2016 marked tough times ahead for queer Americans. Having chosen an openly anti-gay vice president, Mike Pence, Trump signaled to queer Americans that his administration would not be as supportive as Obama's had been. Not only was the election of Trump and the rise of an ultra-conservative fanbase a signal of ominous things to come, but months before his election, the queer community deeply suffered from a terrorist attack, one that would prove to be up until that point the deadliest mass shooting in the history of the United States.[7] On June 12, 2016, a gunman opened fire on a queer nightclub in Orlando, Florida. Fifty people were killed, the majority of whom were queer Latinx folks. It was the deadliest mass shooting in U.S. history and additionally the second deadliest terrorist attack, behind the events of September 11, 2001.[8] The Pulse Nightclub shooting was acknowledged as a homophobic attack based on the popularity and well-known queer status of the nightclub itself. On July 26, 2017, the LGBTQ+ community suffered another blow when President Trump announced his plan, in a series of messages posted to social media platform Twitter, to ban transgender people from serving in the U.S. military.[9]

Despite the heartbreaking and frustrating setbacks queer Americans faced throughout the Trump Administration, film would prove to be more open than ever to the experiences of queer folks. Horror films in particular showcased dozens of queer characters often with dignity and respect to the queer experience. Horror films have always been political, whether extrapolating the intense anxiety of The Cold War in stories of violent alien encounters as in *Invasion of the Body Snatchers* (1956) or having the black hero of a zombie film murdered by white police officers at film's end as seen in *Night of the Living Dead* (1968). The genre examines the American political landscape through a fantastical and horrifying lens. The overall-positive queer portrayals in 2010s horror films could very well be a means to counter the growing hatred and backlash that was aimed toward members of the LGBTQ+ community after the election of Donald Trump and the rise of white supremacist/neo–Nazi movements.

Horror and politics have always been intertwined whether analyzing American racism, societal response to the HIV/AIDS crisis, or police brutality. As part of their marketing campaigns for new films, one of the bloodiest film franchises in history, *Saw*, had organized wildly successful blood donation campaigns since the franchise's inception in 2004. The blood drive, often held around Halloween just in time for *Saw* film premieres, has been a key aspect of the franchise, garnering additional publicity for the infamous torture-porn blood fests that are the *Saw* films as well as giving free movie tickets to donors. In 2017, the campaign took a more political turn, calling out the restrictive blood donation policies that discriminate against queer blood, specifically, queer male blood. These policies have been in effect since the early days of the HIV/AIDS crisis when the Food and Drug Administration (FDA) established a lifetime ban on any prospective male donor who has had sex with a man starting in 1977.[10] This infers that it is "gay blood" that is diseased and therefore unwanted, even though blood donation services are required to screen all participants' blood. The blood drive campaign for *Jigsaw* (2017) spearheaded by Lionsgate studio chief brand officer Tim Palen featured social media influencers with large queer fanbases such as openly gay model Shaun Ross dressed in nurse uniforms. Included on the drive marketing posters was the tagline "All Types Welcome," a direct condemnation of homophobic blood donation regulations. Regarding *Jigsaw*'s LGBTQ+ advocacy, Mark Burg, a producer for the *Saw* franchise stated concretely that "we want this policy changed."[11] This policy was brought to light one year before *Jigsaw* after the 2016 Pulse Nightclub shooting, drawing criticism from more than 100 members of congress including Senator Elizabeth Warren and

Senator Bernie Sanders. In a bipartisan letter from twenty-four U.S. senators led by openly queer congresswoman Tammy Baldwin and Senator Warren, the members called on the FDA to end the discriminatory blood donation deferral policy for queer men:

> During times of tragedy, the American people are quick to demonstrate their resiliency and mobilize in solidarity with victims and affected communities. We have witnessed that compassion as Floridians quickly lined up to donate blood for the wounded. Yet, some of those most touched by this tragedy—members of the LGBT community, who are especially eager to contribute to the response effort—are finding themselves turned away. Due to the FDA's current MSM [men who have sex with men] deferral policy, many healthy gay and bisexual men remain prohibited from donating needed blood.[12]

The *Saw* blood drives resulted in approximately 120,000 pints of blood by 2009. Thanks to advocacy like that from the Saw franchise, the FDA eliminated its ban on queer male blood, though there is a requirement of three months abstinence after gay sexual contact as of 2022. While the Saw franchise is one of the bloodiest, most gruesome, and unforgiving of all time, the promotion of equal opportunity blood donation for queer folks is progressive and hopeful.

Though horror spares few in the thralls of malevolent violence, the genre, more recently, has effectively held a safe space for queer characters to be developed, understood, and taken seriously. Such is the case with *Happy Death Day* (2017) and *Happy Death Day 2 U* (2019) where a reoccurring queer character named Tim receives the chance to acknowledge his sexuality over the course of the two films. He initially appears to be a misogynistic male, but is, as revealed by protagonist Tree, gay. This is similarly done in the 2005 film *Cursed* where a bully named Bo is confronted by Jimmy, a boy he regularly taunts, who tells Bo that he is homophobic for spewing constant gay jokes because he is actually a repressed gay person. Bo later goes to Jimmy's house to tell him he is gay and has a crush on Jimmy. Jimmy rejects him, but they help each other and become friends by the end of the movie.[13]

The revelation of Tim being gay in the *Happy Death Day* series occurs in the first film, and in the second, he is shown lovingly with another man. Tim's appearance is brief in both films. However, these appearances leave a lasting impression on queer viewers for the simple fact that the director chose to include and highlight this seemingly irrelevant storyline to the overall plot. Christopher Landon, who is openly gay and the director of both films, was bullied by his peers as a young man for being perceived as gay and being a misfit.[14] Young

Landon found solace in the macabre, sparking his interest and subsequent dreams of a career in horror.[15] Inserting Tim's story in his films is a nod to all the other queer kids and adults out there, signaling to them that they are seen. Trace Thurman, co-host of the *Horror Queers* podcast, wrote for *Gayly Dreadful* of the significance of Tim's inclusion:

> For queer viewers, seeing themselves represented on screen allows them to not only feel better about themselves, but also contradict the loneliness that they may feel. It's amazing what a simple 5-minutes superfluous subplot in a slasher movie like *Happy Death Day* can do to make someone feel, if only for a moment, that they are not alone in this world.[16]

As America moves forward in the 21st century, queer characters are finally being recognized through film as not an oddity, but as autonomous, complex people. Actor Bex Taylor-Klaus plays Taylor, a female character with a boyfriend, in *Hell Fest* (2018). Though their character is meant to be straight and female-presenting, Taylor-Klaus brought their own queer flavor to the character by not presenting as completely feminine or female, "Audiences responded well to Taylor's hard-femme yet somehow androgynous look," states writer BJ Colangelo for *Bloody Disgusting!*[17] The actor is non-binary, and they present a possibility for the future in film: queer people living their lives without having to explain themselves. "I wanna be able to do everything," explains Taylor-Klaus, and this casting of a non-binary, openly queer individual to play a straight girl subverts the Hollywood trend of casting cisgender, heterosexual folks as queer characters or villains.[18] The fact that Taylor-Klaus was chosen to play this role, as a character who was just one of the gang, is refreshing and a signifier of progress to come. By the late 2010s, queer folks in horror were able to experience more emotion than ever allowed before. They were finally taken seriously within the genre, as well as seen as worthy of full storylines that let them live their queer lives, while still, for example, being changed into werewolves or using witchcraft to bewitch a lover.[19]

Some horror films have decided to confront the homophobia of certain eras of the genre. The horror-comedy satire *The Final Girls* (2015), written by queer men and partners M.A. Fortin and Joshua John Miller, follows a group of teens after having been sucked into the world of the fictional 1980s summer camp slasher flick "Camp Bloodbath," a spoof of the iconic horror film *Friday the 13th* (1980). Complete with stereotypical '80s slasher characters such as the overly-horny misogynistic male and the "girl with the clipboard and a guitar," the film aims at confronting the problematic and often-homophobic dialogue given to many 1980s characters.[20] As the protagonist's friend Chris tries to keep Kurt, the overly-horny misogynistic male, from having sex (as sex summons killer Billy), Chris suggests to Kurt that he should read the articles of his *Playboy* magazine rather than focusing on the nudity.

> KURT: "What are you, a fag? You don't like some nice big hoots, hootin'?"
> CHRIS: "My dads are gay, so shut the hell up."
> KURT: "Yeah right! Gay guys can't have kids. They're too busy going to discos and having sex with each other. It's actually a pretty cool lifestyle."[21]

The film twists Kurt's 1980s homophobia into a possible hidden desire to partake in what he views as a gay lifestyle. Chris only mentions his fathers once, but it places the film in a very contemporary context: post–Marriage Equality (June 2015) and a country that has become more accepting of families headed by queer parents, though there is plenty of work left to do with regards to full equality. *Puppet Master: The Littlest Reich* (2018) echoes this sentiment with the inclusion of a queer female couple. Within minutes of the film's beginning, the women discuss their future together raising a family in 1986 Texas. Unfortunately, these women are murdered by the villain Toulon, who utters "disgusting homosexuals" after overhearing the women's conversation.[22] The film would feature yet another queer female couple later in the story, though their screen-time is limited. Regardless, the inclusion of not one but four queer women is a huge step in any film unrelated to a historical telling of a queer experience.

Don Mancini, the creator of the *Child's Play* franchise, continued his queer inclusion with his 2010s films *Curse of Chucky* (2013) and *Cult of Chucky* (2017). Though neither was theatrically released, both films bring Chucky into a new era of horror that focuses on story rather than slasher gore. *Curse of Chucky* introduces Nica. She is a woman born with a medical condition that tethers her to a wheelchair and is being stalked and attacked by a doll (Chucky). The soul that inhabits the doll is of Charles Lee Ray who was infatuated with Nica's mother before his soul-swapping with a Good Guy Doll in 1988. Nica's family is knocked off one by one by Chucky, including her sister Barb and babysitter Jill. Mancini flips the script with Barb and Jill's storylines as it is initially assumed that Jill is having an affair with Barb's husband, only to be revealed that it is Barb who is sleeping with the babysitter.[23]

Nica's story bleeds into Mancini's next feature *Cult of Chucky*. After Chucky's attacks leave her family dead and her niece missing, sole-survivor Nica is put on trial for their deaths. She is adamant that Chucky, a Good Guy Doll, killed her family. This accusation results in her sentence to be committed to a mental institution for the criminally insane. Terror ensues once Chucky finds where Nica is sent, thanks in part to his former lover Tiffany, now human after the soul-switching voodoo ritual in *Seed of Chucky*. Through another voodoo ritual, a tribe of Chuckys are unleashed on the hospital patients. The film subverts previous Chucky plotlines by finally having Chucky fulfill his desire to enter a human body, but not an expected one. It is Nica's body that he ultimately inhabits. *Cult of Chucky* concludes with Nica, now housing the soul of Chucky thanks to voodoo soul transformation, leaving the hospital and meeting Tiffany face to face, human to human, for the first time since their affair in the 1980s. Nica/Chucky and Tiffany kiss, to which Nica/Chucky realizes his externally-viewed new same-sex relationship and attraction. Tiffany sees beyond Chucky's new female body, for she is in love with Chucky's demented soul rather than its vessel, "Works for me," Tiffany proclaims after their passionate kiss.[24] The film also includes a queer orderly, Carlos, who references his husband in a conversation with Nica in the hospital.

Chucky's soul is in a female body, though this transformation is not meant to signify a transgender experience. Rather, Mancini's goal was to create a new life for Chucky with a partner who does not care whether he was in a male-or-female-presenting body. However, regardless of intent, this queer inclusion is significant to a genre that prioritizes the male killer and slasher. Placing Chucky in a female body with no objection from the historically misogynistic male slasher paves the way for future killers and characters who are not bound to heterosexual/cisgender constructs. In an interview, Jennifer Tilly expresses her excitement for where Mancini is taking the franchise. When reflecting on the final scene of the film where Tiffany and Chucky (now in Nica's body) drive off together, she notes that this scene is a bit of an homage to the 1996 lesbian film *Bound* in which Tilly starred. With regards to Chucky now being in Nica's body, Tilly notes the clear gender-fluid and transgender energy given to the character.[25] Echoing *Seed of Chucky's* foray into genderfluidity and non-binary characters, Nica/Chucky is a step in a more human direction. As a writer and creator, Mancini understands and caters to his queer horror audience. Whether including a gender-fluid doll or wise sissy best friend, Mancini has his audience in mind, and this love is felt and appreciated by myriad queer fans. Vincent Bec, a writer included in the Pride publications for *Gayly Dreadful*, concurs, "Mancini is a gay horror lover and creator who intentionally includes his community in his work, and I feel love and connection when I watch his films because of that."[26] Mancini ensures that his community is included in his art, solidifying a bond between queer creators and queer audiences.

Straight horror directors tend to alienate queer audiences with their queer character and storyline choices. This is not always due to overt homophobia, but rather an ignorance of the violent history of queer folks in America and how queer people respond to these historical triggers in film. This is evident in *It Chapter Two* (2019), directed by Andrés Muschietti. This sequel to *It* (2017), based on Stephen King's iconic 1986 novel, focuses on the parts of the novel which are dedicated to the adult lives of The Losers Club, a group of children who are bonded together by their experiences with bullies, abusive parents, and the terrorization of an evil clown named Pennywise. The film begins with two seemingly random men, Adrian and Don, walking hand and hand through Derry's town carnival. They are in love and discussing their future together outside of Derry, Maine. Soon, they are accosted by teenagers mocking them and hurling homophobic slurs. After verbally defending themselves, and one of them mocking the bullies right back, the couple is attacked. Adrian is viciously beaten, the camera firmly fixed on his face being caved in by the assailants' fists. The beating ends with Adrian being thrown over a bridge. Pennywise soon appears to lend a helping hand to Adrian out of the water. Pennywise subsequently devours his heart, killing him.

Queer audiences turned to the internet to ask others if they had the same feelings after seeing the homophobic attack in theaters: terror, discomfort, and anger. Alas, queer horror fans responded with these same feelings within the opening week of *It Chapter Two*. One viewer reported his experience in a theater to *The Advocate*, where a straight couple behind him and his partner exclaimed "that's gross" as Adrian and Don lovingly kissed on screen. "Seconds later in the movie," he explains, "a group of men echoed these homophobic sentiments, screaming 'faggots' and spitting on the gay couple."[27] It seemed to many queer viewers that the brutal hate crime scene was meant to shock audiences rather than reiterate the scene of which was painted by Stephen King in his 1986 novel. Only the viewers who read King's 1,138-page novel knew of this scene's existence. To all others, the scene appears out of nowhere and is not brought up again for the entire two-hour and fifty-minute film.

King's inclusion of the gay-bashing scene in his book was borne from a real incident in his hometown of Bangor, Maine. In 1984, two years before the publication of King's *It*, Charlie Howard was attacked and killed by a group of teenagers in a homophobic attack.[28] He was walking down the street hand-in-hand with his boyfriend Roy Ogden. As mirrored in *It Chapter Two*, Howard was viciously beaten and thrown from a bridge. King was outraged by the attack and included it in his novel to showcase the evils of humanity. Director Muschetti felt the same in needing to include the scene, citing the scene's relevance to the continuing anti-gay and anti-trans hate crimes in 2019.[29] Good intentions are clear from Muschetti's drive to include the scene. The ignorance, however, lies in camera work and editing. The camera fixed on the attack is brutal to watch. Blood flying, every punch is enough to make an audience wince. This attack is never mentioned again in dialogue, leaving it at face value: a senseless attack meant to shock and startle the audience in the film's opening moments. *It Chapter Two*'s gay couple is used as horror. Adrian's mangled, lifeless body is used as a lasting scare, particularly for queer audiences, and is enough to make the strongest and most open queer couple fearful to hold hands in public lest they too meet Adrian and Don's tragic fate. Kaitlin Reilly posits in a piece for *Refinery29* why the film includes this heartbreaking scene at all:

> The couple in the carnival doesn't feel the need to hide their relationship: They hold hands and kiss because, in 2019, they feel safe doing so. The hate crime suggests that, even in 2019, they could be wrong. It's a disturbing notion, especially in an America that is rolling back protections for LGBTQ+ people. In June [of 2019], the FBI put out a report claiming that anti–LGBTQ+ hate crimes are on the rise. The couple in *IT Chapter Two* are white cisgender men, for trans women of color, the threat of violence has not changed much over the years.[30]

Reilly's comments point to another issue: if this vile homophobic attack can happen to the most arguably safe queer couple, two white cisgender males, where does that leave the remainder of the LGBTQ+ spectrum? Nevertheless, instead of providing visibility for queer people and raising awareness of hate crimes, the hate crime of *It Chapter Two* serves as pornography for homophobes, validating their violent fantasies and fueling queer fears.

The queer men who wrote in *The Advocate* of their homophobic experience while sitting in the theater for *It Chapter Two*, Jonathan Lee and Taylor Drake, felt the powerlessness the film evokes for queer people, and the fire it stokes for homophobes:

> Every time we go out together, we fear our visibility. We fear that walking one inch closer to one another, squeezing our hands for too long, or flirting too loudly might blow our cover and put us in danger of physical or verbal violence. We do not need *It Chapter Two* to remind us that bigotry against the LGBTQ community still haunts America when 18 trans people have been murdered this year, when the [Trump administration] is reversing non-discrimination protections against us, when It was sitting right behind us.[31]

The film attempts to continue some sort of queer resonance in the character of Ritchie, played by comedian Bill Hader. Ritchie, the wise-cracking Loser who hides his emotions behind his comedy, is subtly revealed to be gay. Young Ritchie is fearful of being perceived as gay. After trying to play a video game in the arcade with another young boy, he is mocked by bullies and called a "fairy" and a "fag."[32] Ritchie is seen after the taunts crying on a bench outside. This scene strikes a chord with queer audiences for its portrayal of a young kid so fearful and hurt for being called gay in a small town, and how such taunts can affect the same young kid as an adult, shoving one further into the closet. Adult Ritchie, as Pennywise returns to terrorize each adult Loser with their darkest fears, is confronted again with his hidden queerness. Pennywise confronts him, "I know your darkest secret. Wanna play Truth or Dare? But you don't want Truth, do you?"[33] This is evocative of many a queer child fearful of getting "Truth" in a game of Truth or Dare, afraid of being exposed. The dark secret Pennywise alludes to reignites Ritchie's childhood trauma of being bullied for his perceived queerness.

Unfortunately, *It Chapter Two*'s ending leaves queer audiences, much like from the opening scene, with no catharsis. Throughout the film, there are nods to Ritchie's queerness, but never spoken allowed. The director's choice of verbal omission leaves a bad taste in queer mouths: Muschetti will show a brutal homophobic attack, no holds barred, but not utter a positive word about being queer. The ending shows Ritchie adding to a carving he made as a youth that reads "R + [not revealed]" on a bridge covered with similar etchings devoted to crushes and young loves. Ritchie adds an "E" to signify Eddie, another Loser whom he truly loved as a boy and who died at the hands of Pennywise at the climax of the film.[34] This scene is touching, but only visually. Ritchie never openly discusses his queerness or his romantic love for Eddie. It is only meant to be implied that he becomes proud when gazing upon the grade-school carving of his and Eddie's name on the bridge. Then why not verbally confirm this love, as Adrian and Don had? Jeffrey Bloomer in *Slate Magazine* asks, "[W]hat does it say about this movie that it feels comfortable depicting every crushing blow and desperate cry for help from gay men as they're being bludgeoned but then relies on retro, coded treatment of its only apparently gay principal character, who never gets the dignity of saying who he is?"[35] *It Chapter Two* fails queer audiences, despite its seemingly well-intentioned inclusions. Having a gay-bashing scene to bring awareness to real-life hate crimes is effective *if* there is justice for the oppressed. However, Muschetti did not provide a sigh of relief or echo of triumph for his queer characters, which, in itself, is violent: "the violence of silence and omission," advocate Castiglia and Reed in "Queer Theory is Burning," "is almost as impossible to endure as the violence of unleashed hatred and outright murder."[36] In an era of political dissent and an increase in anti-gay hate crimes, a film with queer violence but no justice or catharsis is maddening to queer audiences. A film with such attributes gives people with anti-gay sentiments titillating ammunition for their prejudices. The same year as the release of *It Chapter Two*, a Straight Pride Parade was held in Boston with openly white supremacist vendors, as a rebuke of the decades of Gay Pride parades.[37] Upset with the growing queer rights movement and increasing openness of sexual orientation and gender identity, straight bigots felt the need to be seen for their heterosexuality, but in a confrontational and slanderous way. Although the turnout for such an event was small, it received mass media coverage, again bringing bigoted minds confirmation of their negative views of queer and transgender folks.

An Ode to Horror's Past (and Hope for Its Future)

Robert Egger's *The Lighthouse* (2019) is the essence of horror's past: sprinkles of thriller, ominous noir, and inevitable Code-era homoerotic subtext. *The Lighthouse*, set in late-nineteenth-century New England, tells the tale of two gruff lighthouse keepers, Ephraim Winslow and Thomas Wake (Robert Pattinson and Willem Dafoe), amid a grueling storm season. The film centers on the often tense, strange, and sensual relationship between the two men, quarantined together on the remote lighthouse property. Shot entirely in black-and-white with shadowy camera angles reminiscent of the great James Whale masterpiece *Bride of Frankenstein*, the tone of *The Lighthouse* is one of ominous mystery where, on the surface, the only mystery to be found is that of Wake, who locks himself away in the lighthouse tower and refuses to let Winslow take a peek at what he does while locked away. However, to those with a keen gay sensibility, the mystery also lies in the subtextual: does Winslow yearn not only for answers to Wake's private lighthouse activities but for Wake himself? Robert Pattinson asserts that his character does so indeed, stating in an interview with *The Huffington Post* that Winslow "sort of wants a daddy."[38] "Daddy" is a term used in the queer male community that denotes the pining of young men toward older, experienced males. Pattinson describes the sensuality of the boss-worker relationship, indicating that there is more than meets the eye when it comes to Wake and Winslow, "there's some kind of [subordinate/dominant] relationship or something where I'm exaggerating in my mind his dominance over me because I kind of want it in a strange kind of way. It always read as a very sensual relationship."[39] The scenes that leap into the realm of romantic attachment, as well as sexual yearning, for the two men are those of drunken nights together, slow dancing, almost kissing, and particularly, when Wake leads Winslow around like a dog, commanding him to bark. Director Eggers supports this underlying "pent-up erotic energy," even including in the script that the lighthouse itself is a phallic symbol, "an erect penis."[40]

Eggers' *The Lighthouse* transcends 2010s horror trends such as jump scares and self-explanatory character arcs in favor of the successful methods of horror's 1930s Golden Age: tension and shadow. The queer subtext, as facilitated by the films of queer horror legend James Whale, is supported by such tension and shadow, the eerie below-the-surface bubbling of queer sexuality, rage, and longing. The two central, and practically sole, characters of Eggers' film are up for interpretation when it comes to their sexuality. An audience can not readily access the inner workings of their minds, but for a queer viewer, their history with creating representation allows for Wake and Winslow to be vessels for queerness. Such a development goes beyond the surface-level characteristics of these two men, much like the early–Hollywood films that trend desperately to keep horror characters from appearing homosexual. Eggers practically celebrates this process of identification and representation-conjuring for queers, where although his script is explicit enough to his actors that these two lighthouse keepers may have hidden desires, a queer viewer can easily indicate the signs they have so long been using for finding representation. In this respect, *The Lighthouse* is an ode to the horror genre's rooted devotion to the subtextual, and essentially, queer viewers. Queer viewers have been essential to the success of the horror genre for this reason: we do not always simply watch a horror movie one time over for cheap scares; rather, we dissect, re-watch, and dissect again to find glimmers of ourselves. With this, comes hope for our future on the bloody silver screen.

Netflix, BIPOC Queers, and Coming Out Narratives

Netflix, an internet-based film and television streaming service, produces a significant amount of content for the queer community. Particularly, Netflix creates content that places BIPOC (black, indigenous, and people of color) in the forefront, including queer BIPOC, some characters being portrayed by openly queer actors. For example, openly gay B.D. Wong is the queer side character Greg in *Bird Box* (2018) and receives an apology from a homophobic neighbor.[41] White and BIPOC queers have also been the stars and protagonists of feature-length films. In 2019, Netflix released two thriller/horror films: *Velvet Buzzsaw* and *The Perfection*. *Velvet Buzzsaw* follows queer art critic and protagonist Mort, played by Jake Gyllenhaal. He openly discusses queer relationships and presents himself as quite queer.[42] Both Greg from *Bird Box* and Mort die in their films, fulfilling the stereotype that the queer doesn't survive. *The Perfection* does the opposite. Lizzie and Charlotte, the film's protagonists, are survivors of a pedophile music instructor and save another little girl from his clutches.[43] They not only survive the film but become their own saviors by working together and triumphing over their oppressors. Not to mention, both women are involved in an extremely intimate love scene and are in love at the film's end. *The Perfection* is a rare film in that both leads are queer women, and one woman is black, Lizzie. She, unlike the black queer men in the *Scary Movie* franchise and the antique dealers in *Blacula*, is not used as comedic relief, nor is she relegated to the sidelines. Russo's *The Celluloid Closet* points to the lack of diversity in mainstream film, where "Hollywood films, content with easy laughs and cheap social comment, have perpetuated a lazy, stereotypical idea of homosexuals in the place of realistic characters who happen to be gay. Homosexuals are a compendium of media-created stereotypes. Gays are a diverse group of real people."[44] In the history of the horror genre, the first openly queer black protagonist in a widely seen film who exists as an autonomous human being without negative stereotypes was not introduced to audiences until 2019 with *The Perfection*. Outside of Netflix, the queer BIPOC, though mainly playing a side character, has been more present than ever.

Queer BIPOC in horror has largely been placed within a romantic relationship with someone of the same sex where their queerness can be affirmed without having clear dialogue to confirm it. *The Puppet Master: The Littlest Reich* (2018), *The Ranger* (2018), and *Unfriended: Dark Web* (2018) all feature queer couples where one partner is a person of color. While *The Ranger*'s queer focus is two male punks, Abe and Jerk, who share little moments of physical or verbal love, *Puppet Master* and *Dark Web* show queer love that is more emotional. *Puppet Master*'s queer female couple discuss their future together, chatting about kids and marriage. *Dark Web*'s queer female couple, Nari and Sarina, announce their engagement to their friends over webchat and air concerns of parental disapproval. Actress Betty Gabriel who plays Nari is also a subtly queer character in Jordan Peele's critically acclaimed *Get Out* (2017). In a quick easy-to-miss scene, Gabriel's character is revealed to have been in a possible romantic relationship with antagonist Rose Armitage based on a photo found in Rose's closet.

Additionally, 2018 granted audiences the opportunity to see a BIPOC coming-out narrative in a horror film. *Truth or Dare* (2018) is a film that revolves around the game Truth or Dare, which a group of friends is forced to play to remain alive. If you don't follow the rules of the game, you are violently killed by your own hand in horrifying ways. Brad Chang, joining B.D. Wong's Greg from *Bird Box* as perhaps the only openly queer people of Asian descent in the history of American horror cinema, is forced to come out to his homophobic father as part of a dare.[45] To his and the audiences' surprise and relief, Brad's father later accepts his son's sexual orientation. Unfortunately, Brad does not survive the game of Truth or Dare, but not because of his "coming-out." *Pitchfork* (2016) also has a coming-out narrative, though with a less sentimental father-son moment. The film centers around a young man, Hunter, as he comes home to his family farm in rural Michigan for the first time since coming out to his homophobic father over the phone. What one would assume would culminate in a dramatic father-son sentimental moment, based on the early-stressing of their tense familial dynamic, turns into a dying father's weak "heart-to-heart" with his gay son as he tells Hunter to "be a man" and mercy kill him.[46]

Though some are more thought-provoking than others, films such as *Truth or Dare* and *Pitchfork* highlight the growing societal exposure of LGBTQ+ folks, especially queer youth, and the struggles they face when coming out to their families. According to the Human Rights Campaign's 2018 LGBTQ Youth Report study, in which over 12,000 queer youth between the ages of thirteen and seventeen participated, only 24 percent of queer youth feel they can securely be themselves around their families, while 48 percent of queer youth who are out to their families are made to feel bad about their sexuality. Additionally, 78 percent of queer youth not yet out to their families often hear negative comments being made by said families, resulting in further stress from the queer child. BIPOC children are more likely than their queer white peers to hear disparaging homophobic or transphobic remarks from family members.[47] While past horror films such as *Bride of Chucky* and *Tammy and the T-Rex* hint or showcase the parent-queer child dynamic and the coming-out process, recent horror films tackle the subject head on, albeit amidst bloody carnage. This does not mean, however, that these narratives are not unproblematic. For the most part, these coming-out experiences for queer characters can and have focused mainly on the reactions of heterosexuals, particularly homophobic parents. The "feel good" element to this narrative seldom lies in the relief of the queer child, finally free from the shadows of the closet and the weight of a secret kept. Rather, the "feel good" moment culminates in a bigoted parent accepting the child—the focus becomes heterosexualized, resulting in the perpetuation of queer as Other. Queer historian Suzanna Danuta Walters perfectly explains the problem of the coming-out film narrative in her book *All the Rage: The Story of Gay Visibility in America* (2001):

> Anguished parents [...] are the staple of [coming out] stories, and, while that tells a sad truth about our experiences, it also serves to move the focus on to the struggle of the parents to "understand" their gay child and learn to "accept" them for "who they are." In the process, gayness still remains something to be "accepted" and "explained."[48]

Rather than the reason for celebration being designated to the self-affirmation of a newly out person, the heterosexual and often bigoted parental reaction to the coming-out of their child becomes the focus of the queer child/character's narrative. Of course, this is a thought pattern for many queer folks if they decide to be open about their sexuality to their families. Questions of acceptance are more than warranted in a world still openly hostile to queerness. But, in a medium dedicated to self-expression such as film (and especially the horror genre), it is disheartening when the subject of the coming-out tale, time and time again, is the parent whose mind needs to be made up about whether they choose to accept their queer child rather than on the newly liberated queer individual. Horror has evolved on outright queerness. However, issues need yet to be addressed in the ways these coming out scenes are written. Input from queer folks must be included in the screenwriting process for the development of queer characters to encompass the complexity of the coming out experience not just for those learning of a loved one's sexuality for the first time, but for the queer person who takes that giant leap from the closet into the unknown.

Ultimately, the 2010s proved that horror is a genre that no longer caters to American homophobic and transphobic sentiments. The genre has become a place where queerness is examined carefully, and true attempts have been made to respect the queer experience. Though films like *It Chapter Two* miss the mark with positive queer representation, responses from horror writers, directors, and actors have been ones of honesty. They exhibit a drive to treat queer characters with empathy. The decade brought fresh queer narratives, ideas, and characters to the bloody silver screen that signify a turn in horror cinema, one that has facilitated the onslaught of queerness in the early 2020s.

Quarantine Streaming: 2020 and 2021

America joined the rest of the world in March of 2020 in a lock-down due to the emerging COVID-19 pandemic. Movie theaters sat vacant for months, with many people not even returning to theaters for the next year, as streaming services took over the film industry to occupy the home audience. Horror fans were crushed to hear that due to the pandemic, horror films like the much-anticipated *Halloween Kills* (2021) and *Candyman* (2021) were pushed back for at least a year to work out streaming deals to facilitate at-home viewing to curb the spread of COVID-19. Though this was indeed unfortunate, lucky queer horror fans were greeted with several horror films, including *Halloween Kills* and *Candyman*, that feature queer characters, and not to mention, an entire film anthology with queer protagonists.

COVID-19 came swift enough to stop the film industry in its tracks. While floundering in the first year of the pandemic, with the thought of losing box office numbers due to theater closings looming, film studios turned to streaming platforms and video-on-demand. One of the first horror movies to swiftly move from theaters to streaming was *Freaky* (2020), which premiered in theaters in October 2020 but moved to streaming two months later. *Freaky* is a slasher comedy helmed by queer filmmaker Christopher Landon (*Happy Death Day*) that features Josh, a gay-best-friend-to-the-protagonist. Having a queer sidekick is nothing new in horror history. However, as stated by non-binary actor Misha Osherovich (Josh) in an article for *Variety* magazine, "My character is a gay best friend, but also a commentary on the gay best friend."[49] Their character, along with other friend-to-the-protagonist Nyla, who is a black girl, were written as autonomous individuals that also serve to put horror's history of marginalization and problematic tropes on display. In one scene, Josh exclaims to Nyla as the slasher that once took the form of Vince Vaughn now inhabits the body of their best friend Millie is on a murderous rampage, "You're black, I'm gay. We are so dead."[50]

Horror cinema has reached a new level of self-awareness that does not aim to alienate marginalized audiences. Iconic slashers such as Candyman and Michael Myers even got in on the action, with David Gordon Green's *Halloween Kills* and Nia DaCosta's *Candyman* including queer male couples, though only one of the couples survived their film's respective massacres. As horror audiences have learned, slashers rarely discriminate against their kills, but what sets these two movies apart is the screen time and character development lent to these couples.

The opus of 2021 queer horror is the widely streamed Netflix trilogy *Fear Street.* The three films, *Fear Street Part One: 1994, Fear Street Part Two: 1978,* and *Fear Street Part Three: 1666* were directed and co-written by Leigh Janiak. Though not queer herself, she and her team of screenwriters devote the entire series to marginalized characters. Low-income households and queer and BIPOC teens are central to the plot of the *Fear Street* films, where characters battle not only several monstrous spectral killers but police oppression, bullying, and a mob on a literal queer witch hunt.

Reclamation is ever-present in the *Fear Street Trilogy,* especially behind the scenes. The three films are inspired by the child and teen-friendly spooky works of R.L. Stine. His *Fear Street* series largely focused on white, suburban, and straight children and teens. Janiak's queer vision for the film adaptation of Stine's stories was intentional. She stated in the *New York Times* that the trilogy was an "'opportunity to tell a story that hasn't been told within that genre very often, if at all.'"[51] This particular story is one of teen lesbian romance that, in Janiak's words, "drove everything" in the overall narrative of the trilogy. Aside from the ghoulish slashers resulting from a town curse hunting the core group of teens, the focus lies not only on the protagonist Deena, who is a queer person of color, but her complicated yet tender relationship with her closeted ex-girlfriend, Sam. Janiak and her fellow writers purposefully subverted Stine's typical storytelling to include voices that have historically been pushed to the margins by the horror genre and made queer and BIPOC issues unavoidable without using tired coming-out tropes or tokenism as placeholders for queer and BIPOC representation. The queer bodies in the *Fear Street Trilogy* are neither fetishized nor expendable; they are not the focus of the horror. The horror, rather, lies in what privileged and ignorant people do to queer lives, not just their bodies, but their emotional and mental well-being.

Queer bodies are no longer a source of horror due to their queerness. For the majority of the twentieth century, queer bodies have been used to shock, scare, and make an audience laugh. They were the punching bags, the sissies, the phantoms and ghosts, the monster under the bed and in the closet—queer horror characters were seldom anything but fodder for American queer fear. Within the past two decades, a new queer age has dawned where queer folks in horror can find empathy from audiences. However, to understand the importance of the decade, past mistakes and triumphs cannot be forgotten. Horror films are time-capsules of their ages. Each film reflects the fears of the era, whether aliens (foreigners), vampires (sexually promiscuous disease carriers), or sadistic serial killers (film menaces that echo the sadism of Ted Bundy or John Wayne Gacy). When looking at the history of horror, queer folks will surely realize for what their bodies were used: violence, comedy, pity, and terror. But if a queer person takes a deeper look, they will also find themselves, as they have in the pages of history, as survivors: final girls, final boys, and final folks in which to place themselves more victoriously than in the monsters American society had tried to stress upon them since *Frankenstein* in 1931. With a deeper understanding of the history of queer bodies in horror, catharsis can be accomplished. This catharsis can be found in the reclamation of painful histories—the ultimate revenge for the misuse of queer bodies in horror.

CHAPTER 7

Catharsis as Revenge

"Much contemporary queer culture uses lesbian and gay heroes from the past to speak to our contemporary struggles with identity and community formation [...] Such tributes to our perverse parents (both textually and cinematically) demonstrate how history can construct our present, but only if we construct our history."—Martha Gever, John Greyson, and Pratibha Parmar, *Queer Looks: Perspectives on Lesbian and Gay Film and Video* (1993)[1]

The Case for Reclamation

"For many lesbians and gays," writes Suzanna Danuta Walters in her 2001 book *All the Rage: The Story of Gay Visibility in America*, "representation was something you *created.*"[2] In 2016, due to a mistake in the film-streaming service's webpage, Netflix named *The Babadook* (2014), an Australian horror film based on a spooky children's book character and a mother's descent into madness, an LGBTQ+ film despite no reference to queerness in its narrative. What started as mass confusion over a possible misunderstanding of the film's plot turned into a glorious embrace for the ghoulish Babadook by members of the queer community. Queer folks have since adopted the dark creature as a queer symbol in a comedic but honest way. Queer folks dress as the Babadook in gay pride parades, create works of art with the Babadook adorned with rainbows, and full discourse of the now-iconic Babadook has surfaced to much internet acclaim. Eren Orbey of *The New Yorker* asserts that "the Babadook's new fabulousness seems to align, quite reasonably, with queer readings of better-known beasts such as Frankenstein and Freddy Krueger. Like those other misunderstood figures, he originated in anonymity, shunned by the traditional folks whom his presence threatened."[3] The re-appropriation of this horror monster is

representative of the need and desire by queer folks for more queer signifiers in popular film, as well as indicative of the queer community's
sense of humor.

In this same vein, queer folks have developed an unusual system of
identification. Historically, queer characters have seldom been heroes,
relegated to villains or useless side characters with little to no backbone. Due to this unfortunate lack of positive representation, queer
folks have largely had to identify with these perceived villainous characters due to their overt or covert queerness (i.e., Dr. Pretorius, Countess
Marya Zaleska, the Babadook). We have become accustomed to identifying with the villain based on the historical fact that film has censored
us and designated us as scapegoats for villainy. As a result, marginalized people, so starved for representation, continue to take these horror
monsters as their own to celebrate as *anti-heroes*, a character that over
the past few decades has become widely popular which whom to identify for their being subversive. Additionally, in an effort to pave the way
for future identification as heroes rather than villains, Final Girls are
being reclaimed from horror films' past. Many of the horror characters
being reclaimed have sufficient reason to be, especially the triumphant
Final Girls, the backbone of the genre since the end of the Universal
monster era (the 1930s-1950s). Final Girls are being taken en masse by
queer folks eager to be embodied by strong, sympathetic, androgynous
victors of oppression, aspects that surely hit close to home for those
across the wide queer spectrum.

Reclaiming the Final Girl

The Final Girl in horror has largely been presented as a straight cisgender white woman. As straight white faces have dominated horror
films since their inception, the appearance of the Final Girl has become
clichéd and assumed. For films with little to no minority representation,
fans of horror who are black, Asian, gay, transgender, Latinx, queer, or
any other race, gender, or sexual orientation other than the stock model
for the sole survivor in horror films have to find themselves within the
characterizations of the Final Girl. Although her appearance may be
deceiving, searching for horror representation beyond the physical can
be rewarding for individuals, especially queer folks. If one looks beyond
the white female face of the Final Girl, personality traits and attributes
can be found to be inspiring and a reflection upon the queer experience.
The Final Girl may just be a pretty face on the outside, but inside she
is teeming with courage, strength, and the tenacity to survive hulking

slashers and high school bullies, attributes many queer folks have developed to endure a queerphobic society.

Carol J. Clover, film and gender scholar and Final Girl expert, dissects what a Final Girl represents in the horror canon. Her book *Men, Women, and Chainsaws: Gender in the Modern Horror Film* develops a theory for what the Final Girl means to a horror film, and what attributes she possesses that make her a feminist hero. The Final Girl tends to be the sole character to be developed psychologically, where she has brains and brawn in times of danger, and ultimately defeats the villain by film's end.[4] Audiences identify with her because she tends to be the only sensible character. Even if she makes mistakes along the way, like running up the stairs when she should sprint out the front door, the Final Girl's humanity is recognized. She is the one to take down the oppressor, and for that, the audience cheers her on. "She is by any measure the slasher film's hero," explains Clover. "The Final Girl has not just manned herself; she specifically unmans an oppressor."[5]

The Final Girl possesses the qualities needed to not only save herself, because it is usually the case that no one comes to her rescue, but also avenge all those killed and abused by the oppressor, the horror villain. Her heroism is not gendered, however. Despite the nickname given to the surviving women of horror movies, the Final Girl is not traditionally or stereotypically feminine. She is a conglomeration of male and female, rendering herself non-binary. As Clover states,

> She alternates between registers [of masculine and feminine] from the outset; before her final struggle she endures the deepest throes of "femininity"; and even during that final struggle she is now weak and now strong, now flees the killer and now charges him, now stabs and is stabbed, now cries out in fear and now shouts in anger. She is a physical female and characterological androgyne.[6]

The idea that the Final Girl is non-binary is revolutionary for the identification by gender-queer folks. Films such as Brian De Palma's *Carrie* allow for identification by the bullied outcasts who seek only to fit in but reach a breaking point of which, unfortunately for Carrie White, there is no return.

In the tragic horror/sci-fi Stephen King tale of Carrie White, Carrie is an insecure girl in high school who has been bullied since childhood by her peers. De Palma's film adaptation begins with the hurling of tampons at Carrie's bleeding body during her first menstrual period in the gymnasium showers and culminates with the dumping of pig's blood upon her crowned head at the prom.[7] Not to mention, Carrie has been seen through the eyes of her religious-zealot mother as a walking sin due to her signification of her mother's fornication, as well as Ms. White's fear of Carrie's telekinesis.

Though not queer herself, Carrie's story echoes the experiences that queer youth have faced for centuries: being told you are sinful for your feelings, demonized by religious parents or churches, and being outcasted by "normal" society for being different. Queer folks have been told by society and those close to them that their queerness is a beast within, like Carrie's telekinesis. When Carrie first realizes her powers, she fears what she might be. However, as the film continues, she practices her powers and grows to appreciate their uniqueness while still yearning to be a part of high school society. She even tells her mother that she is not sinful because God had made her this way.[8] When one embraces their inner "beast," meaning they embrace the parts of themselves that society deems wrong, their loving and enjoying of horror is symbolic of the loving of their queerness. Andrew Tudor in "Why Horror? The Peculiar Pleasures of a Popular Genre" explains, "'Beast within' diagnoses are generally claims applicable to all human beings—to be human [...] is to contain the beast, whatever its specific causation."[9] Queer viewers of films like *Carrie* that experience a protagonist having a "beast within," and using the alleged beast rather than suppressing it, find solace in seeing someone revel in their difference, harnessing inner power, rather than suppressing it as queer youth are told to do. When Carrie, as stated by Joseph Maddrey in *Nightmares in Red, White and Blue: The Evolution of the American Horror Film*, "unleashes the sublime fury of a woman scorned, orchestrating the violent collapse of the mini-society that has no place for her," queer folks get the revenge they have craved after centuries of abuse by various oppressing forces or people.[10] Though Carrie is murderous, queer folks can see and interpret her deadly telekinetic powers as a victory for queers everywhere, and they too can safely place themselves within the fictional carnage. Harry Benshoff, author of *Monsters in the Closet*, elaborates, "Just as some lesbians might find pleasure in the image of the lesbian vampire avenging herself upon straight society [as Countess Zaleska does in her final moments in *Dracula's Daughter* before she is shot down], so might some spectators rally around the queer psycho-killer."[11] In the instance of the queer psycho-killer, as can be represented by Carrie White, they are not celebrated for their murderous leanings, but rather what they represent in the reality for queer folks: the desire to see their oppressors get their comeuppance, and through the bloody silver screen which provides safety, queer spectators can see a mini-victory in a queer killer taking their revenge. Such is the case with Angela Baker in *Sleepaway Camp II: Unhappy Campers* and *Sleepaway Camp III: Teenage Wasteland*.

Benshoff continues, though, by stating that these psycho-queers, and their use as tropes in horror, are used as scapegoats in reality, arguing that

> the resultant connotative and cumulative effect of such images on non-queer spectators remains retrogressive. Even as gay and lesbian people become more visible in "real life," killer queens continue to abound on the screen. And even when the films themselves problematize these figures by linking them to social oppression ... they nonetheless still reaffirm for uncritical audiences the semiotic overlap of homosexual and violent killer.[12]

Here, however, Benshoff makes a case for the reclamation by queer folks of the horror genre and its monsters. Through the understanding of queer-codes, as stressed by Vito Russo, and acknowledging the use of the queer body in horror as horror, queer folks are equipped to place the monsters, as well as the Final Girls, in a place of not violence and bloody-gore, but in a place of understanding, critique, and identification.

    Carrie is an extreme example of revenge of the oppressed, something viewers would probably not wish upon their enemies. Nevertheless, catharsis is found through the rising of the bullied and the oppressed. As stated by author Vivian Sobchack,

> Adolescent Carrie is a pitiful victim of her culture who evokes sympathy [...] whose outrage, however horrific and excessive its expression, is a response to a comprehensive betrayal [of both parent and peers] [...] Carrie's fury is as justified as it is frightening—irrational in its power and force, perhaps, but rationally motivated.[13]

Carrie White's violent revenge soothes the pain of the queer viewer and allows them to safely feel relieved that an oppressed person triumphed. When asked by horror magazine *Scream* whether she feels *Carrie* is a story for the young, bullied, and alienated, "a celebration for these people," Sissy Spacek, star of *Carrie*, said she believes "that everyone at some point in their life felt like Carrie, especially in high school and I think that's why people connected with her. It's healthy to find catharsis through characters in film."[14] Carrie's telekinesis does not only represent revenge, but when her powers are used for good or protection, they offer a positive message to queer viewers, catharsis: who you are is okay and take pride in your inner power/strength despite what the outside world tells you.

    Carrie White is not a textbook representation of a Final Girl. At the film's end, Carrie is brought down by her powers, triggered by the night's scorching events and the attempted murder by her shame-engulfed mother whom she kills in self-defense: boulders, pebbles, and rocks rain

Fragile Carrie White (Sissy Spacek) walks home from school after the traumatic arrival of her first menstrual period in *Carrie* (United Artists, 1976).

down on the home she and her mother share, and Carrie is effectively
stoned to death. This is an ending fit for a classic Universal movie monster (or that of a witch) and what is left of the town is saved from Carrie's wrath, along with the life of Sue Snell, the redeemed classmate who
tried to help a tortured Carrie White. However, Sue is no Final Girl,
though she is the sole survivor of prom night. She did not have a climactic battle scene with the wide-eyed telekinetic Carrie, nor did she
become a hero. Carrie, on the other hand, despite her apparent monstrosity and her death at film's end, signifies all that a Final Girl can be
to queer viewers, and how queer folks can use subtext in otherwise heterosexual film plots to find themselves in horror characters.

The power of the Final Girl, other than her clear skills and smarts
in battle, is the re-appropriation by queer folks of her body as a magnet for subtext. Subtext is extremely powerful with regards to placing one's queer self in the shoes of an on-screen hero. In the story of

Carrie White, by acknowledging her as a victim of child abuse and high school bullying and torment, a queer person can use the subtext to place themselves in Carrie White's world. Her world is a place where queer people have been and will be time and time again. Through her pain, they re-experience and understand their own, but from a safe distance. This also goes for the clear-cut Final Girls like Nancy Thompson in *A Nightmare on Elm Street* who, thanks to Clover's theoretical Final Girl lens, can be viewed in a new light. Nancy Thompson is a young high school student dealing with the bizarre death of her best friend Lisa and chronic nightmares of a burned man in a red and green sweater: child murderer Freddy Krueger.[15] Although she appears to be the cute girl-next-door, Nancy's powers reside not in physical beauty but rather in her courage to take on Krueger in her dreams and her ability to bring him into the real world when no one else would or could. She outsmarts the villain, as well as physically battles her oppressor. Heather Langenkamp, who stars as Nancy in the film, spoke with queer publication *Gay Times* about the importance of her character to queer horror fans. She was shocked at first to find that many young gay men identify with Nancy, who to them is a key character in the movie, more so than Langenkamp originally thought.[16] Additionally, within the context of Nancy's narrative in the first *Nightmare on Elm Street*, queer women can see themselves in the all-American girl-next-door. Nancy, though she has her boyfriend Glen played by young heartthrob Johnny Depp, seldom thinks romantic thoughts of him. They are friends more than anything, offering to protect each other from the malicious Freddy Krueger. Early in the film, Glen tries to initiate sex to a distracted Nancy at her best friend Tina's house (Nancy is comforting Tina while she is home alone and plagued by the fear of the man in her nightmares). When Glen begins to make out with Nancy, she shuts it down, "Glen, not now. We are here for Tina, not ourselves."[17] Glen again alludes to the two having sex later at Nancy's house while there to watch over her as she has a nightmare, to which Nancy rebuffs his insinuation. Nancy is a character with a mission: protect her friends and kill Freddy Krueger. She has no time for teenage activities, which is one of the main attributes of nearly all Final Girls.

The character of Nancy has grown into the Scream Queen legacy and has a cemented status as one of the quintessential Final Girls in all of horror cinema.[18] Similarly, Jamie Lee Curtis, who portrays the young heroine Laurie Strode in John Carpenter's *Halloween* (1978), has solidified herself as an iconic Final Girl.[19] Crystal Williams, a writer featured in *Gayly Dreadful*, a queer independent internet publication, reflects on the significant Final Girl identifications by members of the queer

community, specifically for transgender folks, as seen through the harrowing experience of Laurie at the hands of slasher Michael Myers. For
Williams, Myers' persistence in pursuing his victim, Laurie, was representative of the pressures they felt about abusive family members as
well as an abusive world. "That pressure," Williams explains, "is something I live with on a daily basis [...] but when I experience it in media, it
takes some of that raw tension and fear away from me. [T]here is a calm-
ing and healing nature about experiencing those feelings in something
other than reality."[20] Final Girls like Laurie represent hope in a place of
despair, and triumph in the face of near-death and abuse.

A Nightmare on Elm Street and Halloween are not meant to be
queer. Nevertheless, the character of the Final Girl in each, as well as
across the spectrum of horror, can be used as a vessel for queer experience, oppression, and hope. "'[T]he final girl," explains author Maddrey,
"represents not boyishness or girlishness but monstrous gender, a gender that splatters, rips at the seams, and then is sutured together again
as something much messier that male or female.'"[21] Though the Final
Girl's essence is non-binary, as theorized by Clover, her body becomes a
place in which queer folks can project their experience and find solace
in seeing themselves triumph on screen and seeing their tormentors,
whatever or whoever the tormentor represents to them, die by their own
queer hand. Joshua Anderson, in his essay "The Final Girl: A LGBTQ
Representation," states that "[t]he journey through that confusion [of
coming to terms with your sexuality] is—in essence—the journey that
these final girls take while they are chased and battered almost to the
brink of death. For those of us who grew up in a world where what we
were learning about ourselves was considered immorally or internally
wrong."[22] For decades, queer folks and their bodies have been used by
and for horror. Bruised and bloodied, the bodies of queer horror characters had primarily seen abuse and ridicule, their lives used for evil
deeds or jokes. The increasing identification by queer folks of the Final
Girl signifies the psychological need to repair the damage horror has
inflicted upon queer bodies and minds in the past, and a need for reclamation of a genre that has explicit queer roots, but lost sight of such
roots somewhere throughout the twentieth century. This need for reclamation is a response to the bullying of queer folks from horror films and
society at large.

Mark Patton of A Nightmare on Elm Street 2: Freddy's Revenge has
come full circle in his lifetime with Freddy Krueger. Once holding disdain for the film that made him famous and repulsed by Hollywood, he
now feels that there is a power in Jesse Walsh for himself and queers all
over the world. "I have such compassion for the beautiful young man I

was," Patton explains in *Rue Morgue* magazine (2019). "I wish I could go back and help him navigate the life of an artist."[23] Patton has taken on the affectionate term of "Scream Queen" given to him by queer fans of *Freddy's Revenge* after having once been repelled by the idea. On March 3, 2020, Patton brought his story to the masses with directors Roman Chimienti and Tyler Jensen for the DVD release of their documentary *Scream, Queen! My Nightmare on Elm Street*. The documentary examines Patton's experiences making the infamously gay film, the backlash, his departure from Hollywood, the HIV/AIDS crisis, and the journey with finding peace with the writers of the film that plagued him for decades. Patton acknowledges the power of Jesse for queer fans in his documentary—he reminisces about a young queer horror fan who saw himself in Jesse, the Final Girl, able to conquer the oppressor and "kick Freddy's ass."[24]

It is extremely powerful to find oneself, as a queer person, in a medium that does not always respect people like us. Watching the Final Girl defeat the villain is the ultimate allegory for queer folks to find the courage they need to beat the inner and outer demons that try to strike them down. In addition to finding oneself in the Final Girl, reclamation of characters that for decades meant to oppress queer folks are now

Director Roman Chimienti standing behind Mark Patton who wears his Scream Queen crown in a publicity still for the documentary *Scream Queen! My Nightmare on Elm Street* **(Virgil Films, 2019).**

used as weapons against the oppressor.[25] Catharsis lies in the reclamation of words, actions, and media representations that have been used to harm marginalized populations, and horror has proven itself to facilitate such catharsis. Though, like Jesse Walsh fending off nightmarish Freddy Krueger or Mark Patton reliving the pain of the film's gay codes in *Scream, Queen!*, sometimes it takes going through hell and back to find it.

Testimony: Horror Queers in Their Own Words

Queer fans of the horror genre find themselves among the monsters and Final Girls. Due to the homophobic history of the horror genre despite its queer roots, misrepresentation and lack of representation leave many queer fans in the dark closet of oppression. Additionally, due to the homophobic elements of horror films that use queer bodies and voices *as* horror, some queer folks have forced themselves back into the closet for fear of society's perception of them as the monsters they see on screen. Queer theorist Michel Foucault once suggested that with repression, "'[t]here is not one but many silences.'" "Indeed," continues Benshoff, "homosexual repression—as it might exist within an individual psyche rather within society at large—is still a potent formulation in how one might understand the homosexual and/or homophobic dynamics of many horror films."[26]

When I interviewed queer horror fans for this book, the majority spoke of the oppression felt by the queer community, and importantly the identification with those oppressed in horror films. Monsters and Final Girls alike have been identified by queer folks as manifestations of the cruelty and brutality inflicted on the queer community. They also signify the resilience and bravery of members of the queer community to survive in a world seemingly bent on shoving them back into the shadows.

Through email and the social media platform Instagram, I asked fellow queer fans of horror questions regarding their draw to the horror genre, where they saw themselves in horror films, and how horror reflects moments in queer history.

1. As an LGBTQ+ person, what drew you to horror in the first place?

2. Do you identify with a particular story or character in horror? Why?

3. Based on the history of LGBTQ+ rights in American history, what parallels do you see exhibited in the horror genre?

As to include their voices rather than solely my own, here are selections from their responses, including their pronouns, age, sexual orientation, and favorite horror film.[27]

AJ N.: He/Him/They/She/Her, 33, Gay; Favorite Horror Film: *Candyman* (1992)

When I was younger, horror was a way of shocking me out of my anxiety and depression. It was a fantastic leap into someone else's problems and having to confront them in ways that were either extreme or just flat-out terrifying and impossible. I have not seen a significant increase in representation that doesn't involve trope-ridden storylines. I am still looking for much better representation that actually feels like progress and not like a poorly executed "honorable mention."[28]

Jordan F.: 31, He/Him, Gay; Favorite Horror Film: *The Thing* (1982)

I think my first experience within the horror community was catching the ending clip of Child's Play *(1988) at a restaurant back when I was four. I was reintroduced to the horror genre by seeing ads on TV for* The Blair Witch Project *(1999) and* Sleepy Hollow *(1999). I actively sought out these movies because they were different from the norm I was used to at the ages of nine and ten, like Disney films and Nickelodeon. Once I saw my first horror film, I was hooked on the blood, gore, and terror they brought.*

I feel if there was any character in horror I identify with, it would probably have to be MacReady from The Thing. *Even when shit got to be as extreme as it did for him and the crew of people he worked with, he was able to keep a cool head, for the most part, and work through the problems they faced and protect the planet from the possible threat it could have faced. He handled things probably about as well as I would have.*

The strongest parallels I think of for LGBTQIIA+ rights and a trend in horror is during the AIDS epidemic of the 80s. When looking at the films the horror genre was offering, A Nightmare on Elm Street 2, The Thing, The Blob *(1988), and* The Fly *(1986), a common theme in these movies is an alien or foreign entity invading a person(s) body and disturbing common, everyday life for the character and causing chaos, i.e.* The Fly *or* The Thing, *or disturbing conservative, family values America, i.e.,* Nightmare 2 *or* The Blob.[29]

Evan: 37, Homosexual; Favorite Horror Films: *Alien* (1979), *The Hunger* (1983), *The Wicker Man* (1973), and *The Thing* (1982)

I've always loved monsters. Monster movies are my favorite horror, much more than slasher films.

I usually identify with the monsters. I definitely feel a kinship with Frankenstein's Creature and Clive Barker's Nightbreed *characters. I also feel very empathetically for Carrie and for Dr. Frank-N-Furter from* The Rocky Horror Picture Show.

There's the obvious outsider/misfit narrative of the monsters, but there's also the identification with the way femininity and sexuality are punished in the genre, as well as the femmes taking back power and killing their assailants. There are often issues of which monsters "pass" for "normal" and who cannot pass.[30]

JP W.: He/His, 34, Gay; Favorite Horror Film: *The Texas Chainsaw Massacre* (1974)

Horror has always been in my life. Both my parents are big horror fans, so I was introduced to them at a very early age, everything from the Universal classics right up to the "psychological thrillers" of the 1990s. As I got older, my interest grew and grew, and it finally occurred to me why. So many of these films are based on the idea of ostracization, the understood person shunned for reasons outside of their control and being turned into something monstrous. It doesn't take much to understand why anyone from any marginalized community would find that interesting. Plus, I think a lot of these movies managed to comment on that with a sense of dark humor, unlike so many of those uber-serious dramas, and I love that.

I find the Cenobites relatable, at least in the first two Hellraiser *films before they became unwatchable garbage. I find it interesting how they are treated as monsters, essentially being judged by their appearance, despite their actually being quite neutral and unbiased. They, like myself and all queer people, are angels to some and demons to others.*[31]

Nan: She/Her, 32, Lesbian; Favorite Horror Films: *The Thing* (1982) and *Nightbreed* (1990)

I grew up watching low-budget campy Sci-fi original horror movies and Tales from the Crypt *(1972). I like horror aesthetics (like costuming, makeup, Claymation special effects); the dark storytelling to explore a topic of specific fears, mindset of a culture; and pop culture discussion through the grotesque medium of horror.*

I'm really drawn to supernatural, slasher, and occult horror films. I find it hard to identify with queer people in horror when queer people are demonized, extremely stereotyped, or a subtext [...] But I have enjoyed recent horror movies with queer representation, like Hellbent *and Netflix's* The Haunting of Hill House *(2018).*[32]

I can see the role queer people in American history and horror storytelling shifting slowly towards a more inclusive representation thanks to LGBTQ rights, and queer people getting a voice to tell their renditions. Growing up in the '80s and '90s, the queer representation I saw in horror was a reflection of how gay people were treated. Sleepaway Camp *is an excellent example of a dramatized way that my peers, media, schools, and professionals like* The American Psychiatric Association, *saw homosexuality as a disorder or a disease. As a young gay, watching* Sleepaway Camp *felt like a clear portrayal from the heteronormative horror storytelling that showed two gay fathers endangering their children, a nature vs nurture storyline to force a transphobic misunderstanding of a child murdering their fellow campers. Paired with* The Rocky Horror Picture Show, *displaying queer non-heteronormative people as a threat from another planet, growing up as a gay kid and then as an adult kicked out of my childhood home at 19, working jobs where I was threatened to be fired if [I were] "discovered for being a homosexual," horror films with queer people reflected a lot of shame and confusion, and sent a strong message of queer people [that they are] "other," often badly disordered, not really even human.*

More recently in the last few years with the strides of the LGBTQ+ community, acceptance, and changing the lexicon within the queer community itself (like terms of non-binary, genderqueer, etc.) there seems to be a small shift in horror movies as well. Movies like Jennifer's Body *with a lesbian, although tragic storyline, was a huge shift from* Sleepaway Camp *and how differently queer people were seen in the '80s vs 2000s. Movies like* Hellbent, *a slasher moving featuring gay men and drag queens, and more recently* IT Chapter 2 *opening with the horror and fear of a gay hate crime, is a positive reaction to the rights that the LGBTQ community is gaining in America within the last few years; and offers queer people, directors, and actors, to tell horror. It gives me hope for more queer representation and a more diverse perspective of an LGBTQ+ narrative in the horror genre.*[33]

Anonymous: He/Him/His, 30, Gay; Favorite horror film: *Suspiria* (2018)

I think [I was drawn to horror in the first place] because it was so dynamic and taboo—no other genres were as interesting to me. The characters, particularly the villains, were different but still had power.

The new form of final girl is a character that I'm really drawn to—Susie in Suspiria *(2018), Thomasin in* The Witch *(2015), Dani in* Midsommar *(2019). These are characters that reclaim their agency and power and aren't punished for it. In previous years, they would have been the straight-up villains, but I like that the narrative is changing.*

I think we are still cast as the villains in society—threatening family values, etc. What's interesting is that now, the pushback is also coming from within our community, from sectors that believe we need to assimilate with the heteronormative framework. I see queerness as like being the witch in the woods. You know she's there, and you ignore her existence unless you need something from her. I don't think there is anything wrong with being the "villain"—which is probably why I love the Susies and Danis of the genre![34]

Jeffery: He/Him, 27, Gay; Favorite Horror Movie: *Suspiria* (1977)

Growing up gay, especially in the South, you are often made to feel like you are an abomination. Therefore, when I watch horror films, I can identify with both the monster and the final girl fighting for her life, because I am, by my very nature, both.

Specifically, I love the character dynamic between Freddy Krueger and Nancy Thompson in the original Nightmare on Elm Street *film. Krueger ... carried out revenge on all those that tormented him through their children. Thus, it appeals to my ego and the idea of experiencing revenge on those that tormented me. Nancy, an innocent, spends the entire movie trying to survive, that which is chasing her. For her, it was Freddy; for me, it was bullies.*

I find the idea of zombie films to closely resemble the ways in which gay men were viewed in the late '70s and '80s. At the time, AIDS was an epidemic and rapidly spreading. The same applies to zombies. It's that existential fear of infection.

'90s representation was nonexistent and even today, you would be pressed to find a film that contains a gay character. The only memorable LGBTQ+ character I can think of is Angela from Sleepaway Camp, *a repressed, abused, neglected transgender [person], that was considered a monster and murdered out of torment. So, my feelings are, there isn't much reflection, as there isn't much representation, which I suppose is a reflection itself.*[35]

AJ E.: They/Them, 35, Queer; Favorite Horror Film: *Halloween* (1978)

Growing up, watching and reading horror was an escape, and I loved the luridness of it. I've always loved the otherness of horror and connected to that, even as a queer kid. I identified with the monsters, those who were misunderstood and shunned by society.

I identify with the final girl. Or, in my case, as a non-binary person, the final grrrl.[36] *Specifically, Laurie Strode in* Halloween. *But really, any final grrrl. I identify with the survivor. As someone who has been through a lot of trauma in my own life, it is cathartic to, in these movies and sometimes books, face the trauma and stab it in its fucking face. I have always connected with the strong, resilient underdog type. I think it makes sense, too: I don't know a community more tenacious and resilient than the LGBTQ community.*

I think horror is very, very queer. I think that's why I love it so much! I mean, James Whale was subverting the genre in the 1930s. Bride of Frankenstein *is queer af and he was a gay director at a time when the Hays Code specifically vilified 'deviant' sexuality, including any LGBTQ expressions.*[37] *Despite that, he created these movies in which people could empathize with the monster. There's so much queerness in* The Old Dark House *that it's hard to see how the censors let the film exist in its current form; then again, straight people are very good at ignoring that which is just beneath the surface. Horror has always felt like this bold proclamation of "we're here, we're queer, and we're not fucking going anywhere!"*

I think horror is the one genre that has ALWAYS belonged to us. I think, as queer people, we get used to being 'othered' so much, that we either lean into it or dive back into the closet. I prefer to lean in, a la Dr. Frank-N-Furter. Being a horror fan feels like being with my people. Not all queer people love horror, of course, and there are plenty of straight people into it, too—though I would debate their viewing experience is a bit different from mine—but horror has always been my preferred form of affirming entertainment.[38]

For Your Viewing Pleasure

The following are the American queer horror films referenced in this book, along with dozens of films that missed the cut. After scouring the horror genre, I have found that all of the following films have LGBTQ+ themes and/or characters (both negative and positive), queer-phobic and/or pro-queer dialogue, and several have openly LGBTQ+ actors, writers, and directors. While some of the queer themes and characters exhibited in these films are visible (and audible), as we have learned, one can train themselves to see the subtextual. Since this book's publication, I hope that there will be many more films to include on this list, and perhaps some that were missed or later reclaimed by queer viewers decades after their release. I encourage you to add them.

The 1930s

Frankenstein (Whale, 1931)
Freaks (Browning, 1932)
The Old Dark House (Whale, 1932)

Bride of Frankenstein (Whale, 1935)
Dracula's Daughter (Hillyer, 1936)

The 1940s

Rebecca (Hitchcock, 1940)
The Seventh Victim (Robson, 1943)

The Uninvited (Allen, 1944)

The 1950s

Glen or Glenda (Wood, 1953)
Suddenly, Last Summer (Mankiewicz, 1959)

The 1960s

Psycho (Hitchcock, 1960)
Homicidal (Castle, 1961)
The Haunting (Wise, 1963)

The Fearless Vampire Killers (Polanski, 1967)

The 1970s

Beyond the Valley of the Dolls
(Meyer, 1970)
Multiple Maniacs (Waters, 1970)
Blacula (Crain, 1972)
The Last House on the Left (Craven,
1972)
Love Me Deadly (Lacerte, 1972)
Invasion of the Bee Girls (Sanders,
1973)
The Exorcist (Friedkin, 1974)
The Fun House / Last House on

Dead End Street (Watkins,
1977/1979)
Phantom of the Paradise (De
Palma, 1974)
The Texas Chainsaw Massacre
(Hooper, 1974)
The Rocky Horror Picture Show
(O'Brien, 1975)
Carrie (De Palma, 1976)
Alien (Scott, 1979)

The 1980s

Cruising (Friedkin, 1980)
Dressed to Kill (De Palma, 1980)
Savage Weekend (Paulsen, 1980)
An American Werewolf in London
(Landis, 1981)
Butcher, Baker, Nightmare
Maker / Night Warning (Asher,
1981/1983)
Fear No Evil (LaLoggia, 1981)
Final Exam (Huston, 1981)
Night School (Hughes, 1981)
Student Bodies (Rose, 1981)
The Slumber Party Massacre
(Jones, 1982)
A Polish Vampire in Burbank
(Pirro, 1983)
The Hunger (Scott, 1983)
Sleepaway Camp (Hiltzik, 1983)
Fright Night (Holland, 1985)
A Nightmare on Elm Street 2:
Freddy's Revenge (Sholder, 1985)
Once Bitten (Storm, 1985)
Aliens (Cameron, 1986)

Critters (Herek, 1986)
The Hitcher (Drebit, 1986)
Monster in the Closet (Dahlin, 1986)
Night of the Creeps (Dekker, 1986)
The Lost Boys (Schumacher, 1987)
The Monster Squad (Dekker, 1987)
Redneck Zombies (Lewnes, 1987)
Twisted Nightmare (Hunt, 1987)
Curse of the Queerwolf (Pirro,
1988)
Fright Night Part 2 (Wallace, 1988)
Hellbound: Hellraiser II (Randel,
1988)
Hide and Go Shriek (Schoolnik,
1988)
My Best Friend Is a Vampire
(Huston, 1988)
Night of the Demons (Tenney, 1988)
Sleepaway Camp II: Unhappy
Campers (Simpson, 1988)
Sleepaway Camp III: Teenage
Wasteland (Simpson, 1989)
Warlock (Miner, 1989)

The 1990s

Def by Temptation (Bond, 1990)
Frankenhooker (Henenlotter, 1990)

Maniac Cop 2 (Lustig, 1990)
Nightbreed (Barker, 1990)

Silent Night, Deadly Night 4: The Initiation (Yuzna, 1990)
Troll 2 (Fragasso, 1990)
Poison (Haynes, 1991)
The Silence of the Lambs (Demme, 1991)
Bram Stoker's Dracula (Coppola, 1992)
Jason Goes to Hell: The Final Friday (Marcus, 1993)
Ticks (Randel, 1993)
Interview with a Vampire (Jordan, 1994)
Tammy and the T-Rex (Raffill, 1994)

Hellraiser: Bloodline (Smithee, 1996)
Scream (Craven, 1996)
Scream 2 (Craven, 1997)
Wishmaster (Kurtzman, 1997)
Bride of Chucky (Yu, 1998)
The Faculty (Rodriguez, 1998)
Psycho (Van Sant, 1998)
The Haunting (de Bont, 1999)
House on Haunted Hill (Malone, 1999)
Idle Hands (Flender, 1999)
The Rage: Carrie 2 (Shea, 1999)

The 2000s

American Psycho (Harron, 2000)
Cherry Falls (Wright, 2000)
Leprechaun in the Hood (Spera, 2000)
Psycho Beach Party (King, 2000)
Scary Movie (Wayans, 2000)
Urban Legends: Final Cut (Ottman, 2000)
The Brotherhood (DeCoteau, 2001)
The Brotherhood II: Young Warlocks (DeCoteau, 2001)
Elvira's Haunted Hills (Irvin, 2001)
Ghosts of Mars (Carpenter, 2001)
Hannibal (Scott, 2001)
The Forsaken (Cardone, 2001)
Scary Movie 2 (Wayans, 2001)
Soul Survivors (Carpenter, 2001)
Cabin Fever (Roth, 2002)
May (McKee, 2002)
The Brotherhood III: Young Demons (DeCoteau, 2003)
Freddy vs Jason (Yu, 2003)
Jeepers Creepers 2 (Salva, 2003)
Scary Movie 3 (Zucker, 2003)
Club Dread (Chandrasekhar, 2004)

Dawn of the Dead (Snyder, 2004)
Hellbent (Etheredge-Ouzts, 2004)
Seed of Chucky (Mancini, 2004)
The Sisterhood (DeCoteau, 2004)
Straight from the Crapper (Friedman, Ferrin, Paiko, Spitz, & Kaufman, 2004)
Switch Killer (Hail, 2004)
Bad Reputation (Hemphill, 2005)
The Brotherhood IV: The Complex (DeCoteau, 2005)
Cursed (Craven, 2005)
The Devil's Rejects (Zombie, 2005)
House of Wax (Collet-Serra, 2005)
October Moon (Collum, 2005)
Bug (Friedkin, 2006)
Hatchet (Green, 2006)
Hostel (Roth, 2006)
The Night Listener (Stettner, 2006)
Poultrygeist: Night of the Chicken Dead (Kaufman & Friedman, 2006)
Scary Movie 4 (Zucker, 2006)
Slither (Gunn, 2006)
Yeti: A Love Story (Deyoe & Gosselin, 2006)

Cthulhu (Gildark, 2007)
Days of Darkness (Kennedy, 2007)
The Gay Bed and Breakfast of Terror (Thompson, 2007)
Halloween (Zombie, 2007)
Hostel: Part II (Roth, 2007)
Planet Terror (Rodriguez, 2007)
Suffering Man's Charity/Ghost Writer (Cumming, 2007)
Wrong Turn 2: Dead End (Lynch, 2007)
Return to Sleepaway Camp (Hiltzik, 2008)
Berdella (Taft & South, 2009)

The Brotherhood V: Alumni (DeCoteau, 2009)
Cabin Fever 2: Spring Fever (West, 2009)
Edgar Allan Poe's The Pit and the Pendulum (DeCoteau, 2009)
George: A Zombie Intervention (Seaton, 2009)
The Last House on the Left (Iliadis, 2009)
Night of the Demons (Gierasch, 2009)
Sorority Row (Hendler, 2009)
Stan Helsing (Zenga, 2009)
Jennifer's Body (Kusama, 2009)

The 2010s

Black Swan (Aronofsky, 2010)
The Brotherhood VI: Initiation (DeCoteau, 2010)
The Last Exorcism (Stamm, 2010)
ZMD: Zombies of Mass Destruction (Hamedani, 2010)
"I Was a Teenage Werebear," in *Chillerama* (Lynch, 2011)
"Burn," in *The Summer of Massacre* (Castro, 2011)
Red State (Smith, 2011)
Scream 4 (Craven, 2011)
Wrong Turn 4: Bloody Beginnings (O'Brien, 2011)
Jack & Diane (Gray, 2012)
ParaNorman (Butler, 2012)
Sorority Party Massacre (Jones, 2012)
All Cheerleaders Die (McKee & Siverston, 2013)
The Brides of Sodom (Creepersin, 2013)
Carrie (Peirce, 2013)
Curse of Chucky (Mancini, 2013)
Evil Dead (Álvarez, 2013)

Hatchet III (McDonnell, 2013)
Horns (Aje, 2013)
Scary Movie 5 (Lee, 2013)
A Girl Walks Home Alone at Night (Amirpour, 2014)
"J Is for Jesus," in *ABCs of Death 2* (Ramalho, 2014)
Jamie Marks Is Dead (Smith, 2014)
Kissing Darkness (Townsend, 2014)
Lyle (Thorndike, 2014)
The Taking of Deborah Logan (Robitel, 2014)
Zombeavers (Rubin, 2014)
Condemned (Gesner, 2015)
Cooties (Milott & Murnion, 2015)
The Final Girls (Strauss-Schulson, 2015)
Green Room (Saulnier, 2015)
Hansel vs. Gretel (Demaree, 2015)
Victor Frankenstein (McGuigan, 2015)
You're Killing Me (Hansen, 2015)
The Amityville Legacy (Ferguson & Johnson, 2016)
Home (Lin, 2016)

The Love Witch (Biller, 2016)
The Neon Demon (Refn, 2016)
Pitchfork (Packard, 2016)
Alien: Covenant (Scott, 2017)
Another Yeti: A Love Story: Life on the Streets (Deyoe & Gosselin, 2017)
Better Watch Out (Peckover, 2017)
Cult of Chucky (Mancini, 2017)
Happy Death Day (Landon, 2017)
Annihilation (Garland, 2018)
Bird Box (Bier, 2018)
Hell Fest (Plotkin, 2018)
Killer Unicorn (Bolton, 2018)

Puppet Master: The Littlest Reich (Wiklund, 2018)
The Ranger (Wexler, 2018)
Truth or Dare (Wadlow, 2018)
Unfriended: Dark Web (Susco, 2018)
3 from Hell (Zombie, 2019)
Darlin' (McIntosh, 2019)
Happy Death Day 2 U (Landon, 2019)
It Chapter Two (Muschietti, 2019)
The Perfection (Shepard, 2019)
Velvet Buzzsaw (Gilroy, 2019)

2020s

Bit (Elmore, 2020)
Freaky (Landon, 2020)
The New Mutants (Boone, 2020)
The Scary of Sixty-First (Nekrasova, 2020)
Candyman (DaCosta, 2021)
Fear Street Part One: 1994 (Janiak, 2021)

Fear Street Part Two: 1978 (Janiak, 2021)
Fear Street Part Three: 1666 (Janiak, 2021)
Halloween Kills (Green, 2021)

Chapter Notes

Introduction

1. Abigail Waldron and Jeffrey, "Queer Horror Questionnaire" (September 23, 2019).

2. Elizabeth Ewen and Stuart Ewen, *Typecasting: On the Arts and Sciences of Human Inequality, a History of Dominant Ideas* (New York: Seven Stories Press, 2006), 487.

3. Boze Hadleigh, *The Lavender Screen: The Gay and Lesbian Films—Their Stars, Directors, and Critics* (New York: Citadel, 2001), 14.

4. Harry M. Benshoff, "The Monster and the Homosexual," in *Horror, the Film Reader,* ed. Mark Jancovich (New York: Routledge, 2002), 95.

5. Simon Watney, *Policing Desire: Pornography, AIDS, and the Media*, second edition (Minneapolis: University of Minnesota Press, 1987), 42.

6. Hadleigh, *The Lavender Screen*, 16.

7. *Ibid.*

8. "Lesbian, Gay, Bisexual, and Transgender Health," *Healthy People*, Office of Disease Prevention and Health Promotion, accessed April 2020.

9. Mark Jancovich, *Horror, the Film Reader* (New York: Routledge, 2002), 13.

10. Eric Garber and Lyn Paleo, *Uranian Worlds: A Guide to Alternative Sexuality in Science Fiction, Fantasy, and Horror* (Boston: Hall, 1990), 15.

11. Normality: conformity to the dominant social norms.

12. Robin Wood, "The American Nightmare: Horror in the 70s," in *Horror, the Film Reader*, ed. Mark Jancovich (New York: Routledge, 2002), 31.

13. Alexander Doty, "There's Some-thing Queer Here," in *Making Things Perfectly Queer: Interpreting Mass Culture* (Minneapolis: University of Minnesota Press, 1993), 15.

14. Andrew Tudor, "Why Horror? The Peculiar Pleasures of a Popular Genre," in *Horror, the Film Reader*, ed. Mark Jancovich (New York: Routledge, 2002), 54.

15. Doty, "There's Something Queer Here," 16.

16. Richard Dyer, *Heavenly Bodies: Film Stars and Society* (London: Routledge, 2004), 4.

17. bell hooks, "The Oppositional Gaze: Black Female Spectators," in *Movies and Mass Culture*, ed. John Belton (London: Athlone Press, 1999), 253.

18. *Ibid.*, 255.

19. Joseph Maddrey, *Nightmares in Red, White and Blue: The Evolution of the American Horror Film* (Jefferson: McFarland, 2004), 30.

20. Allison Graham, "'The Fallen Wonder of the World': Brian De Palma's Horror Films," in *American Horrors: Essays on the Modern American Horror Film* (Urbana: University of Illinois Press, 1987), 130.

21. Trace Thurman, "Shove It Down Their Throats—Why Queer Representation in the Media Matters," *Gayly Dreadful* (blog), June 3, 2019, https://www.gaylydreadful.com/blog/2019/6/3/shove-it-down-their-throats-why-queer-representation-in-the-media-matters.

22. Vito Russo, *The Celluloid Closet: Homosexuality in the Movies*, revised edition (New York: Harper & Row, 1987), 92.

23. Brian Pronger, *The Arena of Masculinity: Sports, Homosexuality, and the*

Meaning of Sex (New York: St. Martin's Press, 1990).

24. Christopher Castiglia and Christopher Reed, "Queer Theory Is Burning: Sexual Revolution and Traumatic Unremembering," in *If Memory Serves: Gay Men, AIDS, and the Promise of the Queer Past* (Minneapolis: University of Minnesota Press, 2012), 147.

25. *Ibid.*

26. Anneke Smelik, "Bodies-Without-Organs in the Folds of Fashion: Gilles Deleuze," in *Thinking Through Fashion: A Guide to Key Theorists*, ed. Agnes Rocamora and Anneke Smelik (New York: Bloomsbury Academic, 2015), 169.

Chapter 1

1. Michael Bronski, *A Queer History of the United States* (Boston: Beacon Press, 2011), 104–5.

2. *Ibid.*, 119.

3. Benshoff, *Monsters in the Closet*, 32.

4. William J. Mann, *Behind the Screen: How Gays and Lesbians Shaped Hollywood, 1910–1969* (New York: Penguin, 2002), 123.

5. *Ibid.*, 122.

6. *Ibid.*

7. Benshoff, *Monsters in the Closet*, 32.

8. Russo, *The Celluloid Closet*, 255.

9. *Ibid.*

10. Further analysis can be found in Fiona Sampson's *In Search of Mary Shelley: The Girl Who Wrote Frankenstein* (London: Profile Books, 2018); Fern Riddell, "Does It Matter If Mary Shelley Was Bisexual?" *The Guardian*, November 7, 2019.

11. Mann, *Behind the Screen*, 185.

12. *Ibid.*

13. Benshoff, *Monsters in the Closet*, 39.

14. Caleb Kaltenbach, and Matthew Vines, "Debating Bible Verses on Homosexuality," *The New York Times*, June 8, 2015.

15. Lester D. Friedman and Allison B. Kavey, "It's Still Alive: The Universal and Hammer Movie Cycles," in *Monstrous Progeny: A History of the Frankenstein Narratives* (New Brunswick: Rutgers University Press, 2016), 113.

16. Friedman and Kavey, "It's Still Alive," 116.

17. Russo, *The Celluloid Closet*, 50.

18. Maddrey, *Nightmares in Red, White and Blue*, 101; *Freaks* (1932; Metro-Goldwyn-Mayer).

19. Maddrey, *Nightmares in Red, White and Blue*, 15; the "transvestite" mentioned here will be discussed in Chapter 4.

20. *Ibid.*

21. Lugowski, "Queering the (New) Deal," 5.

22. Hadleigh, *The Lavender Screen*, 20.

23. Benshoff, *Monsters in the Closet*, 36.

24. Russo, *The Celluloid Closet*, 45.

25. *Bride of Frankenstein*, directed by James Whale (1935; Universal City, CA: Universal Pictures, 1999), DVD.

26. Mann, *Behind the Screen*, 164.

27. *Ibid.*, 184–5.

28. *Ibid.*, 187.

29. Friedman and Kavey, "It's Still Alive," 117.

30. *Ibid.*, 125

31. *Ibid.*, 142.

32. *Ibid.*

33. *Ibid.*

34. Russo, *The Celluloid Closet*, 50.

35. Jonathan Katz, ed., "1935: Dr. Louis W. Max; Aversion Therapy (Electric), 'Low Shock Intensities Had Little Effect,'" in *Gay American History: Lesbians and Gay Men in the U.S.A.* (New York: Thomas Y. Crowell, 1976), pp. 164–165.

36. James Curtis, *James Whale: A New World of Gods and Monsters* (Boston: Faber and Faber, 1998), 254–55.

37. *Dracula's Daughter*, directed by Lambert Hillyer (1936; Universal City, CA: Universal Pictures, 2001), DVD.

38. *Ibid.*

39. *Ibid.*

40. *Ibid.*

41. Jonathan Katz, ed., "1933: Dr. La Forest Potter; Psychoanalysis and Hormone Medication, 'Some we would probably kill. Others we would cure,'" in *Gay American History: Lesbians and Gay Men in the U.S.A.* (New York: Thomas Y. Crowell, 1976), 162.

42. *Dracula's Daughter* (1936; Universal Pictures).

43. Benshoff, *Monsters in the Closet*, 80.

44. *Ibid.*

45. *Dracula's Daughter* (1936; Universal Pictures).

46. *Ibid.*

47. *Ibid.*

48. Hadleigh, *The Lavender Screen*, 207.

49. *Dracula's Daughter* (1936; Universal Pictures).

50. Lugowski, "Queering the (New) Deal," 19.

51. Andrea Weiss, *Vampires & Violets: Lesbians in Film* (New York: Penguin, 1993), 90.

52. Weiss, *Vampires & Violets: Lesbians in Film*, 104.

53. Bronski, *A Queer History of the United States*, 124.

54. *Ibid.*

55. Russo, *The Celluloid Closet*, 107.

56. *Ibid.*

57. Leisa D. Meyer, "The Myth of Lesbian (In)Visibility: World War II and the Current 'Gays in the Military' Debate," in *Modern American Queer History* (Philadelphia: Temple University Press, 2001), 273.

58. Rhona J. Berenstein, "Adaptation, Censorship, and Audiences of Questionable Type: Lesbian Sightings in 'Rebecca' (1940) and 'The Uninvited' (1944)," *Cinema Journal* 37, no. 3 (1998).

59. Maddrey, *Nightmares in Red, White and Blue*, 21.

60. Berenstein, "Adaptation, Censorship, and Audiences of Questionable Type," 17–18.

61. *Ibid.*, 21.

62. Bronski, *A Queer History of the United States*, 182.

63. Russo, *The Celluloid Closet*, 102.

64. Judith Butler, "Imitation and Gender Insubordination," in *Inside/Out: Lesbian Theories, Gay Theories*, ed. Diana Fuss (New York: Routledge, 1991), 20.

65. Patrick Higgins, ed., *A Queer Reader* (London: Fourth Estate Limited, 1993), 148.

66. Bronski, *A Queer History of the United States*, 178.

67. Higgins, ed., *A Queer Reader*, 149, 166.

68. Jonathan Katz, ed., "1950–1955: Witch-Hunt; The United States Government versus Homosexuals," in *Gay American History: Lesbians and Gay Men in the U.S.A.* (New York: Thomas Y. Crowell, 1976), pp. 91–105, 91.

69. Bronski, *A Queer History of the United States*, 179.

Chapter 2

1. Maddrey, *Nightmares in Red, White and Blue*, 75.

2. Russo, *The Celluloid Closet*, 107.

3. *Ibid.*, 63.

4. *Ibid.*, 107.

5. *Ibid.*, 107–8.

6. Benshoff, *Monsters in the Closet*, 131.

7. *Ibid.*, 99.

8. *Ibid.*, 84.

9. *Ibid.*, 128.

10. Les Fabian Brathwaite, "Hays'd: Decoding the Classics—'Suddenly Last Summer,'" *IndieWire*, March 31, 2014; Vidal was an openly bisexual man, once proclaiming "that everyone is bisexual"; Judy Wieder, *Celebrity: The Advocate Interviews* (New York: Advocate Books, 2001), 127.

11. Russo, *The Celluloid Closet*, 116.

12. *Ibid.*, 108.

13. *Ibid.*, 116, 118; *Suddenly, Last Summer*, directed by Joseph L. Mankiewicz (1959; Los Angeles: Columbia Pictures, 2000), DVD.

14. Lee Gambin, "You're a Vile, Sorry Little Bitch!" *Fangoria*, 2015, 56.

15. Bronski, *A Queer History of the United States*, 186.

16. *Ibid.*, 190.

17. "The Simple Life of a Busy Bachelor: Rock Hudson Gets Rich Alone," *Life*, October 3, 1955, pp. 129–132.

18. *Psycho*, directed by Alfred Hitchcock (1960; Hollywood: Paramount Pictures, 1998), DVD.

19. Julia Grant, "'A Thought a Mother Can Hardly Face': Sissy Boys, Parents, and Professionals in Mid–Twentieth Century America," in *Modern American Queer History* (Philadelphia: Temple University Press, 2001), 118.

20. Hadleigh, *The Lavender Screen*, 27.

21. Russo, *The Celluloid Closet*, 156.

22. *The Haunting*, directed by Robert Wise (1963; Los Angeles: Metro-Goldwyn-Mayer, 2003), DVD.

23. Patricia White, "Female Spectator,

Lesbian Specter: *The Haunting*," in *Inside/Out: Lesbian Theories, Gay Theories*, ed. Diana Fuss (New York: Routledge, 1991), 157.

24. *Ibid.*

25. *Ibid.*, 161.

26. *Ibid.*, 162.

27. *The Haunting* (1963; Metro-Goldwyn-Mayer).

28. *Ibid.*

29. *Ibid.*

30. Russo, *The Celluloid Closet*, 158.

31. David France, *How to Survive a Plague: The Story of How Activists and Scientists Tamed AIDS* (New York: Alfred A. Knopf, 2016), 18.

32. Bronski, *A Queer History of the United States*, 222.

33. "Trends: Where the Boys Are," *Time Magazine*, June 28, 1968.

34. Maddrey, *Nightmares in Red, White and Blue*, 59.

35. Bronski, *A Queer History of the United States*, 199.

36. Phil Brown, "Still, Waters' Runs Deep," *Fangoria*, November 2012, 27.

37. *Multiple Maniacs*, directed by John Waters (1970; Burbank: New Line Cinema, 2017), DVD.

38. Lady Divine brings up fellow murderer David's involvement with the murder of Sharon Tate. "Had yourself a real ball that night, didn't you?" David retorts that Divine was there as well; *Multiple Maniacs* (1970; New Line Cinema).

39. Brown, "Still, Waters' Runs Deep," 28.

40. *The Last House on the Left*, directed by Wes Craven (1972; Boston, MA: Hallmark Releasing, 2002), DVD.

41. Russo, *The Celluloid Closet*, 162.

42. Benshoff, *Monsters in the Closet*, 180.

43. Robin R. Means Coleman, *Horror Noire: Blacks in American Horror Films from the 1890s to Present* (New York: Routledge, 2011), 121–22.

44. *Ibid.*

45. Red spray paint was used as a substitute for mace which was forbidden to use, according to "The Sexes: The Lavender Panthers," *Time*, October 8, 1973; "The Sexes: The Lavender Panthers," *Time*, October 8, 1973.

46. *The Rocky Horror Picture Show*, directed by Jim Sharman (1975; Los Angeles: 20th Century Fox, 2000), DVD.

47. Hadleigh, *The Lavender Screen*, 133.

48. Russo, *The Celluloid Closet*, 52–53.

49. Queer folks were seen as deviant by Nazi Germany, and many were sent to concentration camps. While homosexual men were branded with a pink triangle on their camp attire, homosexual women had a black triangle, signifying mental disease and their designation as "asocial," sewn on their clothes.

50. Lester D. Friedman and Allison B. Kavey, "Mary Shelley's Stepchildren: Transitions, Translations, and Transformations," in *Monstrous Progeny: A History of the Frankenstein Narratives* (New Brunswick: Rutgers University Press, 2016), 161.

51. *The Rocky Horror Picture Show* (1975; 20th Century Fox).

52. Carol J. Cover, *Men, Women and Chainsaws: Gender in the Modern Horror Film* (Princeton: Princeton University, 1997), 89.

53. *The Exorcist*, directed by William Friedkin (1974; Burbank: Warner Bros. Pictures, 2003), DVD.

54. *Ibid.*

55. *Ibid.*

56. *Ibid.*

57. William Peter Blatty, *The Exorcist* (New York: Harper & Row, 1971), 328.

58. Nick Cull, "The Exorcist," *History Today* 50, no. 5 (May 2000), 47, https://doi.org/https://www.historytoday.com/archive/exorcist.

59. Anita Bryant, "Save the Children," in *A Queer Reader*, ed. Patrick Higgins (London: Fourth Estate Limited, 1993), 239.

60. *Ibid.*

Chapter 3

1. Hadleigh, *The Lavender Screen*, 220.

2. *Savage Weekend*, directed by David Paulsen (1980; U.S.: The Cannon Group, 2015), DVD.

3. *Ibid.*

4. Joe Baltake, "Sleazy 'Savage' Is Sick," *Philadelphia Daily News*, December 1, 1980, p. 23.

5. Bronski, *A Queer History of the United States*, 184.

6. Alex Simon, "William Friedkin: The Hollywood Flashback Interviews," *The Hollywood Interview*, February 12, 2013, http://thehollywoodinterview.blogspot.com/2008/01/cruising-with-billy.html.

7. Darrell Yates Rist, "Fear and Loving and AIDS," *Film Comment* 22, no. 2 (1986), 45.

8. Judith Halberstam, *Female Masculinity* (Durham: Duke University Press, 1998), 180.

9. Alex Simon, "William Friedkin: The Hollywood Flashback Interviews," *The Hollywood Interview*, February 12, 2013, http://thehollywoodinterview.blogspot.com/2008/01/cruising-with-billy.html.

10. Larry Gross, *Up from Invisibility: Lesbians, Gay Men, and the Media in America* (New York: Columbia University Press, 2001), 66.

11. Donald H.J. Herman, et al., "People of the State of Illinois vs. John Gacy: The Functioning of the Insanity Defense at the Limits of the Criminal Law," *West Virginia Law Review 86*, no. 4 (June 1984).

12. *Ibid.*

13. *Ibid.*

14. *Ibid.*

15. *Ibid.*

16. Larry Kramer, "1,112 And Counting," *New York Native*, March 27, 1983, 59; Meyer Lansky was the infamous "Mob's Accountant"; Rabbi Bernard Bergman, known for operating a nursing home empire that gained a reputation for patient neglect, was convicted of Medicaid fraud in the 1970s; Rabbi Meir Kahane was an ultra-nationalist who advocated for militancy to combat anti-Semitism and was convicted of conspiracy to manufacture explosives; the Seattle Slaughters, known as the Wah Mee Massacre, occurred in February 1983 in Seattle, Washington, where three Chinese perpetrators bound, shot, and robbed fourteen people in the Wah Mee gambling club in the Louisa Hotel in Chinatown International District; the North American Man/Boy Love Association (NAMBLA) is an advocacy organization for pedophiles that has tried to align itself with LGBTQ+ organizations for decades, which has been fodder for anti-LGBTQ+ discourse by conservative persons and organizations and aids in perpetuating the myth of correlation between homosexuality and pedophilia.

17. Jancovich, *Horror, the Film Reader*, 13.

18. Benshoff, "The Monster and the Homosexual," 91.

19. Robert Scheer and Gore Vidal, *Playing President: My Close Encounters with Nixon, Carter, Bush I, Reagan, and Clinton: and How They Did Not Prepare Me for George W. Bush* (Los Angeles: Truthdig, 2006), 154.

20. "Part 4—In the Stars," *The Reagans* (New York: Showtime, December 6, 2020).

21. Benshoff, *Monsters in the Closet*, 238; Tom Buckley, "Embodiment of Lucifer," review of *Fear No Evil*, *The New York Times*, 6 February, 1981, C22:1.

22. "Rare Cancer Seen in 41 Homosexuals," *The New York Times*, July 3, 1981; *Fear No Evil* was released in January of 1981.

23. *Butcher, Baker, Nightmare Maker*, directed by William Asher (1981; N/A: Comworld Pictures, 2017), DVD.

24. *Ibid.*

25. On Camera Interview: Steve Easton, *Butcher, Baker, Nightmare Maker*, directed by William Asher (1981; N/A: Comworld Pictures, 2017), DVD.

26. David Koon, "The Woman Who Cared for Hundreds of Abandoned Gay Men Dying of AIDS," *OUT Magazine*, February 28, 2019.

27. *Ibid.*

28. Bronski, *A Queer History of the United States*, 226.

29. France, *How to Survive a Plague*, 91–92.

30. Rocco Thompson, "Final Boy," *Rue Morgue*, July/August 2019, 14–15.

31. *Scream Queen! My Nightmare on Elm Street*, directed by Roman Chimienti and Tyler Jensen (2019; New York: Virgil Films, 2020), DVD.

32. *A Nightmare on Elm Street 2: Freddy's Revenge*, directed by Jack Sholder (1985; Burbank: New Line Cinema, 2000), DVD.

33. *Ibid.*

34. Thompson, "Final Boy," 15.

35. France, *How to Survive a Plague*, 190.

36. Andrew Huff and Matty Zaradich, hosts, "Horror Hookup: Mark Patton of *A*

Nightmare on Elm Street 2!" FriGay the 13th Horror Podcast (podcast), September 5, 2019.

37. *Ibid.*

38. Thompson, "Final Boy," 13.

39. *Ibid.*, 15, 17.

40. *Ibid.*, 17.

41. France, *How to Survive a Plague*, 87.

42. Michaeleen Doucleff, "Researchers Clear 'Patient Zero' From AIDS Origin Story," National Public Radio, October 26, 2016.

43. France, *How to Survive a Plague*, 87.

44. Letter from American Family Association, quoted in *A Queer History of the United States*, 226–27.

45. Marty Fink, "AIDS Vampires: Reimagining Illness in Octavia Butler's 'Fledgling,'" *Science Fiction Studies* 37, no. 3 (2010), 417.

46. German expressionist silent film *Nosferatu* (1922) preceded Tod Browning's *Dracula* (1931). *Nosferatu* is an unauthorized and unofficial adaptation of Stoker's 1897 novel that heavily uses the idea of plague in the story of Count Orlok. *Nosferatu* director F.W. Murnau was himself a queer man; Benshoff, *Monsters in the Closet*, 21.

47. *Ibid.*, 6.

48. Benshoff, "The Monster and the Homosexual," 92.

49. Duy Dang, "A Disease with a Bite: Vampirism and Infection Theories in Bram Stoker's *Dracula*," *Xavier University of Louisiana's Undergraduate Research Journal* 10, no. 2 (April 1, 2003).

50. Fink, "AIDS Vampires," 424.

51. *Ibid.*

52. Thomas Yingling, "AIDS in America: Postmodern Governance, Identity, and Experience," in *Inside/Out: Lesbian Theories, Gay Theories*, ed. Diana Fuss (New York: Routledge, 1991), 293.

53. Rist, "Fear and Loving and AIDS," 46.

54. *The Hunger*, directed by Tony Scott (1983; Beverly Hills: MGM/UA Entertainment Co., 2004), DVD.

55. Michel Foucault, *Discipline and Punish: The Birth of the Prison*, trans. Alan Sheridan (New York: Vintage Books, 1979), 25.

56. Jan Zita Grover, "Visible Lesions:

Images of the PWA," in *Out in Culture: Gay, Lesbian, and Queer Essays on Popular Culture*, ed. Corey K Creekmur and Alexander Doty (Durham: Duke University Press, 1995), pp. 354–381, 363.

57. Fink, "AIDS Vampires," 423.

58. Hadleigh, *The Lavender Screen*, 209.

59. *The Hitcher*, directed by Robert Harmon (1986; Culver City, CA: TriStar Pictures, 2003), DVD.

60. *Ibid.*

61. Scott Drebit, "Drive-In Dust Offs: The Hitcher," *Daily Dead*, November 28, 2015, https://dailydead.com/drive-in-dust-offs-the-hitcher/.

62. Hadleigh, *The Lavender Screen*, 48.

63. *Ibid.*

64. Russo, *The Celluloid Closet*, 300.

65. *Fright Night*, directed by Tom Holland (1985; Los Angeles: Columbia Pictures, 1999), DVD.

66. *Ibid.*

67. *The Lost Boys*, directed by Joel Schumacher (1987; Burbank: Warner Bros., 1999), DVD.

68. Andrew Goldman, "In Conversation: Joel Schumacher," *Vulture*, June 22, 2020, https://www.vulture.com/2020/06/joel-schumacher-in-conversation.html.

69. *The Lost Boys* (1987; Warner Bros.).

70. *The Forsaken*, directed by J.S. Cardone (2001; Culver City, CA: Screen Gems, 2001), DVD.

71. *Blade*, directed by Stephen Norrington (1998; Burbank: New Line Cinema, 1998), DVD.

72. France, *How to Survive a Plague*, 69.

73. *The Monster Squad*, directed by Fred Dekker (1987; Culver City, CA: TriStar Pictures, 2007), DVD.

74. *Once Bitten*, directed by Howard Storm (1985; Culver City, CA: The Samuel Goldwyn Company, 2003), DVD.

75. *Ibid.*

76. Russo, *The Celluloid Closet*, 252.

77. *Ibid.*, 251.

78. Eric Marcus and Vito Russo, "The Film Historian," in *Making History: The Struggle for Gay and Lesbian Equal Rights, 1945–1990, an Oral History* (New York: HarperCollins, 1992), 415.

79. *Sleepaway Camp*, directed by Robert Hiltzik (1983; USA: United Film Distribution Company, 2000), DVD.

80. Justin Hamelin, "Heading off to Camp: An Interview with Felissa Rose," *Mangled Matters*, March 27, 2015.
81. This will be discussed further in Chapter 4.
82. *Sleepaway Camp II: Unhappy Campers*, directed by Michael A. Simpson (1988; Los Angeles, CA: Nelson Entertainment, 2002), DVD; *Sleepaway Camp III: Teenage Wasteland*, directed by Michael A. Simpson (1989; Los Angeles: Nelson Entertainment, 2002), DVD.

Chapter 4

1. "Half-Woman, Half-Man Case," *Yorkshire Post*, August 23, 1930; Intersex is when a body has both male and female sex organs.
2. Jenni Holtz, "Blood, Bodies and Binaries: Trans Women in Horror," *14 East* (DePaul University), January 18, 2019, http://fourteeneastmag.com/index.php/2019/01/18/blood-bodies-and-binaries-trans-women-in-horror/.
3. Haley E. Solomon and Beth Kurtz-Costes, "Media's Influence on Perceptions of Trans Women," *Sexuality Research and Social Policy*, March 2018, 45.
4. *Ibid.*, 37.
5. *Disclosure*, directed by Sam Feder (2020; Los Gatos, CA: Netflix, 2020), Web.
6. Solomon and Kurtz-Costes, "Media's Influence," 35.
7. "Violence Against the Transgender Community in 2018," *Human Rights Campaign*, accessed October 14, 2019.
8. Solomon and Kurtz-Costes, "Media's Influence," 45.
9. Chloe Hadjimatheou, "Christine Jorgensen: 60 Years of Sex Change Ops," *BBC News*, November 30, 2012.
10. "Ex-GI Becomes Blonde Beauty: Operations Transform Bronx Youth," *New York Daily News*, December 1, 1952, 34, sec. 136.
11. Stephen Whittle, "A Brief History of Transgender Issues," *The Guardian*, June 2, 2010.
12. Benshoff, *Monster in the Closet*, 157, 159.
13. *Glen or Glenda*, directed by Ed Wood (1953; Los Angeles: Columbia Pictures, 2000), DVD.

14. *Ibid.*
15. *Ibid.*
16. *Ibid.*
17. Rudolph Grey, *Nightmare of Ecstasy: The Life and Art of Edward D. Wood, Jr.* (Los Angeles: Feral Press, 1992), 62.
18. *Glen or Glenda* (1953; Columbia Pictures).
19. John Semley, "How the Shower Scene from 'Psycho' Slashed Its Way into Legend," Macleans.ca, April 24, 2017; "Itchy & Scratchy & Marge," *The Simpsons*, December 20, 1990; *National Lampoon's Vacation*, directed by Harold Ramis (1983; Burbank: Warner Bros., 1997), DVD.
20. John Phillips, *Transgender on Screen* (New York: Palgrave Macmillan, 2006), 85.
21. *Psycho* (1960; Paramount Pictures).
22. *Ibid.*
23. Roland Barthes, "The Rhetoric of the Imagem" *Image—Music—Text*, sel. and trans. Stephen Heath (New York: Hill and Wang, 1977).
24. *Dressed to Kill*, directed by Brian De Palma (1980; Sonoma County, CA: Filmways Pictures, 2002), DVD.
25. *Ibid.*
26. *Sleepaway Camp* (1983; United Film Distribution).
27. Willow Maclay, "'How Can It Be? She's a Boy': Transmisogyny in Sleepaway Camp," *Cleo Journal* (blog), February 2017.
28. Alison Lang, "Slasher Shocker," *Rue Morgue*, July/August 2019, 16–17.
29. Maclay, "'How Can It Be? She's a Boy,'" *Cleo Journal* (blog).
30. Laura Mulvey, "Visual Pleasure and Narrative Cinema," ed. Leo Braudy and Marshall Cohen, *Film Theory and Criticism: Introductory Readings* (1999), 835.
31. Judith Halberstam, *In a Queer Time and Place: Transgender Bodies, Subcultural Lives* (New York: New York University Press, 2005), 78.
32. Halberstam, *Female Masculinity*, 24.
33. *Ibid.*, 25.
34. Dr. Edith Bracho-Sanchez, "Transgender Teens in Schools with Bathroom Restrictions Are at Higher Risk of Sexual Assault, Study Says," *CNN*, May 6, 2019.

35. *Ibid.*
36. Mulvey, "Visual Pleasure and Narrative Cinema," 835.
37. *Sleepaway Camp II: Unhappy Campers* (1988; Nelson Entertainment).
38. *Sleepaway Camp III: Teenage Wasteland* (1989; Nelson Entertainment).
39. *Curse of the Queerwolf*, directed by Mark Pirro (1988; Hollywood: Pirromount Pictures, 2003), DVD.
40. *Ibid.*
41. Cynthia Lee, *The Trans Panic Defense Revisited (2019).* 57 AM. CRIM. L. REV. 1411 (2020); GWU Law School Public Law Research Paper No. 2019–63; GWU Legal Studies Research Paper No. 2019–63. Available at SSRN: https://ssrn.com/abstract=3481295. Thirty years after the release of *Curse of the Queerwolf*, Lee states that at least twenty-six transgender folks were killed in the United States, the vast majority, 96 percent, being transgender women.
42. *Curse of the Queerwolf* (1988; Pirromount Pictures).
43. *Ibid.*
44. *Ibid.*
45. *Hellraiser: Bloodline*, directed by Alan Smithee (1996; Buffalo: Miramax Films, 2001), DVD
46. Alexander Kacala, "The Handkerchief Code, According to 'Bob Damron's Address Book' in 1980," The Saint Foundation, April 25, 2019, https://www.thesaintfoundation.org/community/hanky-code-bob-damrons-address-book.
47. Susan Stryker, *Transgender History: The Roots of Today's Revolution* (SEAL, 2017), 50.
48. *The Silence of the Lambs*, directed by Jonathan Demme (1991; Los Angeles: Orion Pictures, 2001), DVD.
49. *The Silence of the Lambs* (1991; Orion Pictures).
50. Pamela Demory, *Queer/Adaptation: A Collection of Critical Essays* (London: Palgrave Macmillan, 2019), 58.
51. *The Silence of the Lambs* (1991; Orion Pictures).
52. Phillips, *Transgender on Screen*, 105.
53. *Disclosure* (2020, Netflix).
54. *Aliens*, directed by James Cameron (1986; Los Angeles: 20th Century Fox, 1999), DVD.
55. Thomas Hobbes, "Why Alien's Gender Politics Run a Lot Deeper than Ellen Ripley," *Little White Lies*, May 10, 2017, https://lwlies.com/articles/alien-gender-politics-ellen-ripley-joan-lambert/.

Chapter 5

1. *Poison*, directed by Todd Haynes (1991; New York: Zeitgeist Films, 2011), DVD.
2. Bronski, *A Queer History of the United States*, 226.
3. Means Coleman, *Horror Noire*, 171.
4. *Ibid.*, 171–72.
5. Gwynne Watkins, "Before #OscarsSoWhite: The Forgotten Story of Queer Nation's 1992 Academy Awards Protest," *Yahoo Entertainment*, February 24, 2016.
6. Somini Sengupta, "Hate Crimes Hit Record High in 1992: Discrimination: A County Panel Finds an 11% Increase to 736 Incidents and Says the Figure Might Have Been Higher If All Riot-Related Instances Had Been Included. African-Americans and Gay Men Were the Most Frequent Targets, Report Finds," *Los Angeles Times*, March 23, 1993.
7. Means Coleman, *Horror Noire*, 192–193.
8. Averie Mendez, "Konerak Sinthasomphone: Dahmer's Victim Who Didn't Have to Die," *StMU History Media*, March 9, 2019.
9. *Ibid.*
10. Clive Barker, *Hellraiser* Box Set Liner Notes (Anchor Bay Entertainment, 2004), DVD.
11. Trace Thurman, "The Inherent Queerness of Clive Barker's 'Nightbreed,'" *Bloody Disgusting*, April 24, 2019, https://bloody-disgusting.com/editorials/3556029/horror-queers-nightbreed/.
12. Vicki Lynn Eaklor, *Queer America: A GLBT History of the 20th Century* (New York: New Press, 2011), 198–199.
13. *Scream 2*, directed by Wes Craven (1997; New York: Dimension Films, 1998), DVD.
14. "Hate Crimes Timeline," *Human Rights Campaign*, accessed February 17, 2020.

15. "Westboro Baptist Church," Southern Poverty Law Center (SPLC), accessed March 22, 2021, https://www.splcenter.org/fighting-hate/extremist-files/group/westboro-baptist-church.

16. *Red State*, directed by Kevin Smith (2011; Los Angeles: SModcast Pictures, 2011), DVD.

17. Reimer and Brown, *We Are Everywhere*, 301.

18. *Interview with a Vampire*, directed by Neil Jordan (1994; Burbank: Warner Bros., 1997), DVD.

19. Alice Collins, "Normalizing Queerness Through Vampirism," *Gayly Dreadful* (blog), June 24, 2019, https://www.gaylydreadful.com/blog/2019/6/19/normalizing-queerness-through-vampirism.

20. Halberstam, *Female Masculinity*, 177.

21. *The Faculty*, directed by Robert Rodriguez (1998; Los Angeles: Miramax Films, 1999), DVD.

22. *The Rage: Carrie 2*, directed by Kat Shea (1999; Beverly Hills: Metro-Goldwyn-Mayer, 1999), DVD

23. *Ibid.*

24. Jeffrey Epstein, "Kevin Williamson: Unbound," *The Advocate*, August 31, 1999, 44.

25. Judith Butler, "Imitation and Gender Insubordination," in *Inside/Out: Lesbian Theories, Gay Theories*, ed. Diana Fuss (New York: Routledge, 1991), 19.

26. Michael J. Tyrkus and Michael Bronski, eds., "Rita Mae Brown," in *Gay & Lesbian Biography* (Detroit: St. James Press, 1997), 91.

27. Thomas Waugh, in *Queer Looks: Perspectives on Lesbian and Gay Film and Video*, ed. Martha Gever, John Greyson, and Pratisha Parmar (New York: Routledge, 1993), pp. 141–161, 157.

28. *Tammy and the T-Rex*, directed by Stewart Raffill (1994; Bridgeport, CT: Vinegar Syndrome, 2020), DVD.

29. Amy Villarejo, "1992 Movies and the Politics of Authorship," in *American Cinema of the 1990s: Themes and Variations*, ed. Chris Holmund (New Brunswick: Rutgers University Press, 2008) pp. 84–90.

30. *Bride of Chucky*, directed by Ronny Yu (1998; Universal City, CA: Universal Pictures, 1999), DVD.

31. Mann, *Behind the Screen*, 365.

32. Benshoff, "The Monster and the Homosexual," in *Horror, the Film Reader*, ed. Mark Jancovich, 98.

33. Renee Bever, Michael Kennedy and Brennan Klein, hosts, "Big Dyke Energy," *Attack of the Queerwolf!* (podcast), Fangoria Podcast Network, November 29, 2018.

34. Hadleigh, *The Lavender Screen*, 287–88.

35. *Psycho*, directed by Gus Van Sant (1998; Universal City, CA: Universal Pictures, 1998), DVD; Hadleigh, *The Lavender Screen*, 288.

36. "USA and Torture: A History of Hypocrisy," Human Rights Watch, October 28, 2020, https://www.hrw.org/news/2014/12/09/usa-and-torture-history-hypocrisy#.

37. Alison Mitchell, "The 2000 Campaign: The Texas Governor; Bush Talks to Gays and Calls It Beneficial," *The New York Times*, April 14, 2000, sec. A, p. 26.

38. "Cheney at Odds with Bush on Gay Marriage," NBCNews.com, August 25, 2004, https://www.nbcnews.com/id/wbna5817720.

39. *Freddy vs. Jason*, directed by Ronny Yu (2003; Burbank: New Line Cinema, 2004), DVD.

40. Chris Eggertsen, "How One Homophobic Slur Stained Freddy vs. Jason's' Legacy Forever," UPROXX, May 13, 2016, https://uproxx.com/hitfix/freddy-vs-jason-writers-we-tried-to-keep-kelly-rowlands-homophobic-slur-out-of-the-movie/.

41. *American Psycho*, directed by Mary Harron (2000; Santa Monica: Lions Gate Films, 2000), DVD.

42. France, *How to Survive a Plague*, 146.

43. Sarah Kendzior, "American Psycho Drama," *Fangoria*, April 2000, 40.

44. France, *How to Survive a Plague*, 146.

45. *Hostel*, directed by Eli Roth (2006; Santa Monica: Lionsgate, 2006), DVD.

46. *Ibid.*

47. Enio Chialo and Eli Roth, "Postal Zone: 'Hostel' Responses," *Fangoria*, May 2006, 6.

48. *Ibid.*, 6–7.

49. *Ibid.*, 7.

50. Eli Roth, "Postal Zone: An End to

'Hostel'-ities," *Fangoria*, October 2006, 6.

51. *Hostel Part II*, directed by Eli Roth (2007; Santa Monica: Lionsgate, 2007), DVD.

52. *Wrong Turn 2: Dead End*, directed by Joe Lynch (2007; Los Angeles: 20th Century Fox Home Entertainment, 2007), DVD.

53. "Men on Films," *In Living Color*, April 15, 1990.

54. Essex Hemphill, "In Living Color: Toms, Coons, Mammies, Faggots, and Bucks," in *Out in Culture: Gay, Lesbian, and Queer Essays on Popular Culture*, ed. Corey K Creekmur and Alexander Doty (Durham: Duke University Press, 1995), pp. 389–401, 392–393.

55. *Scary Movie*, directed by Keenan Ivory Wayans (2000; New York: Dimension Films, 2000), DVD.

56. *Scream 2* (1997; Dimension Films).

57. *Scary Movie* (2000; Dimension Films).

58. The Wayans Bros. continued to provide out-of-focus homophobia in the background of scenes in *Scary Movie*'s sequel, *Scary Movie 2*. In a scene between Cindy and Shorty where Shorty tries to teach Cindy how to be cool in their college's main quad, a blurry bright pink Welcome Booth reads "Cum Bum Rush the First Gay Fraternity: Gay Phi A's!" (*Scary Movie 2*, directed by Keenan Ivory Wayans (2001; New York: Dimension Films, 2001), DVD).

59. Richard Plant, *The Pink Triangle: The Nazi War Against Homosexuals* (New York: Holt Paperbacks, 1988), 15–16.

60. *Scary Movie 2* (2001; Dimension Films).

61. *Scary Movie 3*, directed by David Zucker (2003; New York: Dimension Films, 2004), DVD.

62. *Scary Movie 4*, directed by David Zucker (2006; New York: Dimension Films, 2006), DVD.

63. *Ibid.*

64. *Psycho Beach Party*, directed by Robert Lee King (2000; Culver City, CA: Strand Releasing, 2005), DVD.

65. *Ibid.*

66. *Psycho Beach Party* was produced by independent, LGBTQ+ centered company Strand Releasing.

67. Russo, *The Celluloid Closet*, 325–26.

68. Castiglia and Reed, "Queer Theory is Burning," 148.

69. *May*, directed by Lucky McKee (2002; Santa Monica: Lions Gate Films, 2003), DVD.

70. Greg Reifsteck, "Hellbent: Queer Eye for the Dead Guy," *Fangoria*, November 2004, 79.

71. *Hellbent*, directed by Paul Etheredge-Ouzts (2004; Los Angeles: Regent Releasing, 2006), DVD.

72. Reifsteck, "Hellbent," 80.

73. *Ibid.*, 79.

74. *Ibid.*

75. *Ibid.*

76. *Ibid.*, 79.

77. *Switch Killer*, directed by Mack Hail (2004; Las Vegas: Vegas Media Group, 2005), DVD.

78. *Ibid.*

79. *Ibid.*

80. *Seed of Chucky*, directed by Don Mancini (2004; Universal City, CA: Rogue Pictures, 2005), DVD.

81. This line is also included in the gay storyline of Ricky in *Chillerama*'s "I Was a Teenage Werebear"; *Chillerama*, directed by Adam Green, Joe Lynch, Adam Rifkin, and Tim Sullivan (2011; Los Angeles: Image Entertainment, 2012), DVD.

82. *Seed of Chucky* (2004; Rogue Pictures).

83. Vincent Bec, "Don Mancini's Queer Inclusion," *Gayly Dreadful* (blog), June 11, 2019, https://www.gaylydreadful.com/blog/2019/5/27/don-mancinis-queer-inclusion-pride-2019.

84. Noreen Giffney and Myra J. Hird, *Queering the Non/Human* (New York: Routledge, 2016), 278.

85. Michael Rowe, "Bringing Up Chucky," *Fangoria*, November 2004, 31.

86. Chris Azzopardi, "How Did Chucky Get So Gay? LGBT Icon Jennifer Tilly Dishes on Horror Saga's Queerness & Warner Bros.'s Resistance to the Lesbian Love In 'Bound,'" *Pride Source Media Group*, 2017.

87. *Bound* (1996; Gramercy Pictures).

88. Renee Bever, Michael Kennedy and Brennan Klein, hosts, "Big Dyke Energy," *Attack of the Queerwolf!* (pod-

cast), Fangoria Podcast Network, November 29, 2018.

89. *Jennifer's Body*, directed by Karyn Kusama (2009; Los Angeles: 20th Century Fox, 2009), DVD.

90. *Ibid.*

91. *Scream* (1996; Dimension Films).

92. Alyssa Hardy, "Megan Fox Is No Longer Hiding," *InStyle*, July 9, 2021, https://www.instyle.com/celebrity/megan-fox/megan-fox-profile-2021.

93. *Jennifer's Body* (2009; 20th Century Fox).

94. Jossalyn Holbert, "Is *Jennifer's Body* the Bisexual Horror Film We Never Knew We Needed?" *Gayly Dreadful*, June 20, 2019.

95. "Megan Fox Blames Lindsay Lohan for Losing Her Toenails | Let's Unpack That," *InStyle* (YouTube, 2021), https://www.youtube.com/watch?time_continue=5&v=UkTZuhZg16E&feature=emb_title.

96. *Jennifer's Body* (2009; 20th Century Fox).

Chapter 6

1. France, *How to Survive a Plague*, 152–53.

2. *Black Swan*, directed by Darren Aronofsky (2010; Los Angeles: Fox Searchlight Pictures, 2011), DVD.

3. *The Taking of Deborah Logan*, directed by Adam Robitel (2014; Los Angeles: Millennium Entertainment, 2014), DVD.

4. Waylon Jordan, "Adam Robitel Shares His Story of Coming Out and the Power of Visibility in 2019," *iHorror*, July 11, 2019, https://www.ihorror.com/writer-director-adam-robitel-on-coming-out-and-his-road-to-self-acceptance/.

5. *You're Killing Me*, directed by Jim Hansen (2015; San Jose: Wolfe Video, 2017), DVD.

6. Jason LeRoy, "The Binge Interview: Jeffery Self and Jim Hansen on 'You're Killing Me,' Serial-Killing as Sexuality, and Murderous Real Housewives," March 4, 2016, http://www.thebinge.us/the-binge-interview-jeffery-self-and-jim-hansen-on-youre-killing-me/.

7. Ellis, Ralph, Ashley Fantz, Faith Karimi, and Eliott C. McLaughlin, "Orlando Shooting: 49 Killed, Shooter Pledged ISIS Allegiance," *CNN*, June 13, 2016.

8. *Ibid.*

9. Matt Thompson, "How to Spark Panic and Confusion in Three Tweets," *The Atlantic*, January 14, 2019.

10. Dan Avery, "FDA Considers Lifting Restrictions on Blood Donations by Gay and Bi Men," NBCNews.com, December 28, 2020) https://www.nbcnews.com/feature/nbc-out/fda-considers-lifting-restrictions-blood-donations-gay-bi-men-n1252424.

11. Brooks Barnes, "Movie's Ads Protest Rules Restricting Gay Men from Donating Blood," *The New York Times*, September 24, 2017, https://www.nytimes.com/2017/09/24/business/media/saw-blood-donations-gay.html.

12. "U.S. Senators Tammy Baldwin and Elizabeth Warren Lead Bipartisan Call on FDA to End Discriminatory Blood Donation Ban: U.S. Senator Tammy Baldwin of Wisconsin," Tammy Baldwin: United States Senator for Wisconsin, June 20, 2016, https://www.baldwin.senate.gov/press-releases/bipartisan-call-end-discriminatory-blood-donation-ban.

13. *Cursed* (2005; Miramax Films).

14. John Griffiths, "Christopher's Street—Christopher Landon Comes Out as Gay—Interview." *The Advocate*, December 7, 1999.

15. *Ibid.*

16. Thurman, "Shove It Down Their Throats," *Gayly Dreadful* (blog).

17. BJ Colangelo, "Bex Taylor-Klaus Talks 'Hell Fest' and Non-Binary Representation in Horror [Interview]," *Bloody Disgusting!* January 12, 2019.

18. *Ibid.*

19. *Jack & Diane*, directed by Bradley Rust Gray (2012; New York: Magnolia Pictures, 2012), DVD; *All Cheerleaders Die*, directed by Lucky McKee and Chris Sivertson (2013; Los Angeles: Image Entertainment, 2014), DVD.

20. *The Final Girls*, directed by Todd Strauss-Schulson (2015; Culver City, CA: Stage 6 Films, 2015), DVD.

21. *Ibid.*

22. *Puppet Master: The Littlest Reich*, directed by Sonny Laguna and Tommy Wiklund (2018; Los Angeles: RLJE Films, 2018), DVD.

23. *Curse of Chucky*, directed by Don Mancini (2013; Universal City, CA: Universal 1440 Entertainment, 2013), DVD.

24. *Cult of Chucky*, directed by Don Mancini (2017; Universal City, CA: Universal Pictures Home Entertainment, 2017), DVD.

25. Azzopardi, "How Did Chucky Get So Gay?" *Pride Source*.

26. Vincent Bec, "Don Mancini's Queer Inclusion," *Gayly Dreadful* (blog), June 11, 2019, https://www.gaylydreadful.com/blog/2019/5/27/don-mancinis-queer-inclusion-pride-2019.

27. Jonathan Lee and Taylor Drake, "*IT*'s Gay Bashing Scene Serves No Purpose Except as Porn for Homophobes," *Advocate*: September 12, 2019.

28. Jeffrey Bloomer, "*It: Chapter Two*'s Gay-Bashing Scene Exploits a Real-Life Killing for a Cheap Shock," *Slate Magazine*, September 5, 2019.

29. Jacob Stolworthy, "*It Chapter Two* Director Explains Why Film Opens with a Brutal Hate Crime," *The Independent*, August 27, 2019.

30. Kaitlin Reilly, "Did We Need the Hate Crime Scene in *It Chapter Two*?" *Refinery29*, September 6, 2019.

31. Lee and Drake, "*IT*'s Gay Bashing Scene," *The Advocate*.

32. *It Chapter Two*, directed by Andres Muschietti (2019; Burbank: Warner Bros. Pictures, 2020), DVD.

33. *Ibid.*

34. *Ibid.*

35. Bloomer, "*It: Chapter Two*'s Gay-Bashing Scene," *Slate Magazine*.

36. Castiglia and Reed, "Queer Theory Is Burning," 151.

37. Colin Drury, "Organizers of 'Straight Pride' Revealed to Have Far-Right Links," *The Independent*, June 9, 2019.

38. Matthew Jacobs, "'He Sort of Wants a Daddy': Decoding the Homoeroticism in 'The Lighthouse,'" *HuffPost*, October 20, 2019, https://www.huffpost.com/entry/the-lighthouse-homoeroticism-robert-pattinson-willem-dafoe_n_5da9c888e4b0e71d65b801ae.

39. *Ibid.*

40. *Ibid.*

41. *Bird Box*, directed by Susanne Bier (2018; Los Gatos, CA: Netflix, 2018), Web.

42. *Velvet Buzzsaw*, directed by Dan Gilroy (2019; Los Gatos, CA: Netflix, 2019), Web.

43. *The Perfection*, directed by Richard Shepard (2019; Los Gatos, CA: Netflix, 2019), Web.

44. Russo, *The Celluloid Closet*, 248.

45. *Truth or Dare*, directed by Jeff Wadlow (2018; Universal City, CA: Universal Pictures, 2018), DVD.

46. Pitchfork, directed by Glenn Douglas Packard (2016; Flagler Beach, FL: Uncork'd Entertainment, 2017), DVD.

47. "2018 LGBTQ Youth Report," Human Rights Campaign, accessed March 10, 2021, 3–5, https://www.hrc.org/resources/2018-lgbtq-youth-report.

48. Suzanna Danuta Walters, *All the Rage: The Story of Gay Visibility in America* (Chicago: University of Chicago Press, 2001), 200.

49. Matt Donnelly, "How 'Freaky' Evokes Queer and Feminist Power beneath a Slasher Surface," *Variety*, December 4, 2020, https://variety.com/2020/film/news/freaky-vince-vaughn-chris-landon-queer-feminist-12348 46719/.

50. *Freaky*, directed by Christopher Landon (2020; Universal City, CA: Universal Pictures, 2021), DVD.

51. Candice Frederick, "In 'Fear Street,' a Lesbian Romance Provides Hope for a Genre," *The New York Times*, July 16, 2021, https://www.nytimes.com/2021/07/16/movies/fear-street-lesbian-romance.html.

Chapter 7

1. Martha Gever, Pratibha Parmar, and John Greyson, eds., *Queer Looks: Perspectives on Lesbian and Gay Film and Video* (New York: Routledge, 1993), 139.

2. Walters, *All the Rage: The Story of Gay Visibility in America*, 132.

3. Eren Orbey, "The Babadook Is a Frightening, Fabulous New Gay Icon," *The New Yorker*, June 17, 2017), https://www.newyorker.com/culture/rabbit-holes/the-babadook-is-a-frightening-fabulous-new-gay-icon.

4. Carol J. Cover. *Men, Women and Chainsaws: Gender in the Modern Horror Film* (Princeton: Princeton University Press, 1997).

5. Carol J. Clover, "Her Body, Himself: Gender in the Slasher Film," in *Horror, the Film Reader*, ed. Mark Jancovich (New York: Routledge), 79, 81.

6. *Ibid.*, 86.

7. *Carrie*, directed by Brian De Palma (1976; Beverly Hills: United Artists, 1998), DVD.

8. *Ibid.*

9. Tudor, "Why Horror?" 48.

10. Maddrey, *Nightmares in Red, White and Blue*, 60–62.

11. Benshoff, *Monsters in the Closet*, 232.

12. *Ibid.*

13. Vivian Sobchack, "Bringing It All Back Home: Family Economy and Generic Exchange," in *American Horrors: Essays on the Modern American Horror Film*, ed. Gregory A. Waller (Urbana: University of Illinois Press, 1987), pp. 175–194, 182–183.

14. Lee Gambin, "Carrie: Over 40 Years of Memories," *Scream*, 2017, 7.

15. *A Nightmare on Elm Street*, directed by Wes Craven (1984; Burbank: New Line Cinema, 1999), DVD.

16. "It's Just a Nightmare ... Heather Langenkamp Talks Nancy's Nightmare on Elm Street," *Gay Times*, October 30, 2015)

17. *A Nightmare on Elm Street* (1984; New Line Cinema).

18. Scream Queens are similar to final girls but more so focus on the number of horror films an actress has been in. Though Langenkamp has only been in two *Nightmare* films, her character growth and fierce strength earn her the title.

19. *Halloween*, along with Canada's *Black Christmas* (1974), helped to begin the slasher and Final Girl dynamic in horror.

20. Chrystal Williams, "Horror, Fear & Identity," *Gayly Dreadful* (blog), June 28, 2019.

21. Maddrey, *Nightmares in Red, White and Blue*, 66.

22. Joshua Anderson, "The Final Girl: A LGBTQ Representation," *Gayly Dreadful* (blog), June 25, 2019.

23. Thompson, "Final Boy," 14.

24. Andrew Huff and Matty Zaradich, hosts, "Horror Hookup: Mark Patton of *A Nightmare on Elm Street 2!*" *FriGay the 13th Horror Podcast* (podcast), September 5, 2019.

25. *Ibid.*

26. Benshoff, "The Monster and the Homosexual," 96.

27. The questionnaire was posted to my personal Instagram account, Bloody Milkcrate Records, where I post content about horror, and especially horror soundtracks on vinyl. Those who wanted to participate messaged the account with their email address. Of the eighteen people interested, five participated in the questionnaire and sent me their responses. All participants were informed that their responses would be included as part of my graduate thesis, which was adapted into this book, as well as I assured them that though they consented, I would only use first names. I collected participant emails from September 20, 2019, to October 1, 2019, and sent out the questionnaire during this period. I reached out to queer horror fans again in March of 2021 and collected responses. Racial demographic information was not collected for this questionnaire.

28. Abigail Waldron and AJ N., "Queer Horror Questionnaire" (September 23, 2019).

29. Abigail Waldron and Jordan F., "Queer Horror Questionnaire" (March 4, 2021).

30. Abigail Waldron and Evan, "Queer Horror Questionnaire" (September 24, 2019).

31. Abigail Waldron and JP W., "Queer Horror Questionnaire" (March 16, 2021).

32. *The Haunting of Hill House* is a Netflix television series based on Shirley Jackson's novel *The Haunting of Hill House* and both the 1963 and 1999 film adaptations. The series openly discusses and shows Theo, who was the sexually ambiguous but coded-queer character from *The Haunting* (1963) and the openly bisexual character in the 1999 adaptation, as openly queer and further develops her queerness in the series.

33. Abigail Waldron and Nan, "Queer

Horror Questionnaire" (September 20, 2019).

34. Abigail Waldron and Anonymous, "Queer Horror Questionnaire" (March 9, 2021).

35. Abigail Waldron and Jeffrey, "Queer Horror Questionnaire" (September 23, 2019).

36. The use of "grrrl" or its variations is symbolic of the riot grrrl punk feminist movement of the 1990s.

37. Slang for "as fuck," meaning "significantly."

38. Abigail Waldron and AJ E., "Queer Horror Questionnaire" (October 22, 2019).

Bibliography

"AIDS Kills Television Actor." *The Bulletin*. Bend, Oregon. Associated Press. November 18, 1992, 3.

Alexander, Chris. "Curse of Chucky: Don of the Doll." *Fangoria*, October 2013, 40–44.

Als, Hilton, and John Lahr. "The Man Who Queered Broadway." *The New Yorker*, October 9, 2014. https://www.newyorker.com/books/page-turner/man-queered-broadway.

Anderson, Joshua. "The Final Girl: A LGBTQ Representation." *Gayly Dreadful*, June 25, 2019. https://www.gaylydreadful.com/blog/2019/6/25/the-final-girl-a-lgbtq-representation.

"Antony Hamilton; Dancer, TV Actor." *Los Angeles Times*, April 2, 1995. https://www.latimes.com/archives/la-xpm-1995-04-02-mn-49911-story.html.

Arcade, Penny. "The Last Days and Moments of Jack Smith." *Penny Arcade*, January 8, 2014. http://pennyarcade.tv/friends/the-last-days-and-moments-of-jack-smith/.

The Associated Press. "AIDS Takes Life of Actor Tom Villard." *The Eugene Register-Guard*, November 16, 1994.

Aster, Ari, dir. *Midsommar*. New York: A24, 2019. DVD.

Avery, Dan. "FDA Considers Lifting Restrictions on Blood Donations by Gay and Bi Men." NBCNews.com, December 28, 2020. https://www.nbcnews.com/feature/nbc-out/fda-considers-lifting-restrictions-blood-donations-gay-bi-men-n1252424.

Azzopardi, Chris. "How Did Chucky Get So Gay? LGBT Icon Jennifer Tilly Dishes on Horror Saga's Queerness & Warner Bros.'s Resistance to the Lesbian Love in 'Bound.'" *Pride Source*, October 16, 2017. https://pridesource.com/article/83431-2/.

Baltake, Joe. "Sleazy 'Savage' Is Sick." *Philadelphia Daily News*, December 1, 1980.

Barker, Clive. *Hellraiser* Box Set Liner Notes. Anchor Bay Entertainment, 2004. DVD.

Barnes, Brooks. "Movie's Ads Protest Rules Restricting Gay Men from Donating Blood." *The New York Times*, September 24, 2017. https://www.nytimes.com/2017/09/24/business/media/saw-blood-donations-gay.html.

Bec, Vincent. "Don Mancini's Queer Inclusion." *Gayly Dreadful*, June 11, 2019. https://www.gaylydreadful.com/blog/2019/5/27/don-mancinis-queer-inclusion-pride-2019.

Beìrubeì Allan. *Coming Out Under Fire: The History of Gay Men and Women in World War II*. New York: Penguin Books, 1991.

Belton, John. *Movies and Mass Culture*. New Brunswick: Rutgers University Press, 2000.

Benshoff, Harry M. "The Monster and the Homosexual." 1997. In *Horror, the Film Reader*, edited by Mark Jancovich, 91–102. New York: Routledge, 2002.

Benshoff, Harry M. *Monsters in the Closet: Homosexuality and the Horror Film*. Manchester: Manchester University Press, 1998.

Berenstein, Rhona J. "Adaptation, Censorship, and Audiences of Questionable Type: Lesbian Sightings in 'Rebecca' (1940) and 'The Uninvited' (1944)." *Cinema Journal* 37, no. 3 (1998): 16–37. doi:10.2307/1225825.

Berger, Joseph. "Rock Hudson, Screen Idol, Dies at 59." *The New York Times*, October 3, 1985, sec. D. https://www.nytimes.com/1985/10/03/arts/rock-hudson-screen-idol-dies-at-59.html?searchResultPosition=3.

Bever, Renee, Michael Kennedy, and Brennan Klein, hosts. *Attack of the Queerwolf!* (podcast). Fangoria Podcast Network, September 13, 2018.

Bever, Renee, Michael Kennedy, and Brennan Klein, hosts. "Big Dyke Energy." *Attack of the Queerwolf!* (podcast). Fangoria Podcast Network, November 29, 2018.

Black, Allida M. *Modern American Queer History.* Philadelphia: Temple University Press, 2001.

Blatty, William Peter. *The Exorcist.* New York: Harper & Row, 1971.

Bloomer, Jeffrey. "It: Chapter Two's Gay-Bashing Scene Exploits a Real-Life Killing for a Cheap Shock." *Slate Magazine,* September 5, 2019. https://slate.com/culture/2019/09/it-chapter-two-homophobic-killing-charlie-howard-opening-scene.html.

Bracho-Sanchez, Dr. Edith. "Transgender Teens in Schools with Bathroom Restrictions Are at Higher Risk of Sexual Assault, Study Says." *CNN,* May 6, 2019. https://www.cnn.com/2019/05/06/health/trans-teens-bathroom-policies-sexual-assault-study/index.html.

Brathwaite, Les Fabian. "Hays'd: Decoding the Classics—'Suddenly Last Summer.'" *IndieWire,* March 31, 2014. https://www.indiewire.com/2014/03/haysd-decoding-the-classics-suddenly-last-summer-214475/.

Brehmer, Nat. "'No More Mister Good Guy': Chucky's Struggle with Masculinity Throughout the 'Child's Play' Series." *Bloody Disgusting!* June 20, 2019. https://bloody-disgusting.com/editorials/3568071/no-mister-good-guy-chuckys-struggle-masculinity-throughout-childs-play-series/.

Bronski, Michael. *A Queer History of the United States.* Boston: Beacon Press, 2011.

Brown, Phil. "Still, Waters' Runs Deep." *Fangoria,* November 2012, 26–28, 98.

Bryant, Anita. "Save the Children." In *A Queer Reader,* edited by Patrick Higgins, 239. London: Fourth Estate Limited, 1993.

Buckley, Tom. "Embodiment of Lucifer," review of *Fear No Evil. The New York Times,* February 6, 1981, C22:1.

Butler, Judith. *Bodies That Matter: On the Discursive Limits of Sex.* Hoboken: Taylor and Francis, 2011.

Butler, Judith. *Gender Trouble: Feminism and the Subversion of Identity.* New York: Routledge, 2015.

Butler, Judith. "Imitation and Gender Insubordination." In *Inside/Out: Lesbian Theories, Gay Theories,* edited by Diana Fuss, 13–31. New York: Routledge, 1991.

Castiglia, Christopher, and Christopher Reed. "Queer Theory Is Burning: Sexual Revolution and Traumatic Unremembering." In *If Memory Serves: Gay Men, AIDS, and the Promise of the Queer Past,* 145–74. Minneapolis: University of Minnesota Press, 2012. http://www.jstor.org.ezproxy.trincoll.edu/stable/10.5749/j.ctttwqg.7.

"Cheney at Odds with Bush on Gay Marriage." NBCNews.com, August 25, 2004. https://www.nbcnews.com/id/wbna5817720.

Chialo, Enio, and Eli Roth. "Postal Zone: 'Hostel' Responses." *Fangoria,* May 2006, 6–7.

Clover, Carol J. "Her Body, Himself: Gender in the Slasher Film." 1997. In *Horror, the Film Reader,* edited by Mark Jancovich, 77–89. New York: Routledge, 2002.

Clover, Carol J. *Men, Women and Chainsaws: Gender in the Modern Horror Film.* Princeton: Princeton University Press, 1997.

Cohen, Jeffrey Jerome, ed. *Monster Theory: Reading Culture.* Minneapolis: University of Minnesota Press, 1996. http://www.jstor.org/stable/10.5749/j.ctttsq4d.

Colangelo, BJ. "Bex Taylor-Klaus Talks 'Hell Fest' and Non-Binary Representation in Horror [Interview]." *Bloody Disgusting!* January 12, 2019. Accessed March 12, 2019. https://bloody-disgusting.com/interviews/3541105/bex-taylor-klaus-talks-hell-fest-non-binary-representation-horror-interview/.

Collins, Alice. "Normalizing Queerness Through Vampirism." *Gayly Dreadful,* June 24, 2019. https://www.gaylydreadful.com/blog/2019/6/19/normalizing-queerness-through-vampirism.

"Cookie Mueller Dead; Actress and Writer, 40." *The New York Times,* November 15, 1989, sec. B. https://www.nytimes.com/1989/11/15/obituaries/cookie-mueller-dead-actress-and-writer-40.html?searchResultPosition=1.

Corber, Robert J. *In the Name of National Security: Hitchcock, Homophobia, and the Political Construction of Gender in Postwar America.* New Americanists. Durham: Duke University Press, 1993.

Creekmur, Corey K., and Alexander Doty, eds. *Out in Culture: Gay, Lesbian, and Queer Essays on Popular Culture.* Durham: Duke University Press, 1995.

Cull, Nick. "The Exorcist." *History Today* 50, no. 5 (May 2000). https://doi.org/https://www.historytoday.com/archive/exorcist.

Curtis, James. *James Whale: A New World of Gods and Monsters.* Boston: Faber & Faber, 1998.

Dang, Duy. "A Disease with a Bite: Vampirism and Infection Theories in Bram Stoker's Dracula." *Xavier University of Louisiana's Undergraduate Research Journal* 10, no. 2 (April 1, 2003). https://digitalcommons.xula.edu/xulanexus/vol10/iss2/1.

Dawes, Dorian. "*Cult of Chucky's* Twist-ending Takes a Stab at Queerness." *Medium,* October 28, 2017. Accessed April 3, 2019. https://medium.com/@RealDorianDawes/cult-of-chuckys-twist-ending-takes-a-stab-at-queerness-1e21925e3d9c.

Demory, Pamela. *Queer/Adaptation: A Collection of Critical Essays.* London: Palgrave Macmillan, 2019.

Donnelly, Matt. "How 'Freaky' Evokes Queer and Feminist Power Beneath a Slasher Surface." *Variety,* December 4, 2020. https://variety.com/2020/film/news/freaky-vince-vaughn-chris-landon-queer-feminist-1234846719/.

Doty, Alexander. *Flaming Classics: Queering the Film Canon.* New York: Routledge, 2000.

Doty, Alexander. "There's Something Queer Here." In *Making Things Perfectly Queer: Interpreting Mass Culture,* 1–16. Minneapolis: University of Minnesota Press, 1993. http://www.jstor.org.ezproxy.trincoll.edu/stable/10.5749/j.cttttcmx.5.

Doucleff, Michaeleen. "Researchers Clear 'Patient Zero' from AIDS Origin Story." National Public Radio, October 26, 2016. https://www.npr.org/sections/health-shots/2016/10/26/498876985/mystery-solved-how-hiv-came-to-the-u-s.

Douglas, Mary. *Purity and Danger: An Analysis of Concepts of Pollution and Taboo with a New Preface by the Author.* London: Routledge, 2015.

Drebit, Scott. "Drive-In Dust Offs: *The Hitcher.*" *Daily Dead,* November 28, 2015. https://dailydead.com/drive-in-dust-offs-the-hitcher/.

Drury, Colin. "Organizers of 'Straight Pride' Revealed to Have Far-Right Links." *The Independent,* June 9, 2019. https://www.independent.co.uk/news/world/americas/straight-pride-parade-boston-far-right-mark-sahady-john-hugo-chris-bartley-a8950836.html.

Dyer, Richard. *Heavenly Bodies: Film Stars and Society.* London: Routledge, 2004.

Dyer, Richard. *Now You See It: Studies on Lesbian and Gay Film.* New York: Routledge, 1990.

Eaklor, Vicki Lynn. *Queer America: A GLBT History of the 20th Century.* New York: New Press, 2011.

Eggertsen, Chris. "How One Homophobic Slur Stained 'Freddy vs. Jason's' Legacy Forever." *UPROXX,* May 13, 2016. https://uproxx.com/hitfix/freddy-vs-jason-writers-we-tried-to-keep-kelly-rowlands-homophobic-slur-out-of-the-movie/.

Ellis, Ralph, Ashley Fantz, Faith Karimi, and Eliott C. McLaughlin. "Orlando Shooting: 49 Killed, Shooter Pledged ISIS Allegiance." *CNN,* June 13, 2016. https://www.cnn.com/2016/06/12/us/orlando-nightclub-shooting/index.html.

Epstein, Jeffrey. "Kevin Williamson: Unbound." *The Advocate,* August 31, 1999.

Ewen, Elizabeth, and Stuart Ewen. *Typecasting on the Arts and Sciences of Human Inequality, a History of Dominant Ideas.* New York: Seven Stories Press, 2006.

"Ex-GI Becomes Blonde Beauty: Operations Transform Bronx Youth." *New York Daily News,* December 1, 1952, 34 edition, sec. 136.

Fairyington, Stephanie. "Two Decades After Brandon Teena's Murder, a Look Back at Falls City." *The Atlantic,* September 15, 2018. https://www.theatlantic.com/national/archive/2013/12/two-decades-after-brandon-teenas-murder-a-look-back-at-falls-city/282738/.

Filippo, Maria San. "Power Play/s: Bisexuality as Privilege and Pathology in Sexploitation Cinema." In *The B Word: Bisexuality in Contemporary Film and Television*, 95–151. Bloomington: Indiana University Press, 2013. http://www.jstor.org.ezproxy.trincoll.edu/stable/j.ctt16gzcbc.7.

Fink, Marty. "AIDS Vampires: Reimagining Illness in Octavia Butler's 'Fledgling.'" *Science Fiction Studies* 37, no. 3 (2010): 416–32. http://www.jstor.org.ezproxy.trincoll.edu/stable/25746442.

Folkart, Burt A. "Vito Russo; Writer on Homosexual Issues." *Los Angeles Times*, November 9, 1990. https://www.latimes.com/archives/la-xpm-1990-11-09-mn-4031-story.html.

Foucault, Michel. *Discipline and Punish: The Birth of the Prison*. Translated by Alan Sheridan. New York: Vintage Books, 1979.

Foucault, Michel, and Robert Hurley. *The History of Sexuality*. Camberwell, Victoria: Penguin, 2008.

Fox, Alistair. "The New Anglo-American Cinema of Sexual Addiction." In *Transgression in Anglo-American Cinema: Gender, Sex, and the Deviant Body*, edited by Gwynne Joel, 9–24. New York: Columbia University Press, 2016. http://www.jstor.org.ezproxy.trincoll.edu/stable/10.7312/gwyn17604.5.

Fradley, Martin. *Film Quarterly* 64, no. 3 (2011): 73–75. doi:10.1525/fq.2011.64.3.73.

France, David. *How to Survive a Plague: The Story of How Activists and Scientists Tamed AIDS*. New York: Alfred A. Knopf, 2016.

Frederick, Candice. "In 'Fear Street,' a Lesbian Romance Provides Hope for a Genre." *The New York Times*, July 16, 2021. https://www.nytimes.com/2021/07/16/movies/fear-street-lesbian-romance.html.

Freeman, Elizabeth. *Time Binds Queer Temporalities, Queer Histories*. Durham: Duke University Press, 2010.

Friedman, Lester D., and Allison B. Kavey. "It's Still Alive: The Universal and Hammer Movie Cycles." In *Monstrous Progeny: A History of the Frankenstein Narratives*, 104–122. New Brunswick: Rutgers University Press, 2016. www.jstor.org/stable/j.cttlcx3tkb.8.

Friedman, Lester D., and Allison B. Kavey. "Mary Shelley's Stepchildren: Transitions, Translations, and Transformations." In *Monstrous Progeny: A History of the Frankenstein Narratives*, 161–163. New Brunswick: Rutgers University Press, 2016. http://www.jstor.org.ezproxy.trincoll.edu/stable/j.cttlcx3tkb.9.

Fuss, Diana. *Inside/Out: Lesbian Theories, Gay Theories*. New York: Routledge, 2016.

"Gacy Defense Witness Tells of Rape, Torture by Accused." *The Gadsden Times*, February 22, 1980.

Gambin, Lee. "Carrie: Over 40 Years of Memories." *Scream*, 2017.

Gambin, Lee. "They Are Still His Children." *Fangoria*, 2010, 58–62.

Gambin, Lee. "You're a Vile, Sorry Little Bitch!" *Fangoria*, 2015, 56.

Garber, Eric, and Lyn Paleo. *Uranian Worlds: A Guide to Alternative Sexuality in Science Fiction, Fantasy, and Horror*. Boston: Hall, 1990.

Gever, Martha, Pratibha Parmar, and John Greyson, eds. *Queer Looks: Perspectives on Lesbian and Gay Film and Video*. New York: Routledge, 1993.

Giffney, Noreen, and Myra J. Hird. *Queering the Non/human*. London: Routledge, 2016.

Gingold, Michael. *Ad Nauseam: Newsprint Nightmares of the 1980s*. Cleveland: 1984 Publishing, 2018.

Gingold, Michael. "Love Transforms Jack & Diane." *Fangoria*, November 2012, 20–22.

Goddu, Teresa A. "Vampire Gothic." *American Literary History* 11, no. 1 (1999): 125–41. http://www.jstor.org.ezproxy.trincoll.edu/stable/490080.

Goldman, Andrew. "In Conversation: Joel Schumacher." *Vulture*, June 22, 2020. https://www.vulture.com/2020/06/joel-schumacher-in-conversation.html.

Gordon, Michael, Mark S. Price, and Katie Peralta. "Understanding HB2: North Carolina's Newest Law Solidifies State's Role in Defining Discrimination." *The Charlotte Observer*, March 26, 2016. https://www.charlotteobserver.com/news/politics-government/article68401147.html.

Gould, Deborah B. *Moving Politics: Emotion and ACT UPs Fight Against AIDS*. Chicago: University of Chicago Press, 2009.

Grant, Barry Keith, ed. *American Cinema of the 1960s: Themes and Variations*. New Brunswick: Rutgers University Press, 2008. http://www.jstor.org.ezproxy.trincoll. edu/stable/j.ctt5hhxjc.

Grant, Julia. "'A Thought a Mother Can Hardly Face': Sissy Boys, Parents, and Professionals in Mid-Twentieth Century America." In *Modern American Queer History*, edited by Allida M. Black, 117–130. Philadelphia: Temple University Press, 2001.

Greven, David. *Psycho-Sexual: Male Desire in Hitchcock, De Palma, Scorsese, and Friedkin*. Austin: University of Texas Press, 2013.

Grey, Rudolph. *Nightmare of Ecstasy: The Life and Art of Edward D. Wood, Jr*. Los Angeles: Feral Press, 1992.

Griffin, F. Hollis. "The Aesthetics of Banality After New Queer Cinema." In *Feeling Normal: Sexuality and Media Criticism in the Digital Age*, 53–81. Bloomington: Indiana University Press, 2016. http://www.jstor.org.ezproxy.trincoll.edu/stable/j. ctt2005trt.6.

Griffiths, John. "Christopher's Street—Christopher Landon Comes Out as Gay—Interview." *The Advocate*, December 7, 1999.

Gross, Larry. *Up from Invisibility: Lesbians, Gay Men, and the Media in America*. New York: Columbia University Press, 2001.

Gross, Terry, and Mark Griffin. "'All That Heaven Allows' Examines Rock Hudson's Life as a Closeted Leading Man." National Public Radio, December 5, 2018. https://www. npr.org/2018/12/05/673696589/all-that-heaven-allows-examines-rock-hudsons-life-as-a-closeted-leading-man.

Grover, Jan Zita. "Visible Lesions: Images of the PWA." In *Out in Culture: Gay, Lesbian, and Queer Essays on Popular Culture*, edited by Corey K. Creekmur and Alexander Doty, 354–81. Durham: Duke University Press, 1995.

Hadjimatheou, Chloe. "Christine Jorgensen: 60 Years of Sex Change Ops." *BBC News*, November 30, 2012. https://www.bbc.com/news/magazine-20544095.

Hadleigh, Boze. *The Lavender Screen: The Gay and Lesbian Films—Their Stars, Directors, and Critics*. New York: Citadel, 2001.

Halberstam, Judith. *Female Masculinity*. Durham: Duke University Press, 1998.

Halberstam, Judith. *In a Queer Time and Place: Transgender Bodies, Subcultural Lives*. New York: New York University Press, 2005.

"Half-Woman, Half-Man Case." *Yorkshire Post*, August 23, 1930.

Hamelin, Justin. "Heading Off to Camp: An Interview with Felissa Rose." *Mangled Matters*, March 27, 2015. https://mangledmatters.wordpress.com/2015/03/27/ heading-off-to-camp-an-interview-with-felissa-rose/.

Hardy, Alyssa. "Megan Fox Is No Longer Hiding." *InStyle*, July 9, 2021. https://www. instyle.com/celebrity/megan-fox/megan-fox-profile-2021.

"Hate Crimes Timeline." *Human Rights Campaign*. Accessed February 17, 2020. https:// www.hrc.org/resources/hate-crimes-timeline.

Hemphill, Essex. "In Living Color: Toms, Coons, Mammies, Faggots, and Bucks." In *Out in Culture: Gay, Lesbian, and Queer Essays on Popular Culture*, edited by Corey K. Creekmur and Alexander Doty, 389–401. Durham: Duke University Press, 1995.

Herman, Donald H., Helen L. Morrison, Yvonne Sor, Julie A. Norman, and David M. Neff. "People of the State of Illinois vs. John Gacy: The Functioning of the Insanity Defense at the Limits of the Criminal Law." *West Virginia Law Review* 86, no. 4 (June 1984). https://researchrepository.wvu.edu/wvlr/vol86/iss4/8.

Higgins, Patrick, ed. *A Queer Reader*. London: Fourth Estate Limited, 1993.

"History of HIV and AIDS Overview." *Avert*, October 10, 2019. https://www.avert.org/ professionals/history-hiv-aids/overview.

Hobbes, Thomas. "Why Alien's Gender Politics Run a Lot Deeper Than Ellen Ripley." *Little White Lies*, May 10, 2017. https://lwlies.com/articles/alien-gender-politics-ellen-ripley-joan-lambert/.

Holbert, Jossalyn. "Is 'Jennifer's Body' the Bisexual Horror Film We Never Knew

We Needed?" *Gayly Dreadful*, June 20, 2019. https://www.gaylydreadful.com/blog/2019/6/15/is-jennifers-body-the-bisexual-horror-film-we-never-knew-we-needed.

Holmlund, Chris. "Cruisin' for a Brusin': Hollywood's Deadly (Lesbian) Dolls." *Cinema Journal* 34, no. 1 (1994): 31–51. doi:10.2307/1225654. http://www.jstor.org.ezproxy.trincoll.edu/stable/j.ctt5hj6fx.

Holtz, Jenni. "Blood, Bodies and Binaries: Trans Women in Horror." *14 East*, DePaul University, January 18, 2019. http://fourteeneastmag.com/index.php/2019/01/18/blood-bodies-and-binaries-trans-women-in-horror/.

hooks, bell. "The Oppositional Gaze: Black Female Spectators." In *Movies and Mass Culture*, edited by John Belton, 247–64. London: Athlone Press, 1999.

Huff, Andrew, and Matty Zaradich, hosts. "Horror Hookup: Mark Patton of *A Nightmare on Elm Street 2!*" *FriGay the 13th Horror Podcast* (podcast). September 5, 2019. Accessed November 19, 2019.

Hunt, Elle. "The Babadook: How the Horror Movie Monster Became a Gay Icon." *The Guardian*, June 11, 2017. https://www.theguardian.com/film/2017/jun/11/the-babadook-how-horror-movie-monster-became-a-gay-icon.

"It's Just a Nightmare ... Heather Langenkamp Talks Nancy's Nightmare on Elm Street." *Gay Times*, October 30, 2015. https://www.gaytimes.co.uk/culture/14932/its-just-a-nightmare-heather-langenkamp-talks-nancys-nightmare-on-elm-street/.

Jacobs, Matthew. "'He Sort of Wants a Daddy': Decoding the Homoeroticism in 'The Lighthouse.'" *HuffPost*, October 20, 2019. https://www.huffpost.com/entry/the-lighthouse-homoeroticism-robert-pattinson-willem-dafoe_n_5da9c888e4b0e71d65b801ae.

Jancovich, Mark. "'Two Ways of Looking': The Critical Reception of 1940s Horror." *Cinema Journal* 49, no. 3 (2010): 45–66. http://www.jstor.org.ezproxy.trincoll.edu/stable/40800733.

Jancovich, Mark, ed. *Horror, the Film Reader*. New York: Routledge, 2002.

"John Megna, 42, 'Mockingbird' Star." *The New York Times*, September 7, 1995. https://www.nytimes.com/1995/09/07/obituaries/john-megna-42-mockingbird-star.html.

Johnston, David MacGregor. "Kitsch and Camp and Things That Go Bump in the Night; Or, Sontag and Adorno at the (Horror) Movies." In *The Philosophy of Horror*, edited by Fahy Thomas, 229–44. Lexington: University Press of Kentucky, 2010. http://www.jstor.org.ezproxy.trincoll.edu/stable/j.ctt2jck39.18.

Jones, Alan. *The Rough Guide to Horror Movies*. New York: Rough Guides, 2005.

Jordan, Waylon. "Adam Robitel Shares His Story of Coming Out and the Power of Visibility in 2019." *iHorror*, July 11, 2019. https://www.ihorror.com/writer-director-adam-robitel-on-coming-out-and-his-road-to-self-acceptance/.

Jordan, Waylon. "Horror Pride Month: Christopher Landon on Fatherhood, 'Happy Death Day,' & So Much More!" *Horror News and Movie Reviews*, June 1, 2018. https://www.ihorror.com/horror-pride-month-christopher-landon-on-fatherhood-happy-death-day-so-much-more/.

Kacala, Alexander. "The Handkerchief Code, According to 'Bob Damron's Address Book' in 1980." *The Saint Foundation*, April 25, 2019. https://www.thesaintfoundation.org/community/hanky-code-bob-damrons-address-book.

Kaltenbach, Caleb, and Matthew Vines. "Debating Bible Verses on Homosexuality." *The New York Times*, June 8, 2015. https://www.nytimes.com/interactive/2015/06/05/us/samesex-scriptures.html.

Katz, Jonathan, ed., "1933: Dr. La Forest Potter; Psychoanalysis and Hormone Medication, "Some we would probably kill. Others we would cure.'" In *Gay American History: Lesbians and Gay Men in the U.S.A.*, 162–164. New York: Thomas Y. Crowell, 1976.

Katz, Jonathan, ed. "1935: Dr. Louis W. Max; Aversion Therapy (Electric), 'Low Shock Intensities Had Little Effect.'" In *Gay American History: Lesbians and Gay Men in the U.S.A.*, 164–65. New York: Thomas Y. Crowell, 1976.

Katz, Jonathan, ed. "1950–1955: Witch-Hunt; The United States Government Versus

Homosexuals." In *Gay American History: Lesbians and Gay Men in the U.S.A.* 99–105. New York: Thomas Y. Crowell, 1976.

Kendzior, Sarah. "American Psycho Drama." *Fangoria*, April 2000, 38–41, 82.

Kim, Eun Kyung. "Charlie Sheen Reveals He's HIV Positive in TODAY Show Exclusive." *Today*, November 17, 2015. https://www.today.com/health/charlie-sheen-reveals-hes-hiv-positive-today-show-exclusive-t56391.

Koon, David. "The Woman Who Cared for Hundreds of Abandoned Gay Men Dying of AIDS." *OUT*, February 28, 2019. https://www.out.com/positive-voices/2016/12/01/woman-who-cared-hundreds-abandoned-gay-men-dying-aids.

Kramer, Larry. "1,112 And Counting." *New York Native*, March 27, 1983, 59.

Lamb, W. Scott. "20 Years Ago, Bill Clinton Signed Defense of Marriage Act." *The Washington Times*, September 21, 2016. https://www.washingtontimes.com/news/2016/sep/21/20-years-ago-bill-clinton-signed-defense-of-marria/.

Lang, Alison. "Slasher Shocker," *Rue Morgue*, July/August 2019, 16–17.

Lee, Cynthia, *The Trans Panic Defense Revisited (2019)*. 57 AM. CRIM. L. REV. 1411 (2020); GWU Law School Public Law Research Paper No. 2019–63; GWU Legal Studies Research Paper No. 2019–63. Available at SSRN: https://ssrn.com/abstract=3481295.

Lee, Jonathan, and Taylor Drake. "IT's Gay Bashing Scene Serves No Purpose Except as Porn for Homophobes." *Advocate*, September 12, 2019. https://www.advocate.com/commentary/2019/9/12/its-gay-bashing-scene-serves-no-purpose-except-porn-homophobes?utm_source=facebook&utm_medium=social&utm_campaign=commentary&fbclid=IwAR0LBiovR4Wy1f88N22r_y-dDZQUOFBAPmhX69deS1jfyaaq7UU-MOU2EIQ.

LeRoy, Jason. "The Binge Interview: Jeffery Self and Jim Hansen on 'You're Killing Me,' Serial-Killing as Sexuality, and Murderous Real Housewives," March 4, 2016. http://www.thebinge.us/the-binge-interview-jeffery-self-and-jim-hansen-on-youre-killing-me/.

"Lesbian, Gay, Bisexual, and Transgender Health." *Healthy People*, Office of Disease Prevention and Health Promotion, 2020. https://www.healthypeople.gov/2020/topics-objectives/topic/lesbian-gay-bisexual-and-transgender-health.

Levin, Brian, and John David Reitzel. "Report to the Nation: Hate Crimes Rise in U.S. Cities and Counties in Time of Division & Foreign Interference." May 2018. https://www.csusb.edu/sites/default/files/2018%20Hate%20Final%20Report%205-14.pdf.

Levy, Emanuel, Pedro Almodóvar, Terence Davies, Todd Haynes, Gus Van Sant, and John Waters. "Todd Haynes: Deconstructive Queer Cinema." In *Gay Directors, Gay Films? Pedro Almodóvar, Terence Davies, Todd Haynes, Gus Van Sant, John Waters*, 160–99. New York: Columbia University Press, 2015. http://www.jstor.org.ezproxy.trincoll.edu/stable/10.7312/levy15276.8.

Lipsett, Joe, and Trace Thurman, hosts. *Horror Queers* (podcast). *Bloody Disgusting*. January 16, 2019.

Loutzenheiser, Lisa W. "How Schools Play 'Smear the Queer.'" *Feminist Teacher* 10, no. 2 (1996): 59–64. Accessed April 24, 2020. www.jstor.org/stable/40545754.

Lueck, Thomas J. "Ray Sharkey, 40; Actor Often Played Role of Tough Guy." *The New York Times*, June 13, 1993. https://www.nytimes.com/1993/06/13/obituaries/ray-sharkey-40-actor-often-played-role-of-tough-guy.html.

Lugowski, David M. "Queering the (New) Deal: Lesbian and Gay Representation and the Depression-Era Cultural Politics of Hollywood's Production Code." *Cinema Journal* 38, no. 2 (1999): 3–35. http://www.jstor.org.ezproxy.trincoll.edu/stable/1225622.

Maclay, Willow. "'How Can It Be? She's a Boy.' Transmisogyny in 'Sleepaway Camp.'" *Cleo*, February 22, 2017. http://cleojournal.com/2015/08/10/how-can-it-be-shes-a-boy-transmisogyny-in-sleepaway-camp/.

Maddrey, Joseph. *Nightmares in Red, White and Blue: The Evolution of the American Horror Film*. Jefferson: McFarland, 2004.

Man, Glenn. "1975: Movies and Conflicting Ideologies." In *American Cinema of the 1970s: Themes and Variations*, edited by Lester D. Friedman, 135–56. New Brunswick: Rutgers University Press, 2007. https://hdl-handle-net.ezproxy.trincoll.edu/2027/heb.08007.

Mann, William J. *Behind the Screen: How Gays and Lesbians Shaped Hollywood, 1910–1969.* New York: Penguin, 2002.

Mar, Pollo Del. "Oscar-Winner Patricia Arquette Reflects on Late Sister Alexis' Struggle with AIDS Stigma." *Huffington Post,* November 30, 2017. https://www.huffpost.com/entry/oscar-winner-patricia-arquette-reflects-on-sister-alexis_b_5a1fec3ce4b0dff40be036af.

Marcus, Eric. *Making History: The Struggle for Gay and Lesbian Equal Rights, 1945–1990, an Oral History.* New York: HarperCollins, 1992.

Marcus, Eric, and Vito Russo. "The Film Historian." In *Making History: The Struggle for Gay and Lesbian Equal Rights, 1945–1990, An Oral History,* 407–19. New York: Harper Collins, 1992.

McDonough, Jimmy. *The Ghastly One: the Sex-Gore Netherworld of Filmmaker Andy Milligan.* Chicago: Acapella, 2001.

Means Coleman, Robin R. *Horror Noire: Blacks in American Horror Films from the 1890s to Present.* New York: Routledge, 2011.

"Megan Fox Blames Lindsay Lohan for Losing Her Toenails | Let's Unpack That." *InStyle,* YouTube, 2021. https://www.youtube.com/watch?time_continue=5&v=UkTZuhZg16E&feature=emb_title.

"Men on Films." Episode. *In Living Color* 1, no. 1. April 15, 1990.

Mendez, Averie. "Konerak Sinthasomphone: Dahmer's Victim Who Didn't Have to Die." *StMU History Media,* March 9, 2019. https://stmuhistorymedia.org/konerak-sinthasomphone-dahmers-victim-who-didnt-have-to-die/.

Merritt Buttrick AIDS Quilt Block Number 01274. The AIDS Memorial Quilt. The NAMES Project Foundation. Accessed June 15, 2020. http://search.aidsquilt.org/.

Meyer, Leisa D. "The Myth of Lesbian (In)Visibility: World War II and the Current 'Gays in the Military' Debate." In *Modern American Queer History,* ed. Allida M. Black. Philadelphia: Temple University Press, 2001.

Meyer, Richard. "Rock Hudson's Body." In *Inside/Out: Lesbian Theories, Gay Theories,* ed. Diana Fuss. New York: Routledge, 1991.

Mitchell, Alison. "THE 2000 CAMPAIGN: THE TEXAS GOVERNOR; Bush Talks to Gays and Calls It Beneficial." *The New York Times,* April 14, 2000, sec. A.

Morland, Iain, and Annabelle Wilcox, eds. *Queer Theory: Readers in Cultural Criticism.* Basingstoke: Palgrave Macmillan, 2004.

Moyer, Justin Wm. "Danny Pintauro, 'Who's the Boss?' Child Star, Reveals He Got HIV While on Crystal Meth." *The Washington Post,* September 28, 2015. https://www.washingtonpost.com/news/morning-mix/wp/2015/09/28/danny-pintauro-whos-the-boss-child-star-reveals-he-got-hiv-while-on-crystal-meth/.

Mulvey, Laura. "Visual Pleasure and Narrative Cinema." *Film Theory and Criticism: Introductory Readings.* Ed. Leo Braudy and Marshall Cohen. New York: Oxford University Press, 1999: 833–44.

Myers, Steven Lee. "Anthony Perkins, Who Mastered a Frightening Role, Is Dead at 60." *The New York Times,* September 13, 1992. https://www.nytimes.com/1992/09/13/nyregion/anthony-perkins-who-mastered-a-frightening-role-is-dead-at-60.html?searchResultPosition=1&login=smartlock&auth=login-smartlock.

Nutman, Philip. "The Dark Backward." *Fangoria,* March 2001, 26–32.

O'Flinn, Paul. "Production and Reproduction: The Case of Frankenstein." 1983. In *Horror, the Film Reader,* edited by Mark Jancovich, 105–13. New York: Routledge, 2002.

Orbey, Eren. "The Babadook Is a Frightening, Fabulous New Gay Icon." *The New Yorker,* June 17, 2017. https://www.newyorker.com/culture/rabbit-holes/the-babadook-is-a-frightening-fabulous-new-gay-icon.

Palmer, Lorrie. *Journal of the Fantastic in the Arts* 16, no. 4 (64) (2006): 380–84. http://www.jstor.org.ezproxy.trincoll.edu/stable/43310271.

Pariselli, Mark. "Excavating Queer Representation in 'Tammy and the T-Rex.'" *Bloody Disgusting!,* June 26, 2020. https://bloody-disgusting.com/editorials/3621578/excavating-queer-representation-tammy-t-rex/.

"Part 4—In the Stars." Episode. *The Reagans* 1, no. 4. New York: Showtime, December 6, 2020.

Pearson, Wendy. "Alien Cryptographies: The View from Queer." *Science Fiction Studies* 26, no. 1 (1999): 1–22. http://www.jstor.org.ezproxy.trincoll.edu/stable/4240748.

Phillips, John. *Transgender on Screen.* Basingstoke: Palgrave Macmillan, 2006.

Plant, Richard. *The Pink Triangle: The Nazi War Against Homosexuals.* New York: Holt Paperbacks, 1988.

Pronger, Brian. *The Arena of Masculinity: Sports, Homosexuality, and the Meaning of Sex.* New York: St. Martin's Press, 1990.

Pullen, Christopher. "Queer Gazes and Identifications." In *Straight Girls and Queer Guys: The Hetero Media Gaze in Film and Television,* 41–64. Edinburgh: Edinburgh University Press, 2016. http://www.jstor.org.ezproxy.trincoll.edu/stable/10.3366/j.ctt1bgzbtn.8.

Q Lazarus, "Goodbye Horses," written and produced by William Garvey, track number 7 on *Married to the Mob,* Reprise, 1988, compact disc.

Reifsteck, Greg. "Hellbent: Queer Eye for the Dead Guy." *Fangoria,* November 2004, 78–82.

Reilly, Kaitlin. "Did We Need the Hate Crime Scene in *IT Chapter Two*?" *Refinery29,* September 6, 2019. https://www.refinery29.com/en-us/2019/09/8356473/it-chapter-two-adrian-carnival-scene-based-on-real-hate-crime.

Rich, B. Ruby. *New Queer Cinema: the Director's Cut.* Durham: Duke University Press, 2013.

Riddell, Fern. "Does It Matter If Mary Shelley Was Bisexual?" *The Guardian,* November 7, 2019. https://www.theguardian.com/books/booksblog/2019/nov/07/does-it-matter-if-mary-shelley-was-bisexual.

Riemer, Matthew, and Leighton Brown. *We Are Everywhere: Protest, Power, and Pride in the History of Queer Liberation.* California: Ten Speed Press, 2019.

Rist, Darrell Yates. "Fear and Loving and AIDS." *Film Comment* 22, no. 2 (1986): 44–50. http://www.jstor.org.ezproxy.trincoll.edu/stable/43453726.

Rodriguez, Mathew. "Mark Patton on Fighting the HIV Horror Show with Honesty." *The Complete HIV/AIDS Resource. TheBody.com,* October 22, 2013. https://www.thebody.com/article/mark-patton-on-fighting-the-hiv-horror-show-with-h.

Roth, Eli. "Postal Zone: An End to 'Hostel'-ities." *Fangoria,* October 2006, 6.

Rowe, Michael. "Bringing Up Chucky." *Fangoria,* November 2004, 29–33.

Russo, Vito. *The Celluloid Closet: Homosexuality in the Movies.* Revised edition. New York: Harper & Row, 1987.

Sampson, Fiona. *In Search of Mary Shelley: The Girl Who Wrote Frankenstein.* London: Profile Books, 2018.

Scheer, Robert, and Gore Vidal. *Playing President: My Close Encounters with Nixon, Carter, Bush I, Reagan, and Clinton: and How They Did Not Prepare Me for George W. Bush.* Los Angeles: Truthdig, 2006.

Scott, Jay. "Nasty Piece of Homophobic Angst: Logic Takes a Hike in *Hitcher.*" *The Globe and Mail,* February 25, 1986.

Semley, John. "How the Shower Scene from 'Psycho' Slashed Its Way into Legend." Macleans.ca, April 24, 2017. https://www.macleans.ca/culture/movies/how-that-scene-from-psycho-slashed-its-way-through-pop-culture/.

Sengupta, Somini. "Hate Crimes Hit Record High in 1992: Discrimination: A County Panel Finds an 11% Increase to 736 Incidents and Says the Figure Might Have Been Higher If All Riot-Related Instances Had Been Included. African-Americans and Gay Men Were the Most Frequent Targets, Report Finds." *Los Angeles Times,* March 23, 1993.

"The Sexes: The Lavender Panthers." *Time,* October 8, 1973.

Shilts, Robert. *And the Band Played on: Politics, People, and the AIDS Epidemic.* New York: St. Martin's Press. 1987.

Simon, Alex. "William Friedkin: The Hollywood Flashback Interviews." *The Hollywood Interview,* February 12, 2013. http://thehollywoodinterview.blogspot.com/2008/01/cruising-with-billy.html.

"The Simple Life of a Busy Bachelor: Rock Hudson Gets Rich Alone." *Life,* October 3, 1955.

Smelik, Anneke. "Bodies-Without-Organs in the Folds of Fashion: Gilles Deleuze." In *Thinking Through Fashion: A Guide to Key Theorists,* edited by Agnes Rocamora and Anneke Smelik, 169. New York: Bloomsbury Academic, 2015.

Snauffer, Douglas, and Joel Thurm. *The Show Must Go On: How the Deaths of Lead Actors Have Affected Television Series.* Jefferson, NC: McFarland, 2008, 21.

Sobchack, Vivian. "Bringing It All Back Home: Family Economy and Generic Exchange." In *American Horrors: Essays on the Modern American Horror Film,* edited by Gregory A. Waller, 175–94. Urbana: University of Illinois Press, 1987.

Solomon, Haley E., and Beth Kurtz-Costes. "Media's Influence on Perceptions of Trans Women." *Sexuality Research and Social Policy* 15, no. 1 (March 2018): 34–47. Accessed April 19, 2019. doi:https://doi.org/10.1007/s13178-017-0280-2.

Spelling, Ian. "They Must Be Psycho." *Fangoria,* January 1999, 26.

Stolworthy, Jacob. "*It Chapter Two* Director Explains Why Film Opens with a Brutal Hate Crime." *The Independent,* August 27, 2019. https://www.independent.co.uk/arts-entertainment/films/news/it-chapter-2-opening-scene-andy-muschetti-jessica-chastain-release-date-trailer-a9079891.html.

Straayer, Chris. *Deviant Eyes, Deviant Bodies: Sexual Re-Orientations in Film and Video.* New York: Columbia University Press, 1996.

Stryker, Susan. *Transgender History: The Roots of Today's Revolution.* SEAL, 2017.

Sullivan, Terry, and Peter T. Maiken. *Killer Clown: The John Wayne Gacy Murders.* New York: Pinnacle Books, 2000.

Swartzwelder, John. "Itchy & Scratchy & Marge." Episode. *The Simpsons* 2, no. 9, December 20, 1990.

Teachout, Terry. "Opinion | 'The Boys in the Band': A Time Capsule of Art and Identity." *The Wall Street Journal,* August 13, 2020. https://www.wsj.com/articles/the-boys-in-the-band-a-time-capsule-of-art-and-identity-11597353592.

Thompson, Matt. "How to Spark Panic and Confusion in Three Tweets." *The Atlantic,* January 14, 2019. https://www.theatlantic.com/politics/archive/2019/01/donald-trump-tweets-transgender-military-service-ban/579655/.

Thompson, Rocco. "Final Boy." *Rue Morgue,* July/August 2019, 13–18.

Thurman, Trace. "The Inherent Queerness of Clive Barker's 'Nightbreed.'" *Bloody Disgusting,* April 24, 2019. https://bloody-disgusting.com/editorials/3556029/horror-queers-nightbreed/.

Thurman, Trace. "Shove It Down Their Throats—Why Queer Representation in the Media Matters." *Gayly Dreadful,* June 3, 2019. https://www.gaylydreadful.com/blog/2019/6/3/shove-it-down-their-throats-why-queer-representation-in-the-media-matters.

"Trends: Where the Boys Are." *Time Magazine,* June 28, 1968, 91 ed.

Tudor, Andrew. "Why Horror? The Peculiar Pleasures of a Popular Genre." In *Horror, The Film Reader,* edited by Mark Jancovich, 47–55. New York: Routledge, 2002.

"2018 LGBTQ Youth Report." Human Rights Campaign. Accessed March 10, 2021. https://www.hrc.org/resources/2018-lgbtq-youth-report.

Tyrkus, Michael J., and Michael Bronski, eds. "Rita Mae Brown." In *Gay & Lesbian Biography.* Detroit: St. James Press, 1997.

"U.S. Senators Tammy Baldwin and Elizabeth Warren Lead Bipartisan Call on FDA to End Discriminatory Blood Donation Ban: U.S. Senator Tammy Baldwin of Wisconsin." Tammy Baldwin: United States Senator for Wisconsin, June 20, 2016. https://www.baldwin.senate.gov/press-releases/bipartisan-call-end-discriminatory-blood-donation-ban.

"USA and Torture: A History of Hypocrisy." Human Rights Watch, October 28, 2020. https://www.hrw.org/news/2014/12/09/usa-and-torture-history-hypocrisy#.

Villarejo, Amy. "1992 Movies and the Politics of Authorship." *American Cinema of the 1990s: Themes and Variations,* edited by Chris Holmund, 84–90. New Brunswick: Rutgers University Press, 2008. www.jstor.org/stable/j.ctt5hj6fx.9.

Vincentelli, Elisabeth. "Call Charles Busch a 'Drag Legend,' If We Must Use Labels." *The New York Times*, January 10, 2020. https://www.nytimes.com/2020/01/10/theater/charles-busch-lily-dare.html?auth=link-dismiss-google1tap.

Waldron, Abigail, and AJ E. "Queer Horror Questionnaire." October 22, 2019.

Waldron, Abigail, and AJ N. "Queer Horror Questionnaire." September 23, 2019.

Waldron, Abigail, and Anonymous. "Queer Horror Questionnaire." March 9, 2021.

Waldron, Abigail, and Evan. "Queer Horror Questionnaire." September 24, 2019.

Waldron, Abigail, and Jeffrey. "Queer Horror Questionnaire." September 23, 2019.

Waldron, Abigail, and Jordan F. "Queer Horror Questionnaire." March 4, 2021.

Waldron, Abigail, and JP W. "Queer Horror Questionnaire." March 16, 2021.

Waldron, Abigail, and Nan. "Queer Horror Questionnaire." September 20, 2019.

Walker, Michael. "Homosexuality." In *Hitchcock's Motifs*, 248–61. Amsterdam: Amsterdam University Press, 2005. http://www.jstor.org.ezproxy.trincoll.edu/stable/j.ctt46mtpf.28.

Walters, Suzanna Danuta. *All the Rage: The Story of Gay Visibility in America*. Chicago: University of Chicago Press, 2001.

Waters, John. "Introduction." Introduction. In *Hairspray, Female Trouble, and Multiple Maniacs: Three More Screenplays*, vii–xvi. New York: Thunder's Mouth Press, 2005.

Watkins, Gwynne. "Before #OscarsSoWhite: The Forgotten Story of Queer Nation's 1992 Academy Awards Protest." *Yahoo Entertainment*. February 24, 2016. Accessed March 22, 2019. https://www.google.ca/amp/s/ca.movies.yahoo.com/amphtml/before-oscarssowhite-the-forgotten-story-of-201810336.html.

Waugh, Thomas. Essay. In *Queer Looks: Perspectives on Lesbian and Gay Film and Video*, edited by Martha Gever, John Greyson, and Pratisha Parmar, 141–61. New York: Routledge, 1993.

Weiss, Andrea. *Vampires & Violets: Lesbians in Film*. New York: Penguin, 1993.

Wells, Paul. *The Horror Genre: From Beelzebub to Blair Witch*. London: Wallflower, 2000.

"Westboro Baptist Church." Southern Poverty Law Center. Accessed March 22, 2021. https://www.splcenter.org/fighting-hate/extremist-files/group/westboro-baptist-church.

Wetmore, Kevin J. *Post–9/11 Horror in American Cinema*. New York: Continuum International, 2012.

White, Mike. "Cruising Speed." *Fangoria*, May 2014, 18.

White, Patricia. "Female Spectator, Lesbian Specter: *The Haunting*." In *Inside/Out: Lesbian Theories, Gay Theories*, edited by Diana Fuss, 142–72. New York: Routledge, 1991.

Whittle, Stephen. "A Brief History of Transgender Issues." *The Guardian*, June 2, 2010. https://www.theguardian.com/lifeandstyle/2010/jun/02/brief-history-transgender-issues.

Wieder, Judy. *Celebrity: The Advocate Interviews*. New York: Advocate Books, 2001.

Wilkins, Heidi. "Subversive Sound: Gender, Technology and the Science Fiction Blockbuster." In *Talkies, Road Movies and Chick Flicks: Gender, Genre and Film Sound in American Cinema*, 125–48. Edinburgh: Edinburgh University Press, 2016. http://www.jstor.org.ezproxy.trincoll.edu/stable/10.3366/j.ctt1bgzcj0.9.

Williams, Chrystal. "Horror, Fear & Identity." *Gayly Dreadful*, June 28, 2019. https://www.gaylydreadful.com/blog/2019/6/28/zjrdwc4uojl8j8i8gx03eer5a13q15.

Willis, Sharon. "1991 Movies and Wayward Images." In *American Cinema of the 1990s: Themes and Variations*, edited by Chris Holmund, 67–69. New Brunswick: Rutgers University Press, 2008. www.jstor.org/stable/j.ctt5hj6fx.8.

Wilson, Jeff. "Death Certificate Shows 'Brady Bunch' Dad Had AIDS Virus." *Associated Press*. May 19, 1992. https://apnews.com/aea91873be211a21383c87a70142462d.

Wood, Robin. "The American Nightmare: Horror in the 70s." In *Horror, the Film Reader*, edited by Mark Jancovich, 25–32. New York: Routledge, 2002.

Woods, Gregory, and Tim Franks. "Music, Film and Post-Stonewall Gay Identity." In *Film's Musical Moments*, edited by Conrich Ian and Tincknell Estella, 158–68.

Edinburgh: Edinburgh University Press, 2006. http://www.jstor.org.ezproxy.trincoll.
edu/stable/10.3366/j.ctt1r277z.17.

Wyatt, Justin. "College Course File: AIDS, the Mass Media, and Cultural Politics."
Journal of Film and Video 45, no. 2/3 (1993): 91–105. http://www.jstor.org.ezproxy.
trincoll.edu/stable/20688008.

Yingling, Thomas. "AIDS in America: Postmodern Governance, Identity, and Experience." In *Inside/Out: Lesbian Theories, Gay Theories*, edited by Diana Russ, 291–310.
New York: Routledge, 1991.

Film

Aje, Alexandre, dir. *Horns.* 2013; New York: Dimension Films, 2015. DVD.

Allen, Lewis, dir. *The Uninvited.* 1944; Hollywood: Paramount Pictures, 2012. DVD.

Altman, Robert, dir. *Come Back to the 5 & Dime, Jimmy Dean, Jimmy Dean.* 1982; New
York: Cinecom International Films, 2014. DVD.

Álvarez, Fede, dir. *Evil Dead.* 2013; Culver City, CA: Sony Pictures Releasing, 2013.
DVD.

Amirpour, Ana Lily, dir. *A Girl Walks Home Alone at Night.* 2014; Brooklyn: Vice Films,
2015. DVD.

Argento, Dario, dir. *Suspiria.* 1977; Los Angeles: International Classics, 2001. DVD.

Arnold, Jack, dir. *The Creature from the Black Lagoon.* 1954; Universal City, CA: Universal Pictures, 2001. DVD.

Aronofsky, Darren, dir. *Black Swan.* 2010; Los Angeles: Fox Searchlight Pictures, 2011.
DVD.

Asher, William, dir. *Butcher, Baker, Nightmare Maker.* 1981; N/A: Comworld Pictures,
2014. DVD.

Barker, Clive, dir. *Hellraiser.* 1987; London: Entertainment Film Distributers, 2000.
DVD.

Barker, Clive, dir. *Nightbreed.* 1990; Los Angeles: 20th Century Fox, 2004. DVD.

Bender, Jack, dir. *Child's Play 3.* 1991; Universal City, CA: Universal Pictures, 2003.
DVD.

Bier, Susanne, dir. *Bird Box.* 2018; Los Gatos, CA: Netflix, 2018. Web.

Biller, Anne, dir. *The Love Witch.* 2016; Brooklyn: Oscilloscope Laboratories, 2016.
DVD.

Bolton, Drew, dir. *Killer Unicorn.* 2018; Los Angeles: Indican Pictures, 2019. DVD.

Bond, James III, dir. *Def by Temptation.* 1990; N/A: Shapiro-Glickenhaus Entertainment, 2009. DVD.

Booker, Ralph, dir. *Bloodlust!* 1961; Beverly Hills: Crown International Pictures, 2001.
DVD.

Boone, Josh, dir. *The New Mutants.* 2020; Burbank: Walt Disney Studios Motion Pictures, 2020. DVD.

Browning, Tod, dir. *Dracula.* 1931; Universal City, CA: Universal Studios, 1999. DVD.

Browning, Tod, dir. *Freaks.* 1932; Beverly Hills: Metro-Goldwyn-Mayer, 2004. DVD.

Butler, Chris, and Sam Fell, dirs. *ParaNorman.* 2012; Universal City, CA: Focus Features, 2012. DVD.

Cameron, James, dir. *Aliens.* 1986; Los Angeles: 20th Century Fox, 1999. DVD.

Cardone, J.S., dir. *The Forsaken.* 2001; Culver City, CA: Screen Gems, 2001. DVD.

Carpenter, John, dir. *Halloween.* 1978; USA: Compass International Pictures, 1998.
DVD.

Carpenter, John, dir. *The Thing.* 1982; Universal City, CA: Universal Pictures, 1998.
DVD.

Carpenter, John, dir. Ghosts of Mars. 2001; Culver City, CA: Sony Pictures Releasing,
2001. DVD.

Carpenter, Stephen, dir. *Soul Survivors.* 2001; Santa Monica: Artisan Entertainment,
2002. DVD.

Castle, William, dir. *Homicidal*. 1961; Culver City, CA: Columbia Pictures, 2002. DVD.
Castro, Joe, dir. *The Summer of Massacre*. 2011; Philadelphia: Vicious Circle Films, 2011. DVD.
Chandrasekhar, Jay, dir. *Club Dread*. 2004; Los Angeles: Fox Searchlight Pictures, 2005. DVD.
Chimienti, Roman, and Tyler Jensen, dir. *Scream Queen! My Nightmare on Elm Street*. 2019; New York: Virgil Films, 2020. DVD.
Clark, Bob, dir. *Black Christmas*. 1974; CA: Ambassador Film Distributors, 2001. DVD.
Collet-Serra, Jaume, dir. *House of Wax*. 2005; Burbank: Warner Bros. Pictures, 2005. DVD.
Collum, Jason Paul, dir. *October Moon*. 2005; USA: Tempe Entertainment, 2006. DVD.
Cooper, Merian C., dir. *King Kong*. 1933; New York: Radio Pictures, 2005. DVD.
Coppola, Francis Ford, dir. *Bram Stoker's Dracula*. 1992; Los Angeles: Columbia Pictures, 1999. DVD.
Corcoran, Jay, dir. *Life and Death on the A-List*. 1996; USA: Corcoran Productions, 2010. DVD.
Crain, William, dir. *Blacula*. 1972; Los Angeles: American International Pictures, 2004. DVD.
Craven, Wes, dir. *Cursed*. 2005; Los Angeles: Miramax Films, 2005. DVD.
Craven, Wes, dir. *The Last House on the Left*. 1972; Boston: Hallmark Releasing, 2002. DVD.
Craven, Wes, dir. *A Nightmare on Elm Street*. 1984; Burbank: New Line Cinema, 1999. DVD.
Craven, Wes, dir. *Scream*. 1996; New York: Dimension Films, 1998. DVD.
Craven, Wes, dir. *Scream 2*. 1997; New York: Dimension Films, 1998. DVD.
Craven, Wes, dir. *Scream 4*. 2011; New York: Dimension Films, 2011. DVD.
Creepersin, Creep, dir. *The Brides of Sodom*. 2013; N/A: Empire Films, 2013. DVD.
Cumming, Alan, dir. *Suffering Man's Charity*. 2007; N/A: Zuckerman Entertainment, 2009. DVD.
Cunningham, Sean S., dir. *Friday the 13th*. 1980; Hollywood: Paramount Pictures, 1999. DVD.
Dahlin, Bob, dir. *Monster in the Closet*. 1986; New York: Troma Entertainment, 1998. DVD.
de Bont, Jan, dir. *The Haunting*. 1999; Universal City, CA: DreamWorks Pictures, 1999. DVD.
DeCosta, Nia, dir. *Candyman*. 2021; Universal City, CA: Universal Pictures, 2021. DVD.
DeCoteau, David, dir. *The Brotherhood*. 2001; Simi Valley, CA: Artist View Entertainment, 2001. DVD.
DeCoteau, David, dir. *The Brotherhood II: Young Warlocks*. 2001; Los Angeles: Regent Entertainment, 2005. DVD.
DeCoteau, David, dir. *The Brotherhood III: Young Demons*. 2003; Los Angeles: Regent Entertainment, 2005. DVD.
DeCoteau, David, dir. *The Brotherhood IV: The Complex*. 2005; Los Angeles: Regent Entertainment, 2005. DVD.
DeCoteau, David, dir. *The Brotherhood V: Alumni*. 2009; Los Angeles: Regent Entertainment, 2010. DVD.
DeCoteau, David, dir. *The Brotherhood VI: Initiation*. 2010; Los Angeles: Regent Entertainment, 2010. DVD.
DeCoteau, David, dir. *Edgar Allan Poe's The Pit and the Pendulum*. 2009; Los Angeles: Regent Releasing, 2009. DVD.
DeCoteau, David, dir. *The Sisterhood*. 2004; Los Angeles: Image Entertainment, 2005. DVD.
Dekker, Fred, dir. *The Monster Squad*. 1987; Culver City, CA: TriStar Pictures, 2007. DVD.
Dekker, Fred, dir. *Night of the Creeps*. 1986; Culver City, CA: TriStar Pictures, 2009. DVD.

Demaree, Ben, dir. *Hansel vs. Gretel*. 2015; Burbank: The Asylum House Entertainment, 2015. DVD.
Demme, Jonathan, dir. *Philadelphia*. 1993; Culver City, CA: TriStar Pictures, 1997. DVD.
Demme, Jonathan, dir. *The Silence of the Lambs*. 1991; Los Angeles: Orion Pictures, 2001. DVD.
De Palma, Brian, dir. *Carrie*. 1976; Beverly Hills: United Artists, 1998. DVD.
De Palma, Brian, dir. *Dressed to Kill*. 1980; Sonoma County, CA: Filmways Pictures, 2002. DVD.
De Palma, Brian, dir. *Phantom of the Paradise*. 1974; Los Angeles: 20th Century Fox, 2001. DVD.
Deyoe, Adam, and Eric Gosselin, dirs. *Another Yeti: A Love Story: Life on the Streets*. 2017; New York: Troma Entertainment, 2017. DVD.
Deyoe, Adam, and Eric Gosselin, dirs. *Yeti: A Love Story*. 2006; New York: Troma Entertainment, 2008. DVD.
Eggers, Robert, dir. *The Lighthouse*. 2019; New York: A24, 2020. DVD.
Eggers, Robert, dir. *The Witch*. 2015; New York: A24, 2016. DVD.
Elmore, Brad Michael, dir. *Bit*. 2020; Santa Monica: Vertical Entertainment, 2020. DVD.
Etheredge-Ouzts, Paul, dir. *Hellbent*. 2004; Los Angeles: Regent Releasing, 2006. DVD.
Farrands, Daniel, and Kasch, Andrew, dir. *Never Sleep Again: The Elm Street Legacy*. 2010; USA: 1428 Films, 2010. DVD.
Feder, Sam, dir. *Disclosure*. 2020; Los Gatos, CA: Netflix. 2020. Web.
Ferguson, Dustin, and Mike Johnson, dirs. *The Amityville Legacy*. 2016; U.S.: Sinister Studios, 2016. DVD.
Flanagan, Mike, dir. *The Haunting of Hill House*. 2018; Los Gatos, CA: Netflix, 2018. Web.
Fleming, Victor, dir. *The Wizard of Oz*. 1939; Beverly Hills: Metro-Goldwyn-Mayer, 2005. DVD.
Flender, Rodman, dir. *Idle Hands*. 1999; Culver City, CA: Sony Pictures Releasing, 1999. DVD.
Fragasso, Claudio, dir. *Troll 2*. 1990; Hollywood: Epic Productions, 2003. DVD.
Frankenheimer, John, dir. *Prophecy*. 1979; Hollywood: Paramount Pictures, 2019. DVD.
Friedkin, William, dir. *Bug*. 2006; Santa Monica, CA: Lionsgate, 2007. DVD.
Friedkin, William, dir. *Cruising*. 1980; Los Angeles: United Artists, 2007. DVD.
Friedkin, William, dir. *The Exorcist*. 1974; Burbank: Warner Bros. Pictures, 2003. DVD.
Friedman, Gabriel, Chad Ferrin, David Paiko, Brian Spitz, and Lloyd Kaufman, dirs. *Tales from the Crapper*. 2004; New York: Troma Entertainment, 2004. DVD.
Garland, Alex, dir. *Annihilation*. 2018; Hollywood: Paramount Pictures, 2018. DVD.
Gershuny, Theodore, dir. *Silent Night, Deadly Night*. 1972; N/A: Cannon Films, 2013, DVD.
Gesner, Eli Morgan, dir. *Condemned*. 2015; Los Angeles: Image Entertainment, 2016. DVD.
Gierasch, Adam, dir. *Night of the Demons*. 2009; London: Seven Arts Inernational, 2010. DVD.
Gildark, Daniel, dir. *Cthulhu*. 2007; Los Angeles: Regent Releasing, 2007. DVD.
Gilroy, Dan, dir. *Velvet Buzzsaw*. 2019; Los Gatos, CA: Netflix, 2019. Web.
Gray, Bradley Rust, dir. *Jack & Diane*. 2012; New York: Magnolia Pictures, 2012. DVD.
Green, Adam, dir. *Hatchet*. 2006; Beverly Hills: Anchor Bay Entertainment, 2007. DVD.
Green, Adam, Joe Lynch, Adam Rifkin, and Tim Sullivan, dirs. *Chillerama*. 2011; Los Angeles: Image Entertainment, 2012. DVD.
Green, David Gordon, dir. *Halloween Kills*. 2021; Universal City, CA: Universal Pictures, 2022. DVD.
Guadagnino, Luca, dir. *Suspiria*. 2018; Culver City, CA: Amazon Studios, 2019. DVD.
Gunn, James, dir. *Slither*. 2006; Universal City, CA: Universal Pictures, 2006. DVD.
Hail, Mack, dir. *Switch Killer*. 2004; Las Vegas: Vegas Media Group, 2005. DVD.

Hamedani, Kevin, dir. *ZMD: Zombies of Mass Destruction*. 2010; N/A: Typecast Pictures, 2011. DVD.
Hansen, Jim, dir. *You're Killing Me*. 2015; San Jose, CA: Wolfe Video, 2017. DVD.
Hardy, Robin, dir. *The Wicker Man*. 1973; London: British Lion Films, 2001. DVD.
Harmon, Robert, dir. *The Hitcher*. 1986; Culver City, CA: TriStar Pictures, 2003. DVD.
Harron, Mary, dir. *American Psycho*. 2000; Santa Monica: Lions Gate Films, 2000. DVD.
Haynes, Todd, dir. *Poison*. 1991; New York: Zeitgeist Films, 2011. DVD.
Hemphill, Jim, dir. *Bad Reputation*. 2005; Deerfield Beach, FL: Maverick Entertainment Group, 2007. DVD.
Hendler, Stewart, dir. *Sorority Row*. 2009; Santa Monica: Summit Entertainment, 2010. DVD.
Henenlotter, Frank, dir. *Frankenhooker*. 1990; N/A: Shapiro-Glickenhaus Entertainment, 2011. DVD.
Herek, Stephen, dir. *Critters*. 1986; Burbank: New Line Cinema, 1997. DVD.
Hillyer, Lambert, dir. *Dracula's Daughter*. 1936; Universal City, CA: Universal Pictures, 2001. DVD.
Hiltzik, Robert, dir. *Return to Sleepaway Camp*. 2008; New York: Magnolia Pictures, 2008. DVD.
Hiltzik, Robert, dir. *Sleepaway Camp*. 1983; USA: United Film Distribution Company, 2000. DVD.
Hitchcock, Alfred, dir. *Psycho*. 1960; Hollywood: Paramount Pictures, 1998. DVD.
Hitchcock, Alfred, dir. *Rebecca*. 1940; Hollywood: United Artists, 1999. DVD.
Holland, Tom, dir. *Child's Play*. 1988; Beverly Hills: MGM/UA Communications Co., 1999. DVD.
Holland, Tom, dir. *Fright Night*. 1985; Los Angeles: Columbia Pictures, 1999. DVD.
Hooper, Tobe, dir. *Salem's Lot*. 1979; Burbank: Warner Bros. Television Distribution, 1999. DVD.
Hooper, Tobe, dir. *The Texas Chainsaw Massacre*. 1974; U.S.A.: Bryanston Distributing Company, 1998. DVD.
Hughes, Ken, dir. *Night School*. 1981; Hollywood: Paramount Pictures, 2011. DVD.
Hunt, Paul, dir. *Twisted Nightmare*. 1987; N/A: United Filmmakers, 2017. DVD.
Huston, Jimmy, dir. *Final Exam*. 1981; USA: Motion Picture Marketing, 2008. DVD.
Huston, Jimmy, dir. *My Best Friend Is a Vampire*. 1988; Delaware: Kings Road Entertainment, Inc., 2009. DVD.
Iliadis, Dennis, dir. *The Last House on the Left*. 2009; Universal City, CA: Universal Pictures, 2009. DVD.
Irvin, Sam, dir. *Elvira's Haunted Hills*. 2001; USA: The Elvira Movie Company LLC, 2002. DVD.
Janiak, Leigh, dir. *Fear Street Part One: 1994*. 2021; Los Angeles: Netflix, 2021. Web.
Janiak, Leigh, dir. *Fear Street Part Two: 1978*. 2021; Los Angeles: Netflix, 2021. Web.
Janiak, Leigh, dir. *Fear Street Part Three: 1666*. 2021; Los Angeles: Netflix, 2021. Web.
Jones, Amy Holden, dir. *The Slumber Party Massacre*. 1982; Atlanta: New World Pictures, 2000. DVD.
Jones, Justin, dir. *Sorority Party Massacre*. 2012; Los Angeles: Highland Film Group, 2014. DVD.
Jordan, Neil, dir. *Interview with a Vampire*. 1994; Burbank: Warner Bros., 1997. DVD.
Kaufman, Lloyd, and Gabriel Friedman, dirs. *Poultrygeist: Night of the Chicken Dead*. 2006; New York, NY: Troma Entertainment, 2008. DVD.
Kennedy, Jake, dir. *Days of Darkness*. 2007; Santa Monica: Lionsgate Films, 2008. DVD.
Kent, Jennifer, dir. *The Babadook*. 2014; Toronto: Entertainment One, 2014. DVD.
King, Robert Lee, dir. *Psycho Beach Party*. 2000; Culver City, CA: Strand Releasing, 2005. DVD.
Kurtzman, Robert, dir. *Wishmaster*. 1997; Van Nuys, CA: Live Entertainment, 1998. DVD.
Kusama, Karyn, dir. *Jennifer's Body*. 2009; Los Angeles: 20th Century Fox, 2009. DVD.

Lacerte, Jacques, dir. *Love Me Deadly.* 1972; N/A: Cinema National, 2008. DVD.
Laguna, Sonny, and Tommy Wiklund, dir. *Puppet Master: The Littlest Reich.* 2018; Los Angeles: RLJE Films, 2018. DVD.
LaLoggia, Frank, dir. *Fear No Evil.* 1981; Los Angeles: Embassy Pictures, 2003. DVD.
Landis, John, dir. *An American Werewolf in London.* 1981; Universal City, CA: Universal Pictures, 1997. DVD.
Landon, Christopher, dir. *Freaky.* 2020; Universal City, CA: Universal Pictures, 2021. DVD.
Landon, Christopher, dir. *Happy Death Day.* 2017; Universal City, CA: Universal Pictures, 2018. DVD.
Landon, Christopher, dir. *Happy Death Day 2 U.* 2019; Universal City, CA: Universal Pictures, 2019. DVD.
Lee, Ang, dir. *Brokeback Mountain.* 2005; Universal City, CA: Focus Features, 2006. DVD.
Lee, Malcolm D., dir. *Scary Movie 5.* 2013; New York: Dimension Films, 2013. DVD.
Lewnes, Pericles, dir. *Redneck Zombies.* 1987; New York: Troma Entertainment, 2009. DVD.
Lin, Frank, dir. *Home.* 2016; N/A: Inception Group Media, 2016. DVD.
Lustig, William, dir. *Maniac Cop 2.* 1990; Santa Monica: Live Entertainment, 2013. DVD.
Lynch, Joe, dir. *Wrong Turn 2: Dead End.* 2007; Los Angeles: 20th Century Fox Home Entertainment, 2007. DVD.
Malone, William, dir. *House on Haunted Hill.* 1999; Burbank: Warner Bros., 2000. DVD.
Mancini, Don, dir. *Cult of Chucky.* 2017; Universal City, CA: Universal Pictures Home Entertainment, 2017. DVD.
Mancini, Don, dir. *Curse of Chucky.* 2013; Universal City, CA: Universal 1440 Entertainment, 2013. DVD.
Mancini, Don, dir. *Seed of Chucky.* 2004; Universal City, CA: Rogue Pictures, 2005. DVD.
Mankiewicz, Joseph L., dir. *Suddenly, Last Summer.* 1959; Los Angeles: Columbia Pictures, 2000. DVD.
Marcus, Adam, dir. *Jason Goes to Hell: The Final Friday.* 1993; Burbank: New Line Cinema, 2002. DVD.
McDonnell, B.J., dir. *Hatchet III.* 2013; Orland Park, IL: Dark Sky Films, 2013. DVD.
McGuigan, Paul, dir. *Victor Frankenstein.* 2015; Los Angeles: 20th Century Fox, 2016. DVD.
McIntosh, Pollyanna, dir. *Darlin.'* 2019; Orland Park, IL: Dark Sky Films, 2019. DVD.
McKee, Lucky, dir. *May.* 2002; Santa Monica: Lions Gate Films, 2003. DVD.
McKee, Lucky and Chris Siverston, dir. *All Cheerleaders Die.* 2013; Los Angeles: Image Entertainment, 2014. DVD.
Meyer, Russ, dir. *Beyond the Valley of the Dolls.* 1970; Los Angeles: 20th Century Fox, 2006. DVD.
Milligan, Andy, dir. *The Ghastly Ones/Blood Rites.* 1968; N/A: J.E.R. Pictures, 2004. DVD.
Milott, Jonathan, and Cary Murnion, dirs. *Cooties.* 2015; Santa Monica: Lionsgate Premiere, 2015. DVD.
Miner, Steve, dir. *Friday the 13th Part II.* 1981; Hollywood: Paramount Pictures, 1999, DVD.
Miner, Steve, dir. *Warlock.* 1989; Santa Monica: Trimark Pictures, 2004. DVD.
Murnau, F.W., dir. *Nosferatu.* 1922; Germany: Film Arts Guild, 2001. DVD.
Muschietti, Andres, dir. *It.* 2017; Burbank: Warner Bros. Pictures, 2018. DVD.
Muschietti, Andres, dir. *It Chapter Two.* 2019; Burbank: Warner Bros. Pictures, 2020. DVD.
Nekrasova, Dasha, dir. *The Scary of Sixty-First.* 2021; Los Angeles: Utopia, 2022. DVD.
Nelson, Ralph, dir. *Embryo.* 1976; N/A: Cine Artists Pictures, 2003. DVD.

Norrington, Stephen, dir. *Blade*. 1998; Burbank: New Line Cinema, 1998. DVD.
Nyby, Christian, dir. *The Thing from Another World*. 1951; New York: RKO Radio Pictures, 2003. DVD.
O'Brien, Declan, dir. *Wrong Turn 4: Bloody Beginnings*. 2011; Los Angeles: 20th Century Fox Home Entertainment, 2011. DVD.
Ottman, John, dir. *Urban Legends: Final Cut*. 2000; Culver City, CA: Columbia Pictures, 2001. DVD.
Packard, Glenn Douglas, dir. *Pitchfork*. 2016; Flagler Beach, FL: Uncork'd Entertainment, 2017. DVD.
Paulsen, David, dir. *Savage Weekend*. 1980; U.S.: The Cannon Group, 2015. DVD.
Peckover, Chris, dir. *Better Watch Out*. 2017; Plano: Well Go USA, 2017. DVD.
Peele, Jordan, dir. *Get Out*. 2017; Universal City, CA: Universal Pictures, 2017. DVD.
Peirce, Kimberly, dir. *Boys Don't Cry*. 1999; Los Angeles: Fox Searchlight Pictures, 2000. DVD.
Peirce, Kimberly, dir. *Carrie*. 2013; Culver City, CA: Sony Pictures Releasing, 2014. DVD.
Pirro, Mark, dir. *Curse of the Queerwolf*. 1988; Hollywood: Pirromount Pictures, 2003. DVD.
Pirro, Mark, dir. *A Polish Vampire in Burbank*. 1983; Hollywood: Pirromount Pictures, 2006. DVD.
Plotkin, Gregory, dir. *Hell Fest*. 2018; Los Angeles: CBS Films, 2019. DVD.
Polanski, Roman, dir. *The Fearless Vampire Killers*. 1967; Beverly Hills: Metro-Goldwyn-Mayer, 2005. DVD.
Raffill, Stewart, dir. *Tammy and the T-Rex*. 1994; Bridgeport, CT: Vinegar Syndrome, 2020. DVD.
Ramalho, Dennison, and Various, dirs. *ABCs of Death 2*. 2014; New York: Magnet Releasing, 2015. DVD.
Ramis, Harold, dir. *National Lampoon's Vacation*. 1983; Burbank: Warner Bros., 1997. DVD.
Randel, Tony, dir. *Hellbound: Hellraiser II*. 1988; Atlanta: New World Pictures, 2000. DVD.
Randel, Tony, dir. *Ticks*. 1993; Los Angeles: Republic Pictures Home Video, 2013. DVD.
Ray, Nicholas, dir. *Rebel Without a Cause*. 1955; Burbank: Warner Bros., 2002. DVD.
Reeves, Matt. *Cloverfield*. 2008; Hollywood: Paramount Pictures, 2008. DVD.
Refn, Nicolas Winding, dir. *The Neon Demon*. 2016; Culver City, CA: Amazon Studios, 2016. DVD.
Robitel, Adam, dir. *The Taking of Deborah Logan*. 2014; Los Angeles: Millennium Entertainment, 2014. DVD.
Robson, Mark, dir. *The Seventh Victim*. 1943; New York, NY: RKO Radio Pictures, 2005. DVD.
Rodriguez, Robert, dir. *The Faculty*. 1998; Los Angeles, CA: Miramax Films, 1999. DVD.
Rodriguez, Robert, dir. *Planet Terror*. 2007; New York: Dimension Films, 2007. DVD.
Romero, George A., dir. *Night of the Living Dead*. 1968; USA: Continental Distributing, 2002. DVD.
Rose, Bernard, dir. *Candyman*. 1992; Culver City, CA: TriStar Pictures, 2004. DVD.
Rose, Mickey, dir. *Student Bodies*. 1981; Hollywood: Paramount Pictures, 2007. DVD.
Roth, Eli, dir. *Cabin Fever*. 2002; Santa Monica: Lionsgate Films, 2004. DVD.
Roth, Eli, dir. *Hostel*. 2006; Santa Monica: Lionsgate, 2006. DVD.
Roth, Eli, dir. *Hostel: Part II*. 2007; Santa Monica: Lionsgate, 2007. DVD.
Rubin, John, dir. *Zombeavers*. 2014; Los Angeles: Freestyle Releasing, 2014. DVD.
Russell, Chuck, dir. *The Blob*. 1988; Culver City, CA: TriStar Pictures, 2001. DVD.
Salva, Victor, dir. *Jeepers Creepers 2*. 2003; Beverly Hills: MGM Distribution Co., 2003. DVD.
Sanders, Denis, dir. *Invasion of the Bee Girls*. 1973; N/A: Dimension Pictures, 2017. DVD.
Saulnier, Jeremy, dir. *Green Room*. 2015; New York: A24, 2016. DVD.

Schoolnik, Skip, dir. *Hide and Go Shriek*. 1988; Beverly Hills: New Star Entertainment, 2016. DVD.

Schumacher, Joel, dir. *The Lost Boys*. 1987; Burbank: Warner Bros., 1999. DVD.

Scott, Ridley, dir. *Alien: Covenant*. 2017; Los Angeles: 20th Century Fox, 2017. DVD.

Scott, Ridley, dir. *Alien*. 1979; Los Angeles: 20th Century Fox, 1999. DVD.

Scott, Ridley, dir. *Hannibal*. 2001; Beverly Hills: MGM Distribution Co., 2001. DVD.

Scott, Tony, dir. *The Hunger*. 1983; Beverly Hills: MGM/UA Entertainment Co., 2004. DVD.

Seaton, J.T., dir. *George: A Zombie Intervention*. 2009; N/A: Tarvix Pictures, 2011. DVD.

Seigel, Don, dir. *Invasion of the Body Snatchers*. 1956; Los Angeles: Allied Artists Pictures, 2012. DVD.

Shadyac, Tom, dir. *Ace Ventura: Pet Detective*. 1994; Burbank: Warner Bros., 1997. DVD.

Sharman, Jim, dir. *The Rocky Horror Picture Show*. 1975; Los Angeles: 20th Century Fox, 2000. DVD.

Shea, Kat, dir. *The Rage: Carrie 2*. 1999; Beverly Hills: Metro-Goldwyn-Mayer, 1999. DVD.

Shepard, Richard, dir. *The Perfection*. 2019; Los Gatos, CA: Netflix, 2019. Web.

Sholder, Jack, dir. *A Nightmare on Elm Street 2: Freddy's Revenge*. 1985; Burbank: New Line Cinema, 2000. DVD.

Shyamalan, M. Night, dir. *The Village*. 2004; Burbank: Buena Vista Pictures, 2005. DVD.

Simpson, Michael A., dir. *Sleepaway Camp II: Unhappy Campers*. 1988; Los Angeles: Nelson Entertainment, 2002. DVD.

Simpson, Michael A., dir. *Sleepaway Camp III: Teenage Wasteland*. 1989; Los Angeles: Nelson Entertainment, 2002. DVD.

Smith, Carter, dir. *Jamie Marks Is Dead*. 2014; Brooklyn: Verisimilitude, 2014. DVD.

Smith, Kevin, dir. *Red State*. 2011; Los Angeles: SModcast Pictures, 2011. DVD.

Smithee, Alan, dir. *Hellraiser: Bloodline*. 1996; Buffalo: Miramax Films, 2001. DVD.

Snyder, Zack, dir. *Dawn of the Dead*. 2004; Universal City, CA: Universal Pictures, 2005. DVD.

Spera, Rob, dir. *Leprechaun in the Hood*. 2000; Santa Monica: Trimark Pictures, 2000. DVD.

Spierig Brothers, dirs. *Jigsaw*. 2017; Santa Monica: Lionsgate, 2018. DVD.

Stamm, Daniel, dir. *The Last Exorcism*. 2010; Santa Monica: Lionsgate, 2011. DVD.

Stettner, Patrick, dir. *The Night Listener*. 2006; Los Angeles: Miramax Films, 2007. DVD.

Storm, Howard, dir. *Once Bitten*. 1985; Culver City, CA: The Samuel Goldwyn Company, 2003. DVD.

Strauss-Schulson, Todd, dir. *The Final Girls*. 2015; Culver City, CA: Stage 6 Films, 2015. DVD.

Susco, Stephen, dir. *Unfriended: Dark Web*. 2018; Universal City, CA: OTL Releasing, 2018. DVD.

Taft, William, and Paul South, dirs. *Berdella*. 2009; Kansas City: Northeast Film Group, 2010. DVD.

Teague, Lewis, dir. *Cujo*. 1983; Burbank: Warner Bros. Pictures, 2000. DVD.

Tenney, Kevin S., dir. *Night of the Demons*. 1988; USA: International Film Marketing, 2004. DVD.

Thompson, Jaymes, dir. *The Gay Bed and Breakfast of Terror*. 2007; Studio City, CA: Ariztical Entertainment, 2008. DVD.

Thorndike, Stewart, dir. *Lyle*. 2014; Philadelphia: Breaking Glass Pictures, 2014. DVD.

Townsend, James, dir. *Kissing Darkness*. 2014; USA: In the Pink Productions, 2014. DVD.

Van Sant, Gus, dir. *Psycho*. 1998; Universal City, CA: Universal Pictures, 1998. DVD.

Wachowskis, Lana and Lily Wachowski, dir. *Bound*. 1996; Universal City, CA: Gramercy Pictures, 2000. DVD.

Wadlow, Jeff, dir. *Truth or Dare*. 2018; Universal City, CA: Universal Pictures, 2018. DVD.

Waggner, George, dir. *The Wolf Man.* 1941; Universal City, CA: Universal Pictures, 1999. DVD.

Wallace, Tommy Lee, dir. *Fright Night Part 2.* 1988; Culver City, CA: TriStar Pictures, 2003. DVD.

Waters, John, dir. *Multiple Maniacs.* 1970; Burbank: New Line Cinema, 2017. DVD.

Watkins, Roger, dir. *Last House on Dead End Street.* 1979; U.S.: Cinematic Releasing Corporation, 2002. DVD.

Wayans, Keenen Ivory, dir. *Scary Movie.* 2000; New York: Dimension Films, 2000. DVD.

Wayans, Keenen Ivory, dir. *Scary Movie 2.* 2001; New York: Dimension Films, 2001. DVD.

West, Ti, dir. *Cabin Fever 2: Spring Fever.* 2009; Santa Monica: Lionsgate, 2010. DVD.

Wexler, Jen, dir. *The Ranger.* 2018; USA: Shudder, 2018. Web.

Whale, James, dir. *Bride of Frankenstein.* 1935; Universal City, CA: Universal Pictures, 1999. DVD.

Whale, James, dir. *Frankenstein.* 1931; Universal City, CA: Universal Pictures, 2001. DVD.

Whale, James, dir. *The Invisible Man.* 1933; Universal City, CA: Universal Pictures, 2000. DVD.

Wise, Robert, dir. *The Haunting.* 1963; Los Angeles: Metro-Goldwyn-Mayer, 2003. DVD.

Wood, Ed, dir. *Glen or Glenda.* 1953; Los Angeles: Columbia Pictures, 2000. DVD.

Wright, Geoffrey, dir. *Cherry Falls.* 2000; Universal City, CA: USA Films, 2000. DVD.

Yeaworth, Irvin, dir. *The Blob.* 1958; Hollywood: Paramount Pictures, 2000. DVD.

Yu, Ronny. *Bride of Chucky.* 1998; Universal City, CA: Universal Pictures, 1999. DVD.

Yu, Ronny, dir. *Freddy vs Jason.* 2003; Burbank: New Line Cinema, 2004. DVD.

Yuzna, Brian, dir. *Silent Night, Deadly Night 4: The Initiation.* 1990; Santa Monica: Live Video, 2009. DVD.

Zenga, Bo, dir. *Stan Helsing.* 2009; Beverly Hills: Anchor Bay Entertainment, 2009. DVD.

Zombie, Rob, dir. *The Devil's Rejects.* 2005; Santa Monica: Lionsgate, 2005. DVD.

Zombie, Rob, dir. *Halloween.* 2007; New York: The Weinstein Company, 2007. DVD.

Zombie, Rob, dir. *3 from Hell.* 2019; Santa Monica: Lionsgate, 2019. DVD.

Zucker, David, dir. *Scary Movie 3.* 2003; New York: Dimension Films, 2004. DVD.

Zucker, David, dir. *Scary Movie 4.* 2006; New York: Dimension Films, 2006. DVD.

Index

Weaver, Sigourney 117
Weiss, Andrea 38
Weiss, George 101
werewolf 86, 157
West Hollywood Halloween Carnival 142
Westboro Baptist Church 124
Whale, James 22, 24–26, 28, 30–34, 130, 163–164, 184
White, Dan 64
White, Patricia 51
The Wicker Man (1973) 181
Williams, Crystal 177–178
Williams, Tennessee 47
Williamson, Kevin 124, 126, 128–129
Willson, Henry 48–49
The Witch (2015) 183

The Wizard of Oz (1939) 60
The Wolf Man (1941) 112
Wolfe, Steven 142
Women's Army Corps (WAC) 40
Wong, B.D. 164–165
Wood, Ed 100–101, 144
Wood, Robin 12–13
World Trade Center 131
World War II 39–40, 45, 99–100
Wrong Turn 2: Dead End (2007) 136

You're Killing Me (2015) 153–154

Zillman, Dolf 98
Zombie, Rob 135
zombies 75, 121, 155, 183